STRONGER IN THE BROKEN PLACES

STRONGER IN THE
BROKEN
PLACES

NINE LESSONS FOR TURNING
CRISIS INTO TRIUMPH

JAMES LEE WITT
AND JAMES MORGAN

TIMES BOOKS

HENRY HOLT AND COMPANY   NEW YORK

Times Books
Henry Holt and Company, LLC
Publishers since 1866
115 West 18th Street
New York, New York 10011

Henry Holt® is a registered trademark of
Henry Holt and Company, LLC.

Library of Congress Cataloging-in-Publication Data
Witt, James Lee, date.
    Stronger in the broken places : nine lessons for turning crisis into triumph /
James Lee Witt and James Morgan.—1st ed.
        p.   cm.
    Includes index.
    ISBN 0-8050-7000-1 (hb)
    1. Crisis management.   2. Emergency management.   3. Crises.
I. Morgan, James, date.   II. Title.

    HD49 .W58 2002
    658.4'056—dc21   2002020399

First Edition 2002

Designed by Kelly S. Too

Printed in the United States of America
10 9 8 7 6 5 4 3 2 1

For Lea Ellen

CONTENTS

STRONGER IN THE BROKEN PLACES

HANDLING IT

This book, which was one-fourth done on September 11, 2001, when crisis took on a new meaning in our lives, is about handling crisis. It is also, by its very nature, a book about leaders.

We tend to toss the word *crisis* around pretty loosely, to the point that it sometimes covers everything from death to dentures. But my dictionary defines crisis as "a crucial or decisive point or situation; a turning point." Crises *are* turning points—defining moments in our lives when we can choose to lead.

Life does—must—go on, a fact that cuts to the heart of what I mean by "handling crisis." You've heard the old saying about keeping your head while all around you others are losing theirs? That's part of what I mean— maintaining a presence of mind, and a sense of proportion, in the midst of the worst calamities. Some people are constitutionally better equipped for this than others, but there are skills that can be taught—about such things as team building, prioritizing, support groups, and even self-discipline. Remember this above all: Procrastination is the archenemy of crisis management. Sometimes a crisis *becomes* a crisis simply because someone has failed to act.

During my eight years at the Federal Emergency Management Agency (FEMA), we handled 373 major disasters, including fifty-four tornadoes, forty-three floods, thirty-eight hurricanes, four earthquakes, and one terrorist bombing. One thing about having crisis as your job description, you get to see people at both their worst and their best—which is often at the same time. Watching so many ordinary humans deal with extraordinary circumstances, I also absorbed a certain gut-level understanding of why some people are able to manage crisis—practically, emotionally, and spiritually—and others aren't. In a disaster, we tend to think in terms of groups—twenty thousand survivors in a shelter, for example. But that's twenty thousand *individuals* who look at the world through only their own eyes. Crisis management is at heart an individual challenge.

Shortly after President Clinton appointed me director of FEMA, somebody asked me what he had meant by saying I was "a man of uncommon common sense." The truth was, I didn't know how to answer. I admitted as much, and said I would think on it. And so I did.

What I came up with was this: In 1960, when I was sixteen years old, I bought my first car, a 1951 Ford that squawked rubber in all three gears. I gave $250 for it, money I had saved up from baling hay in Texas the summer before. I was very proud of that old car. It was sky blue with a flat-head V-8 and twin pipes, and in it I felt like the coolest boy in all of Dardanelle, Arkansas.

One night leaving the roller rink, just as I speed-shifted from first to second, the engine started making a terrible racket. I was a farmer, not a mechanic, but even I knew what that metal-on-metal sound meant: I had thrown a rod. The car was undriveable, so I got a buddy to hook a chain to my bumper and tow me home. We hauled the Ford down to the barn and parked it under the shed. My dad came out and looked at it. He hadn't been all that big on my buying a car in the first place.

"What you gonna do now?" he said.

"Well, Dad," I said, "I guess I'll fix it."

Now, I need to step back here and make a point, which is, when my car broke down, hiring somebody else to fix it was out of the question. I grew up the son of an Arkansas sharecropper. Until I was fifteen, we had no indoor plumbing and only a coal stove for heat. In the winter my dad would spread sheets of linoleum on the floor to block out the cold air, and to this day I can see that linoleum floating up whenever a harsh wind blew. As the youngest of five children, I started driving a tractor at age six, and I stayed home from school so much, helping Dad in the fields, that I almost flunked first grade. When I did go to school I carried my lunch in a lard bucket. My mother was a housekeeper, at first just for us and then for other people, too, and my brother, sisters, and I helped her as well. She had a garden where she grew all our vegetables, and she canned a lot of things to tide us over in the winter. We raised our own hogs and did our own butchering, milked our seventeen cows every morning, and raised chickens that we traded for the staples we needed, like flour, sugar, and salt. Mother made our clothes out of flour sacks, and I soon learned not to object whenever she asked me to go grocery shopping with her. That way, I at least got to choose the color of my next shirt.

I don't mean to make my early life sound unduly harsh. We were a close family, and we had plenty of good times. Still, by age sixteen, I had seen my father and mother survive not just the expected hardships of farm life, which included the usual drought-failed crops (one year my dad brought in a total of two bales of cotton) and sick animals (until I bought one, we didn't have a car—only a wagon and horses), but also the tornado that turned our house on its foundation when I was five, the fire that destroyed everything we had when I was fifteen, and the other tornado that we escaped only by running to a nearby storm shelter, my mother getting bitten by a snake on the way.

Despite all that, I had never torn apart an engine, but the next morning I set to work on it. I jacked the car up on blocks, took off the heads, took off the oil pan, took out the crank shaft, took out all the pistons and rods—everything till that engine block was clean as a whistle. Then I turned the crank shaft, turned the rods, put in new rod bearings, and put the whole engine back together. I still had a little coffee can full of bolts, but the car seemed to run fine. I never figured out what those extra bolts were for.

For years I didn't realize there was anything particularly remarkable about that event. But what I now see as remarkable is that I knew I *could* fix it. Having watched my parents fight their way through all the bad times, and having endured many dicey moments myself, I've come to believe that uncommon common sense is nothing more than a bone-deep faith in your ability to cope in a bad situation—faith that you *can* decide what to do, you *can* figure out how to do it, you *can* pick up the pieces of your life and go on. It's frightening the first time you have to tap into that confidence at your core. But the more you're tested, the more you can rely on your experience at tapping into it. You don't have to be afraid that it'll fail you. Whatever it is inside us that instills, facilitates, and conveys such confidence, the truth about it is this: It grows, like bark, with every trial you face.

UNFORTUNATELY, COMMON SENSE is a commodity that seems to be in extremely short supply, especially in organizations. Leon Panetta, former congressman and White House chief of staff, says, "Democracy operates either through crisis or leadership." I think you could say the same for corporations, communities, and even families.

Groups don't think; they react. More than that, they fantasize, imagine, fear, fabricate, compete, compensate, placate, and supplicate. With their many arms and legs flailing wildly, they wrestle with illusions. When I joined FEMA, the agency itself was in crisis. Widely known as a do-nothing outfit— the government's "turkey farm"—it was actually in danger of being dismantled by Congress. Originally set up to guard against nuclear war, its most useful role was as a dumping ground for political appointees. But shortsightedness always reveals itself. When Hurricane Hugo hit South Carolina in 1989, FEMA's response was so slow and cumbersome that Senator Ernest Hollings called the agency "the sorriest bunch of bureaucratic jackasses I've ever known." Unfortunately, that wasn't the agency's low point. That came in 1992, when Hurricane Andrew devastated South Florida. FEMA was so inept in acting that people were still living in tent cities more than a year after the storm.

So to me, my task as director was clear: to slash red tape and redefine how the federal government responds to crises in its citizens' lives. But as I jumped into my job with both feet, I found I was having a hard time getting my people to open up—to me or to one another. Then one day an employee told me that when he would go to parties in Washington and people asked where he worked, he would mumble or slur his words—anything but to say "FEMA." That's when I realized that my *first* job was to boost this agency's morale.

I started wandering the halls, talking and listening to people and having regular brown-bag lunches with employees all over the building. Most of them had never seen a FEMA director before, much less sat around talking with one. Sometimes we didn't discuss anything but their families and the latest ball game, but that was okay. The main thing was for them to learn to trust me and their other colleagues—but mainly to trust themselves. People are so afraid to fail that they often shut down and do nothing. Failure is part of life. Try something, and if it doesn't work, try something else. I encourage imagination and discourage predictability. At first, whenever I would suggest something new, inevitably someone would pipe up with, "But we've never done it that way. . . ." I got so tired of hearing that that I had a sign made up for my desk. It says, "When entering this office, DO NOT SAY, 'WE'VE NEVER DONE IT THAT WAY BEFORE!'"

Once I felt the employees were on track, we started working to streamline the agency's operations. Today I'm proud to report that in March 2000, the Mercatus Center at George Mason University published a study called *Learning from the Leaders: Results-Based Management at the Federal Emergency Management Agency.* "FEMA has won widespread praise for its reinvention efforts," wrote the study's author, senior research fellow Jerry Ellig. "Lawmakers who once talked of abolishing the agency now compliment it."

Our road to success was strewn with obstacles. Unbelievable as it sounds, FEMA had never had a strategic plan. Its managers had never sat down to establish goals. So one of the first things we did was go away together and talk about what our purpose was and what we needed to do to fulfill that purpose. We simplified the paperwork so disaster victims can get help in days, not weeks or months, and by telephone instead of through the mail. We set up instant community relations programs for survivors. We all but eliminated our original focus on nuclear war and instead began focusing on the far likelier natural disasters.

More important than anything else, though, we shifted the agency's thinking away from simply dealing with a disaster after it's happened to trying to prevent it, or at least to lessen its impact. On the most practical level, disaster management professionals divide their work into four phases: response, recovery, preparedness, and mitigation. Response is the most reactive. Say a tornado tears through a community, wreaking havoc and perhaps death for miles. In the response phase, you go out and look at the situation and see what's needed, from blood supplies to bottled water to shelter (not to mention ministers, psychologists, and financial counselors). Response is crisis management in its most stripped down, most basic, most unimaginative form. It's getting the victims the help they need as fast as you can.

Recovery is returning the victims to some sense of normalcy. That being the case, recovery is as much a goal as it is a process. From the long-range standpoint, recovery will certainly require financial assistance and may necessitate psychological counseling. Short term, it involves everything from debris removal to clothing donations to house rebuilding. I also find that it helps to give people a place to attend church services, even if their house of worship has been blown to kingdom come.

Preparedness is the pivotal step between recovery and prevention. In the case of floods, after a few of them, your experience tells you that another one *is* going to wash over you someday, so you set in place the procedures to follow when that bad day finally arrives. By then you've got a pretty good sense of what you need to be stockpiling—freshwater, say, and sandbags— and what emergency services you need to have on standby. In August 1993, FEMA even took the then-revolutionary step of deploying trucks, crews, and supplies (generators, cots, chainsaws, water, bedding, tents) to Raleigh, North Carolina, in *anticipation* of Hurricane Emily's arrival on the North Carolina coast. Sometimes hurricanes don't follow the routes or schedules the forecasters have mapped out for them, and if Emily had missed North Carolina we would've been criticized for jumping the gun and wasting taxpayers' money. But Emily did hit, and we were heroes because we were prepared.

In the end, though, mitigation—which means to moderate in force or intensity—should be the goal of every crisis manager. Why prepare to clean up more efficiently after a disaster when you can prepare to lessen its effect in the first place? I learned that a long time ago in Yell County, Arkansas, when I was county judge, the official in charge of the roads. We had a big flood that washed away thirty-three of the county's wooden bridges, which put us in quite a fix. When FEMA came to survey the damage, they would only pay us to replace the same kinds of bridges we had. "That's crazy," I said. "Are you telling me that you'd rather replace wooden bridges over and over instead of building bridges that won't wash away?" They wouldn't budge. So we took the money they gave us and raised extra money to build new bridges out of steel and concrete. That was almost twenty years ago. Every one of those bridges is still standing. Mitigation is the ultimate application of common sense to the challenges the world throws our way.

CHOOSING WHICH STORIES to tell in this book wasn't an easy task. I've seen a lot of heroics at places like Northridge, California; Oklahoma City; Xenia, Ohio; and Grand Forks, North Dakota. I've seen individuals surprise themselves with their decisiveness and save their communities in the process. I've seen long feuds healed in the crucible of disaster, and I've seen people find faith when they didn't even know they were missing it. In the end, though, I chose these particular stories because they seemed best to illustrate the lessons I've come to believe are particularly important to managing crisis with courage, with confidence, and with competence, no matter what obstacles lie in our path. I've paired them with a handful of stories from the more familiar terrain of the corporate world, so you can see the power of these principles when the walls aren't literally crumbling around you.

In times of crisis, there's nothing more important than knowing who you are, where you come from, what you believe, and where you're going. That kind of groundedness provides you an internal compass that can't easily be rocked by outside forces, be they the large disasters like an earthquake or a fire; the more "manageable" events such as corporate downsizing, dangerous products, lawsuits, or imploding relationships or business strategies; or even personal events such as divorce or the death of a loved one, which can affect projects and work in a profound way.

Obviously, being true to yourself doesn't necessarily mean going it alone. Far from it. Time and again in the following chapters, you'll see examples of strong people reacting to tough times by relying on others. But if there's a common thread here, I suppose it's a strong sense of self—which inevitably leads to that business of uncommon common sense.

I

PREPARING FOR
CRISIS

1

FIND YOUR ROOTS

Know-how comes from knowing what matters

MALIBU, CALIFORNIA
OCTOBER 1993

For most of his life, David Weil has begun his days gazing at the Pacific Ocean. It's an enviable way to jump-start a morning. "There's something about a view," Weil says. "If you can look out over an unlimited horizon, and complement that with dolphins, whales, morning fog, sunrises, sunsets—if you have that kind of vista to wake up to and to come home to in the evening, it's very serene. It's like a big comforter that you pull on over yourself. Wherever you are, it gives you a feeling of well-being and tranquility."

I don't think I've ever heard a more eloquent testimonial to the soothing effects of life at the shore. It's a life connected to nature, ruled in some essential way by the quiet rhythms of the earth. The often raucous and insistent rhythms of the man-made world ultimately pale in comparison. No wonder so many people have made their homes in places where nature is most unbridled—at the beach, on riverbanks, perched high on mountains or hills with views of verdant valleys or shimmering seas.

David Weil moved to Malibu in the late 1950s, when he was eight. His mother, Carol, had remarried, and David's new stepfather, Matt Rapf, was the producer of such TV shows as *Ben Casey* and, later, *Kojak*. They lived in various houses in what had been known since 1928 as the Malibu Movie Colony, an oceanfront enclave a few miles up the coast from Los Angeles. Besides providing the obvious pleasures for a young surfer like David, this was charmed ground. David rode his bike on the same roads and swam in the same foamy surf that had been christened by such early stars as Clara Bow, Ronald Colman, Harold Lloyd, Gary Cooper, and Barbara Stanwyck; by the '50s and throughout the '60s, David's neighbors had included the likes of Rod Steiger, Paul Newman, Liz Taylor, and Richard Burton. In the earliest days, lots could only be leased, thirty-foot slices going for one dollar per oceanfront foot per month; then, in the late '30s, Malibu lots were offered for sale. From that day to this, the residential area known generally as Malibu has been synonymous in the public's imagination as a playground for movie and music stars and other wealthy personalities from the entertainment world.

But long before the first limo containing the first movie mogul rolled through the gates, this property was considered a very desirable place to live. In 1592, when a Spanish explorer named Juan Rodriguez Cabrillo stopped off for a fresh drink of water, he was stunned by the area's dramatic rise from sea level to mountain vistas—and by the bustling and prosperous towns populated by a healthy and handsome Native American tribe. These were the Chumash Indians, who historians reckon had prospered here for some four thousand years. According to *The Malibu Story,* published by the Malibu Lagoon Museum, the Chumash's main village was nestled at the foot of one of the large canyons, approximately where the Malibu city offices stand today. They called this place Humaliwo, which meant "where the sea sounds loudly." But all through what are now called the Santa Monica Mountains, the Chumash had established pockets of community marked by dome-shaped grass huts. During the day, the women and children ground acorns for mush and kept the home fires burning. As pink evening fell, curls of smoke rising from the huts made a welcome sight for the men returning from a day at sea, their red canoes jam-packed with swordfish, abalone, clams, and pieces of steatite, or soapstone, chinked from quarries on nearby islands and brought home to be shaped into bowls and artwork such as carvings of whales.

The only downside to this idyllic life was that the land the Chumash occupied was designed by nature to burn occasionally in order to begin the regenerative process. "As home to a chaparral ecosystem, the Malibu area hosts one of the most combustible types of brush in existence," wrote *Daily Bruin* staff writer Phillip Carter in 1996. "Chaparral consists of many small, woody plants that are full of oils and are extremely flammable. These plants also tend to occur in very dry climates, and are drought resistant." Citing then-UCLA biologist Jeff Smallwood, Carter wrote, "But the vegetation's most dangerous trait is its tendency to burn every 15 to 45 years in its own reproductive cycle."

When the land burns regularly, as it's supposed to do, there's not enough growth to generate the huge walls of flames—fanned by the bellowslike Santa Ana winds—that the area has seen in recent years. But, said Smallwood, when humans build in these areas, not only do they increase the chance of fires, they disrupt the natural process. Small fires are generally extinguished right away, allowing great quantities of old dry brush to build up. Combine that with the region's high-velocity winds and the north-south-running canyons, and you've got a formula for disaster. "That creates very, very hot fires that also move extremely rapidly," Smallwood told Carter. Yet in those benignly beautiful windows of time between nature's housecleanings, the sparkling sea and the clear blue sky are enough to make even the most cautious of us fall in love.

IN HIS EARLY fifties now, David Weil is managing partner of the elite Los Angeles law firm O'Melveny & Myers, with offices in a Century City skyscraper, right next door to the Century Plaza Hotel. Those who know him well can probably still see some of the young surfer in him. He's trim, owing to his daily morning ritual of jogging along the beach before work. His hair is graying, but full. He seems to be a man not given to small talk, which makes his comments about the soothing aspect of Malibu all the more eloquent. But, then, something that close to the heart couldn't really be considered small talk.

Weil left Malibu in 1968 to go to college, after which he worked a few years before deciding to get a law degree. For that, he moved all the way across the continent, to Washington, D.C. It was at Georgetown Law School that he met his future wife, Annette. She was from New Orleans' Garden District, a close-knit area of fine old homes whose prime views were of Doric columns, pink azaleas, and ghostly streetcars gliding along the boulevard. Annette's law school specialty was corporate securities, and at first she and David thought they would live in Washington. That suited Annette fine. "I was used to a small town," she says. "Los Angeles is not a small town." So in 1980 when David announced that he wanted to go home to California and practice entertainment law, Annette was a bit uneasy about what she was in for.

Annette Weil is Jackie Kennedy thin and elegant in that same unpretentious patrician way. She stopped working as a lawyer when she and David started their family, so on a mild winter Monday in Malibu she's dressed in faded jeans, a white cable-knit sweater, and tennis shoes. Her husband is at work, her two children—sixteen-year-old Derek and fourteen-year-old Holly—are at school, and she's agreed to talk about life in Malibu. And about what happened to that life in October 1993.

Malibu was a surprise to her. "It really has a sense of community," she says. "You can pretend that you're not living in a booming metropolis." The Malibu she's talking about isn't the fabled beachfront Movie Colony. Early on, settlers to the area jumped the Pacific Coast Highway (PCH) and built houses among the peaks and canyons of the Santa Monica Mountains. The houses tend to be close together on lots that dip and slant and rise and fall, and the roads through the neighborhoods are by necessity narrow and winding. Many of the earliest houses are very small, and there is no sewer system—everyone's on septic tanks. Until recently, water pressure was a problem the higher you got up the hill.

On the other hand, the slow twisty roads and the cozy jumble of houses create a distinctive kind of homeyness: not city living, certainly, nor typical suburban sprawl. Mix in views of the sparkling blue Pacific framed by tumbling vines of bright tropical flowers, and you have a place that is as close to the Mediterranean villages of Italy and France as any we have in the United States.

"Our house was built in the 1950s," says Annette, referring to the house the Weils lived in during the 1993 fires, "and there was nothing spectacular about it but the view. The neighborhood was great, though. Our next-door neighbor on one side was a teacher at Santa Monica College, and on the other side was Ali MacGraw. Across the street was a man who worked in a hardware store. I remember one time when my daughter was a baby, she got her leg caught in her crib and we couldn't get it out. I ran across the street and said to him, 'I want you to come quick and bring a saw.' He jumped up and was on his way. Two doors down from Ali was Ashley Judd—this was before she was famous. Holly used to go to her house and bake cookies with her. So it was nice, with all kinds of people."

On the morning of October 26, 1993, David woke up early and went for his run. When he was dressed and leaving for work, he told Annette, "Keep your eyes open." Something about the day, he says now, seemed strange. "The weather conditions were exactly what we've come to associate with fire danger—hot, dry, windy in October, November, December. In the past two or three weeks, there had been very serious fires farther south in Laguna Beach. So there was already a sensitivity to fires throughout southern California."

After David left, Annette drove Derek and Holly—then eight and six— to school in Pacific Palisades, a short distance east of the PCH. That morning she stayed at school, helping Holly's first-grade teacher take the class for an outing in the park. "One of the other mothers said to me, 'You know, there's a fire in Malibu. You should go home.'

"'Nah,' I said. 'There was one last week, too. It's nothing, don't worry about it.'

"'Well, maybe you ought to call somebody and check.'"

The woman's persistence convinced Annette to phone a neighbor. "This lady I called was probably the reason David didn't take this fire seriously at first," says Annette. "When I was in the hospital giving birth to my first child, she called us one morning at five A.M. saying there was a fire on the other side of the mountain and that David better come home. He rushed over but could only get as far as Topanga Canyon Boulevard; after that the streets were blocked off. So he hitchhiked a ride on a fire truck. When he got home, he climbed up on the roof to water down the house with the hose, but the water had been cut off. Still, nothing happened. The fire never came over the hill.

"So this time I called the same neighbor, and she said, 'Yes, absolutely, you have to come home.'"

Annette could almost hear David's eyes rolling when she phoned to tell him what she was doing. "You're crazy," he said. "She's an alarmist. She did this to us before. Why are you bothering?"

Annette's station wagon was the very last vehicle allowed through before emergency crews put up roadblocks. As she negotiated the winding road to their house, she could see the dark smoke cloud emanating from somewhere beyond the ridge. At home, the air was thick and choking. Once inside, she phoned David. "Why are you doing this?" he said. "It'll never come over the mountain."

When they hung up, David sat staring out his seventh-floor office window toward the ocean. It wasn't terribly rare to see smoke rising from the mountains, but this cloud looked unusually menacing. Meanwhile, Annette hurried around the house packing suitcases with clothes, children's photos, and the stuffed animals they slept with. Once the bags were in the car, she carted out an armload of David's suits and threw them across the suitcases. Just as she was about to round up the dog and two cats, the phone rang. It was David, who had phoned the sheriff. "Get out of there!" he shouted.

"I'm not done," Annette said.

"I don't care. *Get out!*"

School was shutting down, so they agreed that David would pick up the kids and they would meet up at a friend's house in Pacific Palisades. Annette finished up as quickly as possible, given the tactical and logistical problems of corralling a couple of cats for a car trip. "One of them, Sparky, doesn't travel well," Annette says with admirable understatement. Finally she got the car loaded and started toward the Palisades, but the road was barricaded. She turned back the other way.

Annette's day deteriorated from there. First, many of the canyon roads were also closed, so the only thing to do was take the PCH to up near Oxnard and then double back on the interstate. About two hours into the trip, the dog, Oreo, threw up on the car seat and the gearshift. Sparky howled, drivers honked, and David—who was watching his neighborhood go up in flames on TV—kept calling Annette and asking where she was and why it was taking her so long.

"When I get there," Annette hissed at him through the cell phone, "I'm getting out of this car and *you're* cleaning it up."

Some five hours after she'd left their house, she pulled into their friends' driveway. By then, the sight of her family, alive and unhurt, made the crazed journey she'd just endured seem perfectly reasonable.

THAT THE WEILS can find something laughable about that day is a testament to their resilience, which is in turn a testament to their values.

I'll never forget my landing in Malibu. It was probably the night of the day the Weils had to evacuate, or maybe a night later. Then-governor Pete Wilson and I flew over the area in a Black Hawk helicopter, sparks from that inferno licking at us from all sides. As our pilot fought to hold steady among the swirling air currents, the sky was blue-black with a raging orange strobe pulsating on the horizon. The lower we got, the better we could see the actual flames starting to come up over the mountain. We put down at Pepperdine University, just west of where the Weils' house was, and for a time we thought we might have to evacuate, too. Then they secured the area and we were able to make that our base.

During that long night, the governor and I heard heartbreaking stories from some homeowners and many firemen. One man told us his house had burned and his children had been given shelter in the home of a family he didn't even know. The firefighters told tales of weary frustration—the fire trucks couldn't maneuver through the narrow mountainside streets, the water pressure was woefully inadequate, the cedar-shake houses so carefully nestled among beautiful but flammable landscaping were doomed to be consumed by flames. The firefighters could only stand by and watch, their fallback goal to prevent the fire from leaping the PCH and igniting the houses on the shore. "A lot of people on the mountain think they cut off the water up here in order to save the Colony," says Annette. "Anyway, that's the rumor."

At about three-thirty A.M., I had just wrapped a *Today* show interview with Bryant Gumbel in the oceanfront parking lot of Duke's restaurant when I got word that CNN was ready for me at their makeshift studio on top of the mountain. We slowly made our way up, and even though I had been in the area for hours, nothing had prepared me for what I saw next. All the houses were gone. All the trees were incinerated. It looked like a picture out of a horror movie. The chimneys were all that remained, smoke slowly circling up around them from the charred ground.

We were still there when the sun started coming up, and the scene only got stranger. Smoke hung heavy on the mountain and in the canyons, and the fire gave everything a sick orange glow. This wasn't the vibrant throbbing energy we'd encountered coming in on the Blackhawk; this was quiet and still and deathlike. This was the aftermath. And I'll never forget, as I was standing there trying to concentrate on making sense of this disaster for CNN's viewers, I caught sight of a stone fireplace chimney with a diamond-shaped cutout in it. Maybe something had once been mounted in that space, or maybe it was just part of some stonemason's design. But while I was talking, the sun began to shine right through that man-made hole, and I felt a chill go down my spine.

IT WAS A couple of days before the Weils could confirm that their house had indeed burned. The only things that survived were their chimney and a swing set in the backyard. In the meantime, they had moved into the Century Plaza Hotel. "Of course the kids loved it," Annette says. "Daddy could walk to work, there were swimming pools all over the place, and across the street were fifteen movie theaters. But the thing they liked best was that the TV had speakers in the bathroom. They didn't want to leave."

It has to be acknowledged that this isn't the usual recovery situation. The Weils aren't typical of the people standing in line to apply for FEMA disaster loans. And yet their personal resources don't in any way negate their trauma or their loss. Disaster, as I've seen time and again, is an equal-opportunity destroyer. It is—no pun intended—a great leveler. And while David and Annette Weil may have been spared the spiraling fears about postevent finances, to me the remarkable thing about them was that they didn't once wring their hands and ask, "Why us?" They didn't moan and wail and play victim. "To us," says Annette, "the important thing was that everybody was safe. Our children were never in any danger. We didn't lose any pets. I managed to get the children's photographs. The rest of it, and I know this sounds trite to say, was just stuff."

The hard truth is, a lot of people pay lip service to that sentiment in the wake of a disaster, but in their heart of hearts they feel like martyrs. The Weils didn't. They actually believed in those corny words about if the family's all right that's all that matters. David does admit to a certain "pain-in-the-butt factor" involved in dealing with the loss of most of their earthly possessions, but everyone experiences that. Often, in fact, it's the practical post-disaster demands that tip some people into personal self-pity.

The Weils' acquaintances couldn't understand their attitude. Their house had been reduced to two feet of ash—the only things they retrieved, from the vicinity of Derek's room, were a scorched penny and some crystallized marbles, which they later had encased in lucite as a memento—and yet they didn't seem devastated. "You know what?" says Annette. "You can burn my house down every day for the rest of my life; and as long as my family's okay, it's fine with me. The hardest part of this was convincing people that it was ultimately no big deal."

One of the first things they did was go to Nordstrom's and buy everyone some clothes. "Nordstrom's was great," says David, marveling at the fact that the store gave them a 50 percent discount. David e-mailed everyone in his office telling them they were okay. "I said I still had some suits, but wasn't sure about socks." He was being funny, but soon "everybody in the office was sending me socks."

"And every day at school, somebody brought old toys for Derek and Holly," says Annette. "We suddenly felt like the latest charity, and we didn't want that. I had a hard time telling people no, because they wouldn't believe me. One day my best friend and I were at the store and we ran into another mother we knew. I was buying, you know, six pairs of shorts and ten T-shirts and twenty pairs of socks and all. This woman said, 'Let me give you Josh's bicycle.'

"'No thank you,' I said. 'When Derek's ready, we'll get him another bike.'

"'How about my china?' she said.

"'No, I really don't need it. . . .'

"And she took my friend aside and said, 'You know, she's in shock. She really doesn't know what she's saying.'"

Annette hastens to add that they weren't insulted, or anything like that. "People wanted to help, but they just didn't know what to do. The offers that mattered, that meant something, were when Derek's oldest friend gave him the teddy bear he'd slept with all his life. Or when the mother of one of Holly's friends gave us her daughter's sheets, which were just like Holly slept on and which I couldn't find anymore. Or when one of the teachers at school offered to baby-sit while David and I went and took care of things."

After a week at the Century Plaza, the Weils moved into a furnished beachfront house that David's mother, a Realtor, had found for them. It didn't suit them, and before long they leased a new house in Malibu, over near Pepperdine. That Christmas they sent out photo holiday cards showing David, Annette, Derek, and Holly smiling—entirely convincingly—before the lonely chimney of their burned house. The greeting was, SEASON'S BEST TO YOU AND YOURS. "We wanted to make a statement," says David: "We're still here." Annette's only regret was that she didn't think of hanging a stocking from their backdrop's scarred stones.

A LITTLE OVER eight years later, you can still see the overgrown remains of foundations, patios, driveways, and, of course, the chimneys that dot the mountainside like tombstones. Conducting a tour of her former neighborhood, Annette tells about a woman whose husband—now her ex—managed to save their house by ignoring the roadblocks and persuading firemen to dump what water they had onto his roof and walls. "He saved their house, but it made things very difficult for her. People would drive by, see all the devastation, and say, 'Why did your house survive and so-and-so's didn't?' Plus it was scary after they divorced, because she was living here all alone in a graveyard."

The fire changed Malibu irrevocably, say the Weils. Elderly residents simply moved away, because they didn't have what David calls "the horizon of time" to deal with the hassles of rebuilding. And neighbors like the schoolteacher and the hardware man—people who bought their small houses very early on, for maybe $25,000—couldn't afford to rebuild. Malibu had simply become too expensive. "So the only people who can live here now," says Annette, "are the ones who can afford to spend a million dollars."

You can tell which houses were built soon after the fire. They tend to be huge modern boxes painted in colors that evoke the Caribbean, or maybe the Italian Riviera. There's a tint of showbiz about them—they're *productions*, brought to you by stellar casts of architects, interior decorators, landscape designers, structural engineers, and—certainly not least—high-powered financial strategists. Sensitive to such ostentation, the officials who dictate Malibu's zoning and standards have closed the window on bright-colored mansions, decreeing that no house be larger than thirty-four hundred square feet and that new structures blend in color with the mountain—so, as Annette puts it, "the people on the beach won't be offended."

There was a brief moment when the Weils considered moving from Malibu, but not for any of the reasons you might suspect. As Derek and Holly got older, their schools would be farther away. David and Annette discussed the growing inconvenience of living so far out—and then said to heck with it. Malibu was home. With that decided, they began planning to rebuild in the same spot as before. They owned two lots, and David's idea was to put up a four-thousand-square-foot house straddling the lots. "The zoning board wouldn't allow it," he says, still baffled, "even though we would have one smaller house, compared to two totaling sixty-eight hundred square feet, with half the cars and half the traffic." Listening to David, you get the feeling that this long-running wrangle ranked high on his postfire "pain-in-the-butt" list.

In the end, they sold their lots and began looking for a place to buy. Annette got her real estate license and went knocking on doors, asking people if they were interested in selling. That's how they bought the house they're in now, a modern white box that cascades down the mountain. Maybe this is a lucky house—it was spared in the big fire of 1993, while the lone chimney of a neighbor stands not thirty yards away.

Such close reminders don't seem to faze the Weils, even after the loss of their house. "You get used to it," says David, meaning you get used to the chance of fires—even the *probability* of fires. Fires are a part of life, and you learn that there are times to fight a fire and times to let it burn and focus on what really matters. And then he tells a story that goes a long way toward explaining such an attitude. "Malibu has always had fires," he says. "When I was a kid, in one of our first houses in the Colony, I had a room that looked out on the mountains, away from the beach. I remember one night in the middle of the night opening my window and seeing the entire hillside in flames. This must've been late fifties, early sixties. To some extent it's just a natural consequence of the weather conditions in southern California, because in the fall when the Santa Ana winds blow, the wind turns around and it blows from the valley over the hills toward the ocean. It's a very hot, dry wind, and it blows very hard. It doesn't take much naturally—or, unfortunately, with arsonists, unnaturally—to start a fire miles away and have it blow right down toward the beach.

"But living close to the beach, we never fear for our lives. We always assume you can walk out on the beach, and, if you had to, you could get in the ocean. And if you have your loved ones and your pets and things around you, you can take care of what matters."

On this Monday in Malibu, with the window-framed ocean sparkling in the sun, Annette tells a story of her own. "In our old house, we had two watercolors of the Malibu coast by a Spanish painter, Ramone Moscardo. One looked up the coast, the other down, and they seemed as though they had been painted from our house, even though they weren't. We had found them in a local gallery, and they were huge—seven feet by ten feet, something like that.

"After the fire, I found myself missing them. We tried to find the artist, but couldn't. Then, a couple of years later, he came back to the area for an exhibition. We bought one of his paintings, an oil of the Spanish coast, and I told him what had happened and asked if we could commission him to paint a painting from where our house used to be. So he came up and did that painting over there."

She points to a shimmering pastel on the wall just off the dining room. "He was wonderful," she says. "We stood out where the house had been, with all the chimneys and foundations between us and the sea. He asked if we wanted the chimneys in it, or did we want houses. 'How about some trees?' he said."

In the end, he produced a painting from the vantage point of just above the house. Ultimately, you don't see much of the house itself. Instead, the picture zeroes in on what's important: In the foreground are two children, a boy and a girl, playing on a backyard swing set. Beyond them the Malibu hills slant down to where a spit of coast slices into the blue Pacific, the late-day sun bathing the world in a veil of pink.

YOU MAY BE thinking, What can the story of a family who lost almost everything they had teach me about preparing my business and myself for crisis? It's a real-life parable, the first of nine that I'm going to tell you in this book, and it really does go to the roots of crisis management. You see, knowing your values—and I mean that both in literal and in figurative ways—is the crucial first step in preparing for a crisis.

The first mistake people often make in responding to a crisis is in trying to fix everything, respond to everything, all at once. Managing a crisis effectively requires decisions. In fact, *crisis* comes from the Greek word for decision, and it helps to think about any crisis that way, as a series of decisions that you have to make quickly, under intense pressure, and with little chance to reflect or research. Whether or not you plan ahead, some things, a project, a relationship, will get lost in the middle of a crisis. Knowing your values is the only way you can ensure that you're the one who is making the decision about what exactly gets lost. And what is too important to sacrifice. Is it your brand reputation? Is it the partnership you've spent years building? Is it the people you've spent years training, developing, mentoring, and managing? Is it the ideas they come up with, or the machines they run, or the people they know? You should know the answer immediately. Not just the big-picture version of the answer, but the way that answer plays out project by project, client by client, product by product, and so on.

They call it triage in medicine, the act of making split-second decisions about the priority of treating one medical case over another one. It's also a group process. There's not just one doctor or emergency medic at a disaster site who is assessing all of the patients. An entire team does it; everyone knows the system of priorities. So once you start to plan for a crisis, by identifying your values and knowing how they will guide your decisions down the road, you have to remember that you can't be the only person making those decisions. Everyone needs to know the values and the plan, inside and out.

I was county judge back in the early 1980s when someone started putting cyanide in bottles of Tylenol in Chicago, and to this day I remember how impressed I was with the way the managers at Johnson & Johnson handled what could've been a disastrous situation for their business. They didn't dillydally, backpedal, stonewall, or spin. They immediately pulled all their product off the shelves, and even—against the advice of their nervous attorneys—from some assembly lines. Their actions quickly became *the* classic business case study of crisis management.

As I've become more enmeshed in management, I've learned that they were able to act so decisively, and with such unity, because of something called the Johnson & Johnson "credo"—their *written* statement of the values the company holds inviolate (mainly, putting the health of their consumers first). That's impressive enough, but consider the following statements by Thomas

Donaldson, director of the Wharton Ethics Program, that appeared as part of an interview in the Wharton business school magazine: "Johnson and Johnson had at the time—as it still does—credo challenge sessions. The company brings managers together a couple of times a year to ask questions about the credo and if they want to change any of the values. Few if any changes are made, but in the process of testing the credo, incredible buy-in occurs."

The clear message is this: Core beliefs, like muscle, respond to exercise.

SOMETIME AFTER SEPTEMBER 11, I read a piece in the *Wall Street Journal* by Howard Paster, CEO of Hill and Knowlton public relations. He ended his article with a line I particularly like: "When the satellite-TV truck is pulling into the corporate parking lot, it is too late to discuss theories of crisis management."

In early 1999, the International Olympic Committee (IOC) was caught up in a scandal involving the acceptance of cash, vacations, and other gifts from organizing committees of cities vying for future Games. Once the spotlight shone on the IOC, it revealed a culture of greed and profligacy, of life as a junket. The IOC had to look deep inside the organization and find ways to communicate their values through new rules and reforms. It's a great example because in this case many of the people they were trying to influence were volunteers or community members of cities that were bidding on the Games, so they weren't all going to go through a performance review. You have to remember that the people you partner with become an extension of your own business and reputation. But just because they aren't on your payroll doesn't mean they can't sacrifice something you value on your behalf.

The IOC's first steps are small, but they go straight to the heart of its mission: To contribute to building a peaceful and better world by educating youth through sport practiced without discrimination of any kind and in the Olympic spirit, which requires mutual understanding with a spirit of friendship, solidarity, and fair play. Doesn't sound like junkets and bribery, does it? Junkets are now forbidden. An outside ethics commission will monitor members—taking the place of the performance reviews a company could use with its employees—keeping a special eye on contributions to regional and national sports associations, who may be hoping to influence votes, rather than building a spirit of fair play. Cities who want to host the Olympic

Games now have to buy into the IOC's mission, and sign contracts outlining ethical rules for contacting members, presenting proposals, and other issues. Active athletes will be recruited to become IOC members, and at least one active athlete will sit on the executive board. The IOC had run so far afield from its values that back in 1999, *Time* magazine reported one American athlete, Bob Ctvrtlik, as saying that "a year ago they would have laughed you out of the room had you suggested an athlete serve on the executive board." It's a reality check when you see that your day-to-day decisions don't fit your values. If a crisis hits, you're looking at the makings of a scandal or a meltdown.

Though the committee ultimately passed these wrenching reforms in time to reestablish the Olympics' reputation prior to the Sydney Summer Games in 2000, I remember thinking that the IOC took the hard way to learn a pretty easy lesson.

It's interesting, though, to see how they found their core values and have started to exercise those muscles—hopefully enough so that the next time the TV truck comes to their parking lot there won't be a scandal brewing. It may seem obvious these days, but the thing that Johnson & Johnson and the IOC both stumbled onto was that ethics, more so than "just" the bottom line, needed to be at the core of their decision making. Making right decisions, in the good or bad sense, was the right decision for their business.

I'm not suggesting that the bottom line isn't important, either generally or to these two organizations. But they chose to communicate their core values to their employees (or volunteers, as is often the case for the IOC) in terms that don't tally up in dollars and cents. It's because their reputations— what you could call the track record of their decision making—are too important to lose. If Johnson & Johnson's name didn't immediately convey safety and health, no amount of flashy packaging, competitive pricing, or even product innovation could keep the business thriving. The decisions that their customers and partners cared about more than anything else weren't, actually, the ones about the cost of a pill. Along the same lines, if the IOC allowed the selection of a city for the Games to be synonymous with backroom negotiations and bribery, that reputation could undermine their deals with corporate sponsors, who underwrite over 30 percent of the cost of each Olympics. (In fact, it nearly did.)

What impressed me about the story of David and Annette Weil in

Malibu was their unshakable conviction about what's important in life. In a crisis such as the one their family endured, that kind of bedrock core belief enabled them to stay centered. Knowing what you believe takes work. Generally speaking, you're not going to be exercising the right muscle group by gorging on sitcoms or blindly chasing the almighty dollar.

And as the case of Johnson & Johnson so elegantly proves, techniques of introspection and self-examination can be incorporated into the life of an organization. At FEMA, before we could outline our strategic plan, we first had to define who we were and what our mission was. In 1993, after much discussion and debate, we agreed that our mission was to "reduce the loss of life and property and protect our institutions from all hazards by leading and supporting the nation in a comprehensive, risk-based emergency management program of mitigation, preparedness, response, and recovery."

This mission marked a new FEMA in three crucial ways: First, just by spelling it out we had done something revolutionary. Before, the agency's mission was so vague that in 1992 when its viability was being challenged, one person interviewed described FEMA as "a check-writing agency, an intelligence agency, a social service agency and insurance agency, with a fire administration thrown in."

Second, we now stated unequivocally that we dealt with *all* hazards, eliminating confusion created by our earlier incarnation as coordinator of the U.S. response to nuclear war. In his report on our results-based management, George Mason University's Jerry Ellig wrote, "One 20-year FEMA veteran said, 'There are people here I've met in the past five or six years that I'd never met before, because they were always locked behind closed doors doing contingency planning.' With the end of the Cold War, the old mission was obsolete."

Finally, the mission statement emphasized reducing loss of life and property, which pretty quickly gets you to preparation—not simply response and recovery—as the overriding theme.

In the end, though, it's all about performance under pressure. Your core values, your core beliefs—they will reveal you in the light of a disastrous day. At FEMA, once we had our mission statement, we outlined the values inherent in that statement, and we made them the backbone of our operation. Those values included customer service, which we emphasized from the top down. Every employee went through mandatory two-day customer-relations training, and after every disaster we conducted surveys with our customers—victims, state and local emergency teams, and other federal and nonprofit agencies. Customer service was a critical factor in all employee performance evaluations. Other values were public stewardship, stressing preparation and prevention projects that made for prudent management of tax dollars; creativity and innovation, especially new, more efficient ways to act on our values; and continuous improvement, focusing on cost reduction and various productivity goals.

In his FEMA study, Ellig wrote, "A clearly stated mission often reveals that an organization must build or acquire new competencies to fully accomplish its goals. . . . FEMA achieved positive results in the 1990s with largely the same career staff it had in the 1980s. 'We knew our jobs,' an employee commented. 'It's just the way we were permitted to implement things that made us look like asses.'"

WHEN NEWLY ELECTED president Bill Clinton was going through his transition period prior to inauguration, Little Rock became for a brief moment something akin to the center of the free world. At least it looked that way to us Arkansans. Every day, people whose faces we'd only seen on TV would show up at the airport and promptly be whisked away to the governor's mansion. They seemed very busy, and mighty important.

In the midst of all this craziness, President-elect Clinton had phoned me at my home in Wildcat Hollow, outside Dardanelle. "James Lee," he said, "do you remember that night in my office when we talked about what you'd want to do if I got elected?" Of course I remembered. He'd been going through some papers when the subject of running for president came up. "I think you'll run and I think you'll win," I told him.

"Do you really?" he said. "What would you like to do if I did?"

"I'd like to be director of FEMA."

"We could really help people, couldn't we," he said.

That was what he was calling about—the transition team needed my résumé and other paperwork for the FEMA appointment.

A few weeks later I got a call from some lawyer, I don't even remember his name. "I'm calling on behalf of President Clinton," he said, "to offer you the position of deputy director of FEMA."

"Is that what the president told you to offer me?" I said.

"That's what the transition team is offering you," he said. I felt my jaw clinch.

"Well, he asked me to apply for the position of director, and that's what I did. If I'm going to move my family to Washington, I want to be responsible for what I do. So if that's what you're offering me, I'm going to have to turn it down."

A couple of nights later, the lawyer called again. "I think we've made a mistake," he said. As I graciously accepted, it occurred to me that being underestimated (which is a whole lot better than being overestimated!) is much easier to take when you know yourself and your own rock-bottom values. That's true every single day, but in a time of crisis, self-knowledge is crucial. Even when it's a personal crisis of confidence, one that's imposed by the prejudgments of the people above and around you.

Finding your roots, the values that are too important to rip out from under your organization, comes first—and long before a crisis hits, if you're going to be successful. Know-how does come from know-why. To build the triage plan your company needs to make decisions and exercise your "core-value muscles" you should:

> • **IDENTIFY, COMMUNICATE, AND PRACTICE YOUR VALUES.** Remember those questions I asked a few pages back, about what your company can't afford to sacrifice? You and everyone in your offices should know exactly what it is that you value, and why and how you value it. What is irreplaceable, expensive to replace or fix, difficult to replace or fix, easy and cheap to replace or fix? This type of seemingly simple priority planning can inform your day-to-day work and long-term strategies even when you aren't in a crisis, but it's when you are in a crisis that the decision tree gets compressed, truncated, and strained. If your workers aren't making decisions based on your company's priorities when things are easy, what's going to happen when sales plummet, a factory gets cut off from your supply chain, a client threatens a lawsuit? And while you may prioritize your values by the bottom line, and build your plans based on it, you should communicate your values in terms that don't require number

crunching on hundreds, if not thousands, of spreadsheets by a staff of accountants; crises don't wait for you to calculate.

• **REASSESS YOUR MISSION STATEMENT, AND WHAT IT MEANS TO INDIVIDUAL PROJECTS, CLIENTS, AND PRODUCTS, ON A REGULAR BASIS.** Your mission statement should be the clearest pointer to your values and an indicator of the decisions the company will make. If you think of it solely as a marketing tool for the outside world, your employees will get the message that your image—which is different from your reputation—is the most valuable thing the company's got. Let advertising and marketing sell your company to your customers and rewrite your mission statement to guide your company's decision making. Decision making creates your reputation, what outsiders expect from you based on your previous actions rather than from your current promises. This isn't a one-time-only performance. Companies, competition, the way you do business, and your values change. When you aren't facing crises, an annual reassessment session of top managers will keep you in good housekeeping; every six months may make more sense when you're expanding or shifting your operations. If you don't control the mission statement for the whole company, write a mission statement for your division, department, or staff.

• **PRACTICE TRIAGE.** Just like emergency workers practice disaster scenarios, sometimes filling a football field or an entire university with victims of hypothetical tornadoes and earthquakes, you can exercise your "core-value muscles" by incorporating a what-if component to your meetings on product development, client relations, and other areas. With each decision, apply a snap test against your values even if you're going through a 360-degree intensive evaluation. If your quick values decision doesn't match your longer process, you should reassess the way you're communicating your values (the mission) and the priorities themselves. Practicing can be something as simple as consciously prioritizing the order in which employees return calls and e-mail messages based on values rather than on how noisy the caller is, how senior the caller is, how long they've sat on the message, or how easy it is to wrap up the question.

• **GIVE YOURSELF REGULAR "KNOW-WHY" PERFORMANCE REVIEWS.** The best way to make exercising your core values an important component in everyone's day is to let them know you're paying attention. Their normal performance reviews should, of course, be tied to the company's mission statement and values. But, either in those reviews or in a separate meeting, talk through specific moments when the person had to make a decision, whether in a crisis situation or a less harried time frame, and what factors went into the decision. In fact, it's often better to dissect a moment when they made a decision that fits your core values, because then the emphasis is on the know-why rather than the know-how. You should also give yourself, as a manager, a performance review on how well you're keeping the core beliefs at the front of people's decision making. When new projects get pitched, are you discussing how and where they fit into your company's priorities? When new clients get signed up, are you doing the same? Reviews are especially useful after a crisis hits, because that's when you start to prepare, and fine-tune, for the next time. Later, when I discuss recovery, I'll talk about the importance of collecting information for new plans. After you've picked up the pieces, review the decisions that got made: Were the decisions consistent with your mission statement and your core values? If so, were they, in retrospect, the right decisions? What got lost, and was it, in fact, replaceable or fixable?

• **GET YOURSELF A TRACTOR.** Once you've got your values in place, it's time to build the know-how around the know-why. What do people need to make these decisions happen? I'm not talking about their knowing exactly what they have authority over, though that's one of the ingredients. A tractor is a tool, and all the decisions in the world aren't going to get a field plowed fast enough—or as fast as possible—unless you've got one. If your top priority is keeping your relationships with all your other clients solid when one of them is making a stink, what resources do you have to have on hand the second the crisis explodes? If your top priority is mending your relationship with your unhappy client, what resources would you need then? Prepare a risk assessment that maps your values to the types of crises that might affect them and then identify the resources you need to have on hand to handle the situation. If you can't afford to sacrifice that project or client, you must find a way to afford the tractors that will help you keep them.

You've got your roots in place, and next you've got to be sure that the furthest branches will be ready to respond to a crisis.

2

MARKET THE STORM

In a crisis, you do what you have to do—but
it's better to do what you planned *to do*

To me, there's something perversely reassuring about a satellite photo of a hurricane. When you're on the ground in the middle of a wet and howling wind, the whole thing is grainy and amorphous, like a bad dream you can't quite get your mind around. But when you step back and study a photograph of the hurricane taken from miles above, you see its recognizable fan-blade shape and its center "eye." That perspective helps me accept the storm as another of nature's endless creations. It also makes for one heck of a compelling marketing image.

Not long ago, my wife, Lea Ellen, and I went to Carolina Beach, North Carolina, to attend a groundbreaking ceremony for the new city hall. The last time I had seen this island was in the fall of 1996, when then-governor Jim Hunt and I conducted a flyover inspecting the damage from Hurricane Fran. Back then, the devastation was astonishing, not just on Carolina Beach, but along Kure Beach to the south and on up to the barrier island beaches of Wrightsville and Topsail. This time, it was good to see Carolina

Beach looking laid-back and loose, the way a beach community is supposed to look.

Yet everywhere we went, the decor of choice seemed to be aerial hurricane photos. In one motel lobby, a portrait of 1999's massive Floyd was the focal point of the room, and commanding attention on a restaurant wall was a poster featuring color-enhanced pictures of six different hurricanes. The motif struck me as a bit odd, considering that beachfront themes usually run to celebrations of sun, sand, and surf.

And then it hit me—we were *succeeding*. About midway through my tenure as FEMA director, it dawned on me that we had to introduce the idea of disaster preparedness and mitigation through a sustained marketing campaign, the way you might sell Gap khakis or Nike shoes. The point was to embed an image in the minds of the consumers. In order to do that, we had to do something revolutionary. We had to *market the storm.*

NEW HANOVER COUNTY in southeastern North Carolina is a 185-square-mile area that takes in Wilmington and the oceanfront beaches around it, including the Pleasure Island communities of Carolina and Kure Beach. Being right on the Atlantic coast, the area has a long and rich history of hurricanes. According to Jay Barnes, author of *North Carolina's Hurricane History,* its first recorded storm was in 1524, when Italian explorer Giovanni da Verrazano found his ship tossed so violently that he named the area Cape of Feare. In the late 1800s, there was a twenty-year period when the region was wracked four times by two major hurricanes in a single season. Some residents, turning inward for answers, were certain that the storms were punishment for their having allowed dancing on Sundays.

In those days before radar and twenty-four-hour weather channels, people often had no idea a hurricane was approaching. Suddenly—or so it seemed—the sky would cloud up, the wind and rain would blow, and the tide would surge over everything that got in its way. "Hundreds of North Carolinians have perished in rapidly rising storm tides," writes Jay Barnes, who tells how "sailors and islanders watched the skies for double moons, sundogs, and the scarlet aura of a summer sunrise. Remember the adage, 'Red sky at morning, sailors take warning, red sky at night, sailors delight . . .'?" Barnes also tells how people monitored animal behaviors as possible warnings for approaching storms. "It's been told that shorebirds gather and live-stock wander in the days preceding a hurricane. Keen observers watched the rhythm of the ocean's swells as another method of predicting incoming cyclones."

Of the ferocious hurricane of 1879 (a man who weathered the storm in a lighthouse measured winds at 168 miles per hour, the highest ever recorded in the state), Barnes tells in his lectures a story he claims documents the first-ever incident of hurricane relief. As the story was recounted by Marty Minchin in the *Wilmington Morning Star,* an elite group of wealthy swells—including the governor of North Carolina—were vacationing together at the ritzy Atlantic Hotel in the South Carolina resort of Beaufort. Seeing that a storm was rising, the hotel's management went around politely knocking on doors to reassure the guests that there was no cause for worry, they experienced coastal storms all the time. Then the waters began invading the hotel's lobby and first floor, and scores of pajama-clad rich people began leaping (most safely) from windows into the flooded streets below. The North Carolina governor, "who made it back to Raleigh wearing a borrowed Army uniform about seven sizes too small and a pair of galoshes, wrote a check and sent it to devastated Beaufort—the first government hurricane relief."

In the twentieth century, the 1950s were a particularly harsh period. Scores of storms hit the area, and in one two-year span New Hanover County was battered by no fewer than seven hurricanes, including the infamous Hazel of 1954. The naming of hurricanes had begun the year before, an effort to manage storm tracking and eliminate confusion in historical reference. Naming also provided another very valuable benefit—it "branded" the storms so that people would have a convenient way of thinking about them. In marketing terms, it gave them a "handle." "Often these storms developed their own personalities," writes Jay Barnes, "which are forever linked to the names they received. This personification of disaster may help us better understand and cope with the emotional scars left by hurricanes."

If the name Hazel makes you think *witch,* you're not far off the mark. Until Fran came along, Hurricane Hazel was considered the greatest natural disaster ever to affect North Carolina. Enhanced by the unhappy coincidence of the storm's striking during October's full moon, the time of the highest lunar tide of the year, Hazel's eighteen-foot storm surge washed over everything in sight. The storm battered virtually the eastern half of the state, leaving nineteen people dead and some two hundred injured.

And then there was a sustained period of relative calm, during which people seemed to forget.

Dan Summers, director of emergency management for New Hanover County, well recalls how ill prepared he was the first time he had to go up against a hurricane. "When I came on board, in 1984, I was a county employee, but my offices were in a city building. When they moved me, the furniture belonged to the city. So I had a desk, no chair, one phone line, and a part-time assistant. A week later, Hurricane Diana hit. It was the first time in twenty-two years that a hurricane had made landfall in New Hanover County. This community had lost all its savvy in dealing with storms. In local government as well as in my industry, we have to fight complacency."

Fortunately or unfortunately, depending on how you look at it, Summers and his team haven't had much opportunity to be complacent lately. Since 1989's powerful Hugo ripped through South Carolina and into the heartland of North Carolina, the eastern United States has endured a dozen years of major storms. "Our county has had six hurricanes in eight years," Summers says. "Emily, Bertha, Fran, Dennis, Bonnie, and Floyd." Meteorologists have predicted that this active period might go a total of twenty years, which means nearly another full decade of violent weather.

TO REACH THE towns of Carolina Beach and Kure Beach, you must first cross the Snows Cut Bridge that links Pleasure Island to the mainland. Civilization, which gravitates to the Atlantic Ocean side of the peninsula, seems to take a more commercial tack in Carolina Beach. I haven't counted, but there appear to be more motels, more condos, more apartment houses there than in Kure. Heading south on Highway 421, which in Carolina Beach is called Lake Park Boulevard, you eventually leave the commercial clutter and enter a stretch of single-family beach homes with manicured lawns. In Kure Beach, Highway 421 becomes South Fort Fisher Boulevard, named for the Civil War–era fortification near the bottom of the peninsula. The commercial center of Kure Beach is small and quiet. Then you pass more nice homes and a series of condos, which quickly gives way, on the ocean side, to a thick stand of wind-bent trees. With their twisted limbs, they look like a dance troupe performing some mad hurricane ballet. After that, there's the North Carolina Aquarium and then Fort Fisher, whose commemorative plaque bears this legend: "The largest earthen coastal fortification in the Confederacy. Original construction commenced May 1861 and continued until December 1864, when the fort came under federal assault. Fort Fisher kept Wilmington open to blockade runners, providing a lifeline of critical supplies for the Confederate armies. The two largest land-sea battles in history until that time took place here, December 24th and 25th and January 13th–15th, 1865, resulting in the fall of the fort."

Some 130 years following that final military battle, a group of civilian generals found themselves engaged in another struggle for the integrity of the island. Just two months before, on July 12, 1996, they had withstood an assault by Hurricane Bertha, whose ninety-two-mph winds and six-foot storm surge had caused an estimated $22 million in damage. And yet, as a report analyzing the emergency response to Bertha put it, "While Bertha was certainly a significant event for New Hanover County, clearly a stronger storm could have been far more damaging, and the county and its municipalities need to continually maintain an awareness of their vulnerability to more severe hurricanes."

Not quite eight weeks later, on the morning of September 4, the National Hurricane Center in Miami issued hurricane warnings for the border between North and South Carolina. Recognizing that New Hanover County was squarely in the bull's-eye depicted by that warning, Dan Summers and his team decided it was time to "go green." They declared a state of emergency and began setting up the emergency operations center, or EOC. "The way Fran was bearing down, we knew it was going to be a big event," Summers says.

The main focus of the EOC, a big conference space across the hall from Summers's office, is a block of many tens of gray modular tables pushed together so that it appears that a battleship is sitting in the middle of the room. By reconfiguring these tables into a giant horseshoe, the space can be quickly converted from a conference room to a command post. "Once we've reformatted the room, we put in telephones and faxes and radios," says Summers. "Then about forty people representing all the public service agencies—police, fire, EMS, health, hospital, highway patrol, Coast Guard, National Guard, emergency management, amateur radio, public information officer, United Way, 911, prisons, Red Cross, Salvation Army, social services— they all come in and take their places around the table, on both sides, with me in the center coordinating the movement of information. It's elbow to elbow, and it gets very crazy very fast. During Hurricane Fran, I was in this room for eleven days."

While the EOC was being set up, Summers pulled together the elected officials of the towns of Wrightsville Beach, Carolina Beach, and Kure Beach. "The way it works, I brief all those elected officials, set the stage, and make recommendations. They give the nod, sign the declaration order, give me other powers and authorities that I need to carry that out. Basically, they approve it, they activate it, and then, Dan, you go handle it." With the necessary powers in hand, Summers ordered an evacuation of the coastal communities to begin that evening at six P.M., with completion by the next morning. That next day—Thursday, September 5—was when the National Hurricane Center was predicting Fran's landfall in New Hanover County.

As the news went out across the airwaves, residents left their offices and jammed the expressways on their way home to pack. But no matter how hard you market the storm, some people either don't get the message, choose to disregard the message, or are unable to heed the message. In New Hanover and surrounding counties, several households ended up ignoring the evacuation order. One was a man we'll call Ken Jones. A restaurateur whose business was doing badly, he was well known to Carolina Beach police. "We used to get a lot of calls with him threatening to commit suicide," says Chief Mark Dunford. As Fran churned out in the Atlantic, Jones elected to weather the storm in his second-story condo on the north end of Carolina Beach.

Another resister had altogether different motives—she wanted to evacuate but waited too late. Fourteen-year-old Nina Blackwell, who lived with her ailing grandparents and her uncle in a Carolina Beach house thirty-five yards from the ocean, somehow wouldn't hear the evacuation order until Thursday morning.

Finally, there was the experience of elderly Georgia Greene, who lived alone in a mobile home near Surf City, a barrier island community just up the coast from Wrightsville Beach in neighboring Pender County. Whether or not Mrs. Greene was able to respond, I'm assuming her county also ordered evacuation. Anything else would've been pure madness.

◆ ◆ ◆

IT MUST BE a lonely feeling to look out your window and watch the loaded-down cars snaking toward the exits while you stay behind monitoring the weather on TV. Beginning Wednesday evening and continuing all through that night, anyone left on the beaches could hardly miss the caravans moving inland. It wasn't just the shoreline residents who fled. "Even in communities far from the coast, hundreds of families went to local shelters for protection from threatening winds and rising water," writes Jay Barnes. "The American Red Cross operated 134 shelters in fifty-one counties, housing 9,426 people on the night of the storm. In all, according to National Weather Service reports, almost a half-million residents in North and South Carolina evacuated during Fran."

Young Nina Blackwell and her family weren't among them. Their evacuation was complicated by the fact that Nina's grandfather was an invalid. Even so, apparently no one in her household had heard about the evacuation order prior to Thursday morning. Nina, whose story was written up in *National Geographic for Kids,* said she woke up that Thursday to what looked like a normal day on Carolina Beach. By midmorning, having gotten the message to leave the coast, she began furiously packing. "She wished her family had called emergency officials about her elderly grandfather, who was blind, ill, and in a wheelchair. The officials could have moved him to a safe place."

But Hurricane Fran was blowing in too fast. Soon the sky over the North Carolina coast had turned dark and ominous. By noon at the EOC in downtown Wilmington, Dan Summers could check off his growing list the fact that the county's Department of Social Services had opened four shelters and that the now-mandatory evacuation had been completed. Also, a few blocks away in the County Building, the Media Center had opened for business, making sure the necessary public information and instructions were disseminated in a timely fashion.

On Carolina Beach, the then-editor of the Pleasure Island newspaper, the *Island Gazette,* had returned from a vacation to find his work cut out for him. Bumming rides through shut-down streets with police and fire officials, Shawn M. Underwood began a compelling stream-of-consciousness narrative of Fran's attack on the island: *"Snows Cut Bridge, it was reported, would stay open as long as it was safely passable. . . . By Thursday most of the structures closest to the ocean had been boarded up and were now wait-ing for the storm. . . . Heavy squalls would blow in, but none of the winds were really sustained. By noon, however, winds were picking up and remain-ing intact, as the outer edge of this huge system began to make landfall. . . ."*

At this point, the storm was still a hundred miles offshore.

All day long the Weather Channel tried to pinpoint the area where Fran would make landfall. Early predictions said it would be near Myrtle Beach, South Carolina, some seventy miles southwest of New Hanover County, but every revision moved the target farther north. *"Shortly after one P.M., Car-olina Power & Light crews were already repairing lines downed in the gust-ing winds, in an apparent attempt to keep pace with the storm. . . . Kure Beach Police had already cordoned off the south end of the town from K Avenue, and wind and rain was gusting in. Huge waves were already batter-ing the remaining pilings of the Kure Pier, and water splashed up onto the foot of K Avenue as waves broke against the bulkhead there. . . ."*

Near the top of the island, Nina Blackwell had realized it was too late to evacuate her grandfather, so the family hunkered down and hoped for the best. *"By two P.M., water was washing over the north end of Carolina Beach, and the tide was still rising. There were small piles of sand where the washover was the most prevalent, and small streams running beneath sev-eral of the oceanfront condominiums and homes on pilings. The sound was angry and churning, and a tarp on the top of Sweetwater Café's second floor had already been shredded by the wind gusts. . . ."*

In midafternoon, cable TV service began failing throughout the island, and soon so did the electricity. Nina Blackwell tried to resuscitate an old portable radio, but the batteries were dead and she had no reserve supply. Fortunately, the phones still worked, so she called a friend in Kure Beach who held the radio up to the phone so she could listen. The Weather Service was still unsure about when Fran would make landfall, but the location was becoming increasingly clear. *"At six P.M., a member of the Carolina Beach Volunteer Fire Department reported that the lake had met the marina, and the police and fire departments had taken on four feet of water. Debris and branches were flying everywhere. . . . The wind was now blowing steadily . . . trees bent almost to the ground."*

Fran made landfall in New Hanover County Thursday night around eight-thirty. Accompanied by 115+-mph winds and torrential rain, the storm pushed a powerful twelve-foot surge of water onto the shore, washing away some houses and cars, and eroding beaches. It was about this time that the police began hearing from Ken Jones, who was panicking in his north-end condo. Floating cars were banging into the outside of his second-floor wall, and he was afraid his building was going to collapse. The police—who had dispatched a couple of officers in a two-and-a-half ton military pickup, only to have them step out into neck-deep water—told Jones they couldn't do anything for him at that point. Frantic, he began phoning the TV stations.

At Nina Blackwell's house on the beach, a wave crashed in through the ocean-side back door. When Nina's grandmother opened the front door to sweep out the water, the dueling forces of wind and sea suspended her in the doorway, half in and half out. As the downstairs began flooding from front and back, Nina and her uncle Jimmy tugged on Nina's grandmother and finally pulled her to safety. But the sea had surrounded the house. Nina and Jimmy had to figure some way to get the old people to the second floor before water filled the downstairs room.

Shawn M. Underwood: *"The eye came ashore around nine P.M. with one last fury of wind and rain, and a still calmness enveloped the island. Intensely humid air blanketed the area, but the rain and wind had stopped for the time being. Reports said the eye came up the Cape Fear River, which put Pleasure Island right in the northeast quadrant of the storm—the worst for both intensity and storm surge. . . . Power lines and trees littered the roads on the backside of the island. Travel was next to impossible with the maze of debris . . . and the deep darkness from a powerless city. . . ."*

Meanwhile, up the coast in Surf City, who knows what private hell Georgia Greene was living through? Friends later reported checking on her by phone at ten P.M. When they called back an hour later, there was no answer.

DAN SUMMERS HAS a videotape taken from his truck on the morning after. Through the windshield we catch a glimpse of a surprisingly sunny sky, but the view is bumpy and jerky as Summers and a TV photographer maneuver through the afflicted area, dodging downed trees and electrical wires, detouring around misplaced automobiles, and slipping on sand-duned roads that an outsider might've easily mistaken for beaches.

Like a pitiless army, the storm had ripped through New Hanover County and marched hard north into a region where so many fleeing coastal residents had gone to seek shelter—the Triangle area of Raleigh, Durham, and Chapel Hill. "Not since Hazel's visit in 1954 had the Raleigh area been subjected to the kind of flooding and wind damage it endured through Fran," writes Jay Barnes. "As the hurricane's collapsing eye approached the region, massive trees tumbled and power lines popped and sizzled. Inside their now-dark homes, almost a million Triangle residents could only sit and listen to the whirling winds outside, waiting fearfully for the next thunderous crash of pine or oak."

After the eye had passed through New Hanover County, the back end of the hurricane had proved to be less organized than the front. Nina Blackwell and her uncle Jimmy had crawled out a downstairs window and up an outside staircase to the second floor, from which they were trying to rig up a rope system to lift Nina's grandparents to safety. Just at that moment the wind stopped. The storm was over.

Back in the EOC now, Dan Summers and his emergency team were operating under a presidential declaration of a major disaster, which made federal resources available throughout the state. This is the moment emergency management prepares for—not the event, but its aftermath. The job is an intense juggling act of information and response, some of it profound in its prosaicness. This is an exercise in deconstructing civilization. What do we need? Ice, drinkable water, portable toilets, temporary showers, hot meals, dry clothes, electrical power, phone hookups, more cots, extra blankets. All this requires communication, coordination, cooperation—the essences of civilization operating in its surface absence.

In the days following Fran's visit, Shawn M. Underwood reported from the violently shifted ground of Pleasure Island: "*A tour of the north end showed destruction on a scale little Bertha could never have imagined. The North Pier was completely gone, and several houses had been moved from their foundations. . . . The lower levels of many were inundated with sand. . . . One house was sitting in the middle of Canal Drive. . . . Though some structures looked intact from the road, if you looked through the front windows you could see the ocean. . . .*"

Dan Summers says that in the long, exhausting days to come, he would order all phones in the EOC turned off for fifteen minutes two or three times a day. He was criticized for this, but the continuing response was only as stable as the people in the EOC. "We had to put the disaster on hold occasionally," Summers says.

Underwood: *"The National Guard rolled into town around one* P.M. . . . *Troops fanned out over the island, from the north end down, and penetrated the backside neighborhoods. . . . Carolina Beach officers, along with those from Charleston, South Carolina, and New Hanover County, were also patrolling with every vehicle they could muster. The north end could only be patrolled with four-wheel drive. Two officers kept an almost constant vigil on ATV four-wheelers. . . ."*

Every few hours, Summers would go around the EOC and encourage people to tell something funny. They began doing an ongoing Letterman act—"Top 10 Ways You Can Tell New Hanover County Is Recovering from Hurricane Fran."

Underwood: *"Curator Paul Barrington, who'd spent the night of the storm at the aquarium, said he watched a four-foot wall of water sweep across the parking lot as the storm surge came ashore. . . . In the wee hours of the morning, around two* A.M., *he went in the water in search of an alligator that had escaped. . . . Paul had to chase down the gator, who had found refuge on a floating piece of debris. . . ."*

Meanwhile, the bill for Hurricane Fran was taking shape: Damaged homes—7,213; estimated cost $190 million. Damaged businesses—711; estimated cost $46 million. Damaged utilities—Bell South: $8 million; CP&L: $95 million. Debris removal—302,257 tons vegetative, 217,257 construction debris: $15.3 million. Forestry value of timber destroyed: $12.5 million. Economic impact on tourism: $150 million.

And, of course, there were the human casualties. No deaths in New Hanover County, but twenty-four throughout North Carolina. This eventually included Georgia Greene, whose Surf City neighbors discovered her mobile home twisted into scrap metal on Friday, September 6. Mrs. Greene wasn't in it. They found her later in the morning clinging, as she had all during that unspeakable storm, to a mattress floating in a marsh. She was rushed to a hospital in Wilmington, where she died the next day.

SPRINGTIME ON PLEASURE Island. On any given weekend, you can find fun things to occupy your time—the Azalea Garden Tour, the Fireman

Barbeque, the Clyde Beatty Circus, the Walk of Art, the Pleasure Island Chowder Cook-Off. The *Island Gazette* is filled with photos of T-ball, softball, and baseball teams, all posed like team pictures immemorial—one knee on the turf, well-oiled glove folded over, curved bills shading eyes squinty in the sun. Endless summer. Pages and pages of Realty ads beckon—"Vacation all year round! Beautiful views of ocean from your front deck. This immaculate home is waiting for you!"

Before he retired as director of the National Hurricane Center in Miami, Max Mayfield participated in the FEMA history project, a collection of interviews with people connected with the disaster business. When asked what he would tell people about hurricanes, this is what Mayfield said: "I would say that we have a bigger hurricane problem now than we've ever had before. . . . With the development that we've had along the Gulf and Atlantic coasts, we have more people at risk than ever. Not only do we have more people, we have nicer and more expensive homes. So the damage from hurricanes is going to continue to go up. What I'm really afraid of is that we are already building toward a real catastrophe here, and people really need to understand that hurricane threat. They need to know their vulnerability to a hurricane. They need to know exactly what to do before the hurricane gets here. . . ."

Fifteen months after Fran hit, FEMA named New Hanover County one of seven pilot communities in Project Impact, a program designed to break the damage-repair, damage-repair cycle and instead help communities become "disaster resistant." Under terms of the agreement, FEMA provided some $1 million in seed money for efforts aimed at reducing the potential damage from disasters.

"What it did," says Dan Summers, "is it gave emergency management a trademark. While we were struggling along trying to do things for disaster prevention and mitigation, Project Impact was the booster shot we needed to get in front of the right folks in Congress, the right elected officials. We took the funds FEMA made available and leveraged them, allowing us to put on the world's largest hurricane preparedness expo three years in a row. On a Saturday in June, we had ten thousand people show up to get hurricane information and talk with experts. We have a group of senior citizens that go into the schools and put on skits about hurricane preparedness. They're hilarious. Under Project Impact, we have computer technology we never had before. We have generator transfer switches at all of our shelters so that we can run our shelters a hundred percent under generator power. Instead of rewiring the building, we just plug and play. We have school buildings that are better reinforced. We taught architects and engineers more about wind-load construction, so as a result of Project Impact, our local architects and engineers have a better skill set. We did dozens of projects like that."

When Lea Ellen and I were in Carolina Beach last fall, enjoying a sandwich under a poster of Hurricane Floyd, I remembered a funny story Dan Summers had told me. "We learned the hard way how to deal with the TV networks," he said. "They like to set us up, and we've gotten more savvy about that. During Floyd, a production team for the one of the major morning shows had been tracking the storm all the way up the coast. One of their guys called and wanted us to meet them at the pool deck at the Hilton and do an interview before the storm made the last turn. The production crew, their eyes looked like road maps. They had been up all night, and they were whupped. And they were looking for something big."

They sat Dan down and told him they were doing a piece on shelter conditions, and they wanted his take on them. "I said, well, there are some difficulties. But on the other hand, we don't have a loss of life, we don't have structural failure. No, not everybody got a cot, but those who were elderly did, and we've got more supplies coming. I didn't paint a rosy picture, but a survival picture. Which I thought was fair."

They said, okay, thanks, went to a commercial, and then pulled what they labeled "The Happy Family." "They got this rough-looking guy in and said, 'So how bad were the conditions at the shelter, and how did your kids possibly survive, and were there enough Red Cross workers, and was the county adequately supporting this?"

The man thought for a moment. Dan glared at the monitor, waiting for the inevitable. "Well," the man said finally, "I have to be honest with you. It's a little scary, and the sandwiches last night were a little cold." Short pause. *"But we had the best ham and eggs for breakfast this morning, and biscuits and juice and coffee!"*

The Happy Family kept on. "We were a little nervous at first," the man said, "but, you know, everybody was really *nice*! They just tried to *take care of us!*"

They finished the interview; the producer flung her clipboard across the set and looked squarely at Dan. "You people," she said, practically spitting the words at him, "run the most boring disaster I've ever seen!"

AS NEW HANOVER County's Dan Summers has demonstrated time and again, honest communication is the lifeblood of crisis management. Whether you're one person in trouble or a corporation of thousands, the process boils down to this: First, communicate with yourself. Then communicate with others who can help you.

That's not as simple as it sounds. Take communication with yourself, for example. Most of us, at one time or another, have tried to pull the wool over our own eyes—usually when the alternative is to see clearly how excruciatingly culpable we are in the crisis at hand. If you don't admit to yourself (individually or as an organization) exactly what the problem is, your chances of solving it are greatly diminished.

I think those people who continually try to deceive themselves must come out of an environment in which blame is a blood sport. If you have a stern and unbending father and a congenitally disapproving mother (for whatever their reasons), you're not going to feel very free to admit you made a mistake. People like that learn as children to point the finger elsewhere when something goes wrong. Eventually they grow up to work in business (with a stern and unbending CEO and a congenitally disapproving COO), and the only thing different is the French cuff on the pointing hand.

As you'll see in other chapters, when I got to FEMA, creating an open and forgiving work environment was one of the first things on my agenda. There's a lot of intentional indirection and obliqueness and obfuscation in government, especially the federal government, and I wanted to change that. Just after I was confirmed, I traveled to Miami to survey the lingering situation created by Hurricane Andrew. This was eight or nine months later and people were still living in a tent city, which nobody wanted me to see. I'm talking about federal, state, and local officials who, I suppose, thought that if they did something to better these victims' situation, the people wouldn't want to try to get back on their own. Anyway, they tried every way possible to keep me from going in there. But I went, and it was disgusting.

When it rained, the kids would get terribly sick. There are a lot of government officials who don't want to see such things, because then it turns into a complex issue: What do you do—something, or nothing? If you do something, how does that affect your career? If you do nothing, how does that affect your sleep at night? I closed down the tent city and brought in FEMA trailers for the people to live in. It wasn't a perfect solution, but it was the most humane one I could come up with.

If you want people to be straight with you, then you have to make it clear—top to bottom, inside out—that that's really what you want. My goal at FEMA was to improve communications in five key areas—with Congress, with state and local governments, with agency employees, with disaster victims, and with the news media. I've talked elsewhere about how we went about opening up communications within the agency. With Congress, as soon as I took office I began a series of meetings with the chairs of all twenty-six committees that had a stake in FEMA, as well as with every member of Congress whose state was affected by the 1993 floods. When there was a disaster in the making, I got on the phone and told the appropriate member of Congress what FEMA could do for his state if they needed us. This communication continued all the way to the staff level, with congressional staffers regularly invited to various of our briefings, and during disasters, with our staff phoning congressional staffers with updates. As Jerry Ellig of George Mason University wrote in his study of our results-based management, "The overall goal is to proactively convey useful information to Congress in a way that advances FEMA's mission, rather than simply responding to congressional requests or deflecting attention altogether."

As for state and local governments, we found that some of FEMA's most spectacular failures had been due to a lack of communication: During major disasters, state and local officials had expected the agency to simply move in and take charge; and when the agency didn't hear from them through a formal disaster declaration, it was assumed that they didn't need FEMA's help. The result was a competence gap that hurt disaster victims and made FEMA look like—well, like bureaucratic jackasses, as Senator Hollings said. To fix things, we instituted intense grassroots interaction among us and our state and local counterparts, we made sure our regional directors got to know governors and their staffs, and we were on the phone with them making a plan even before any disaster was formally declared. For me, as a former state and local official, this was one of the most rewarding facets of our communications strategy.

Except, of course, for our dealings with the victims themselves. After I got to the agency, we chose a large group of disaster victims and surveyed them about how FEMA had performed—the application service, our sensitivity, and so on. In addition to the changes we knew to make without asking (for example, reducing the time between application and relief check from months to days, if not hours), we listened to the victims and made adjustments to our process accordingly, and I wrote them a letter telling them so. One of our most effective communication tools was a newsletter called *Recovery Times.* It had been just a small sliver of a thing, but we really pumped it up. During the Midwest floods, *USA Today* helped us print and distribute it wherever their paper was sold. *Recovery Times* worked because it got real disaster information out in a hurry. It wasn't just some little mimeographed sheet of paper with announcements like "Food station open from 8 to 4." It had clip-and-save phone numbers for everybody from insurance companies to the health department to the IRS and FEMA. But it also gave tips on what you should and shouldn't try to salvage if you're rebuilding. It told people how to store and preserve their family photographs and other heirlooms. And it took the tack of, Now that you've got your house back together, what can you do to mitigate against a future flood in your home? So it was part current information, part preparedness, and part mitigation.

OUR EXPERIENCES INSIDE and outside FEMA can apply just as well to other organizations. For any group, the point is to open up and interact. Quit thinking about making mistakes or attaching blame. Simply fix your eye on what you're trying to accomplish and talk openly and often with those who can help you get the job done—your spouse, your children, your friends, your neighbors, your employees, your colleagues, your suppliers, your board of directors, your customers. And, of course, yourself.

Communication, when it's working, can help you know when a crisis is coming—sometimes early enough to prevent it. Take the example of General Motors Corporation, that watched with the rest of us as their competitor Ford Motor Company and the tire maker Bridgestone/Firestone were caught up in a massive product recall and public relations disaster. GM already had in place a stringent monitoring program for testing the performance of tires in the real world, one that had a system of early-warning flags for identifying defects and poor performance. They had also been the first in the auto industry to cover tires in their limited warranties. While that made it easy for consumers to make complaints and get replacement tires, it also gave GM a wealth of data about tires that had made it through its tire and wheel laboratory. When car buyers were having problems with their tires, GM dealers—rather than the owners' local garage—were more likely to hear about it and could pass it on to the corporate headquarters.

Having your hands on that type of information gives you a heads-up on problems before they get to crisis levels. GM was also able to insulate itself from Ford's crisis because it knew how Bridgestone/Firestone tires were performing on their vehicles. Early on, GM discovered that a small number of their cars might suffer from the same defect as the tires supplied to Ford. They knew, according to Brooke Lindbert, the director of the company's Tire and Wheel Systems, because their "warranty system caused dealers to return three tires to GM, which we then sent to Firestone for further analysis. It was the examination of these three tires, together with other Firestone data that helped Firestone in its analysis and conclusion that there should be a recall." GM's recall affected fewer than 5,000 car owners; Ford was eventually forced to recall more than 21 million tires and pay $1 billion to car owners who won a class-action lawsuit against the company. That's the difference an early warning system can make.

The media, though—now *that's* a communication subject all its own. I've seen corporations go about their everyday work doing most everything right, then a crisis hits, reporters come knocking, and these perfectly upstanding corporate managers clam up and hide out like children who messed up the living room.

We live in an age when reputations can be made or lost by the simple act of appearing before a TV camera. That's power. My feeling is, use that power to further your own mission. When I was at FEMA, I read a story about a database software company called Sybase. In 1997, the company was riding high, having turned the previous year's $70 million loss into a $15 million profit. But just before CEO Mitchell Kertzman and his management team were able to bask in the public announcement of the good news, word came from abroad that a handful of employees in Japan had inflated sales figures that now needed to be drastically restated. The bottom line was, Sybase now had a $55 million *loss* for the year.

I love the Sybase case study write-up in *Reputation Management:* "The lawyers, like lawyers everywhere, were against it. Keep your heads down, they advised. Lay low. Say as little as possible. There will be lawsuits. Remember that anything you do say will be taken down and used in evidence against you. There's no law that says you have to be open with and honest with the media, or with the public."

Fortunately, CEO Kertzman didn't take his lawyers' advice. "He knew the lawsuits would come regardless of whether he opened up or clammed up. He wanted to make sure the company's shareholders—and other key stakeholders—understood that Sybase was handling its crisis with absolute integrity. He wanted employees to know that an isolated, if costly, incident on the other side of the world was no reflection on them. . . ."

To that end, Kertzman did something truly gutsy. Not only did he make himself available to analysts, shareholders, and the media, he even invited *San Francisco Chronicle* reporter Jon Swartz to spend a day with him as Kertzman and Sybase's chief financial officer worked on the crisis. During that day, Kertzman had tough conference calls with both analysts and the media, and Swartz sat in the background taking notes. One media caller asked Kertzman what effect this situation would have on the company's reputation. "We won't be making any T-shirts about it," Kertzman said.

A commitment to telling the truth and a touch of self-deprecating humor—this is always a good recipe for media relations. Reporter Swartz listened and watched and wrote a story that was kind to Sybase. It depicted a company up against the wall but determined to do right.

I don't know why more managers don't understand that the media doesn't have to be an adversary—it *can* be an ally. During the Northridge earthquake, we took newspaper reporters and a *60 Minutes* crew with us, letting them into meetings that traditionally they had been kept out of. Here we are in a huge disaster, the first tense meeting between the state and federal officials, and the state director asks my public affairs guy, "Who are all these people in here?"

"They're reporters," said Morrie.

"Well, get 'em out of here!" the state guy said.

To which Morrie explained that we wanted them there to see and hear how we do our work and what we're up against. "If there's something you don't want to say with them there, then don't say it. But we have nothing to hide." *Sixty Minutes* did an incredible piece. The *Washington Post* did a great piece. *People* magazine did a terrific piece. And that led to other great and positive pieces, and eventually those became a drumbeat. And that drumbeat put FEMA in a good light, which made people on Capitol Hill take notice, which greased the wheels for some of the things we desperately needed, which in turn went to help the victims of disasters, which led to other positive press.

Communication isn't always marketing, but marketing is always communication. And by aggressively "marketing the storms" at FEMA, we raised the public's level of awareness and elevated the public dialogue about disaster and the crisis management goals of preparedness and mitigation. In that way, the media was our invaluable ally in saving American lives.

In summary, then, here are the points to communicate about communication:

- **COMMUNICATION BEGINS AT HOME, SELF TO SELF.** If you're lying to yourself about how bad things are, or about how bad things could get, your employees will do the same. Marketing the storm means getting people accustomed to a state of crisis preparedness, so they're not taken off guard. When you're drawing up crisis prevention plans, delve deep into your greatest fears. It's a great exercise for getting yourself into a crisis-alert mind-set, but it's a useful exercise, too. I've seen disasters take a turn for the worse because one person or one team took on too much, and hadn't imagined a situation in which most or all of the worst-case scenarios happened at once. Set limits for what you can do in a crisis. Let others know your limits, and get them to set their own. If you find that when you add it all up you don't have enough resources, you'll have to refigure your plans.
- **COMMUNICATION IS MORE THAN JUST TALKING—IT'S THE HONEST AND OPEN EXCHANGE OF PERSONAL VIEWS.** Let others know you speak the truth and want to hear the truth. Step one is making it clear that communicating in a crisis isn't a matter of choice, it's a requirement. The biggest obstacle to

truth-telling is the fear of having the truth come around and get you fired once the dust settles. Performance evaluations shouldn't be a choke-hold on good, honest communication. You can set the standard for honest exchange by pointing to times when a report that a project was in jeopardy, a crisis was looming, or a response plan was short-circuiting turned a bad situation around. You can set an even higher standard by rewarding people for making those reports. Ask people to offer up ideas for how you and they might fail in a crunch, even if they think your crisis plan is foolproof. Then rework your plan to beat those ideas. Once they've gotten comfortable playing the hypothetical devil's advocate and seen that you really don't want someone who will applaud the status quo, you'll be well on the way to sparking honest and open exchanges. Don't let a crisis stop them.

• **CREATE A ROCK-SOLID COMMUNICATION INFRASTRUCTURE.** Don't leave communication entirely up to people's memory. You know you're in a tough spot when the TV networks seem to know everything faster than you or your people do. Unfortunately, that can often happen in a crisis. Why? In a crisis, people forget who, what, when, how, and why they're supposed to tell someone else just about everything: a problem that they're busy trying to fix or one that they've conquered, a threat that they can imagine down the road but seems unlikely and unimportant compared to the immediate messes in their laps, even the information that they usually report like clockwork every day and that can give you advance warning of a resource crunch or a meltdown in your plans. You can't rely on memory in a crisis. I find that the best communication plans go in both directions and work on a timeline. Updates should be due at regular intervals, regardless of progress. They should be quick to provide, and that means forget about the etiquette of business memorandums and the premium on complete sentences and perfect spelling. Employees should have a series of specific questions to answer, including a chance to offer up their one-word or one-paragraph assessment of whether the plan needs to be changed (or if they've already done so on their own). What should they be reporting? The order of their priorities, what resources they need and don't have, where they are on a line between crisis and crisis resolution, what obstacles they've encountered and see coming along the way.

• **DON'T WAIT FOR OTHERS TO COMMUNICATE.** In addition to having employees supply information, managers should ask for quick, informal reports from employees who may be caught up in responding to a crisis—or sometimes, waiting for you to tell them what to do. What's the fastest, easiest way for people to share information? It may be your company e-mail, but you need to have a plan in place that gets to people who aren't sitting in front of their computers (not always the best place to be in a crisis) or that gets to them when the e-mail's down. Identify a manager or information coordinator for each employee or team; the coordinators for all the teams—if you have more than one working at a time—should know long before the crisis how to reach one another to share information and revise your crisis response if you need to. This goes for communication outside your department and your company, too.

• **MAKE EARLY-WARNING ALERTS PART OF YOUR COMMUNICATION SYSTEM.** People often make the mistake of thinking that the rules of crisis communication only apply once the storm hits. There's a reason why we have a system of watches and warnings for storms. Those alerts get people ready. Since something like three-quarters of business crises—at least the ones that make the news—start off small, according to the Institute for Crisis Management, early-warning flags can make a big difference. Unfortunately, it seems that the sorts of crisis that can hit businesses, like the recent recession for one, come on suddenly these days. One way for getting early flags is to keep people on continuous watch, rewarding them for early reports of how their own work is going off course rather than chastising them for falling behind. Another way to handle it is to analyze information about potential crises the same way you'd analyze information about how effective your regular marketing is. You should know if complaints from clients or consumers or employees are on the rise, if delays or crunches are becoming more frequent whether or not they make a difference to the end-buyer, if sales in other industries are on a slope downward, if your competitors are outpacing you, or if your suppliers or partners are having difficulties with other companies. And your employees should know exactly what you consider to be a possible crisis so they can be on the lookout for you.

• **LET THE MEDIA BE YOUR MARKETING ALLY.** It's funny how companies and the government tend to think of the media only as the enemy. Even when they're trying to use the media, they call it spin-doctoring, as though they've got to heal a TV or newspaper scratch before it becomes infected. But there's nothing better than the media for getting out a story. Take a lesson from Sybase and find out, before a crisis hits, which reporters are most likely to find interest in the behind-the-scenes action of putting a crisis down or the success story that comes out of your crisis. Find time to pitch your crisis prevention plan—not just the possibility of a crisis—to the media and "market the storm" to the biggest possible audience. You'll be telling your employees and your community just how real and how serious you consider the threat, whether it's a turndown in sales or the collapse of your major partners. What if the TV networks *do* seem to know everything faster than you do? Gather up their information and use it. Thank them for it. Find out where they're getting their information and tap the sources since they're good ones. If an employee is the source, find out if the breakdown is one of communication—you're just not getting the information fast enough—or of morale—you're just not getting the information—and work with the employee to find a solution. In either case, it's your job to make sure everyone and everything is working to get the crisis under control.

Now, it's time to see how these tools get put into action when you're trying to prevent, respond to, and recover from a crisis.

II

PREVENTING
CRISIS

3

A RIVER'S GONNA GO
WHERE A RIVER'S GONNA GO

Sooner or later, you have to take responsibility for your own life

PATTONSBURG, MISSOURI
JULY AND AUGUST 1993

For 160 years, eight full generations, they wrestled with the alternate blessing and curse of their birthplace. Water, in all its fickle moods, was the dom-
inant theme in their lives, from the amiable ripples that powered mills and
transported goods, to the suddenly raging currents that exacted insanely
high fees for its services. Had they known at the beginning what they know
now, the city fathers of Pattonsburg, Missouri, might well have named their
town Jekyll and Hyde.

The saga began in Virginia in the early years of the nineteenth century. A
restless cabinetmaker named Matthew Patton had caught the bug of adven-
ture, a condition nigh to an epidemic in those days. Patton, with his wife,
Polly, in tow, had first moved to Ohio, then Indiana, territories known as the
Far West. But they weren't far enough west for Patton. In 1835, he and Polly
pulled up on the banks of what is now Big Creek, a picturesque stream in
western Missouri that feeds into the Grand River a few miles to the south.
This seemed to Patton a perfect spot for a business venture. Soon he was

joined by his younger brother William, and together they built a saw- and grist mill.

Three years later the water took its first casualty. A family traveling west stopped for the night at Big Creek, and in the evening the mother went to the stream to wash clothes. When she returned to their covered wagon, she found that her three-year-old daughter was missing. Footprints led to the water's edge, and the next day the child's body was recovered. Until then, the Patton enclave had had no use for a cemetery. Now they did, and a man named O'Keefe volunteered a piece of his ground overlooking the Pattons' mill. In time, he donated three acres there to the community. That's still where Pattonsburg's own are laid to rest.

With business booming, in 1843 the Patton brothers platted out a town roughly between Big Creek and the cemetery. With a community growing, they decided they also needed a bridge across Big Creek. It washed away before being finished, and for a long time they didn't try another one. Instead, travelers needing to cross the creek forded the stream at the point where the bridge had been planned.

In 1844, the area was hit by the worst flood anyone there had ever seen. The Grand River, described by early trappers as "a clear, cool stream abounding with fish," had changed with the coming of agriculture. As forest gave way to crops, and as more and more topsoil washed away, the river often became a rushing muddy mess, each flood more intense than the one before.

The 1844 flood destroyed the Patton mill. The Pattons didn't rebuild, but a man named David Groomer stepped in to fill the void. Groomer dreamed big. Not for his mill a mere creek; he planned to locate two and a half miles south, on the Grand itself. While building was in progress, the riverbank caved in and killed three workers. Groomer tried again and eventually established a grist mill on the east side of the Grand and a sawmill on the west.

THE COMING OF the railroad threatened to turn Pattonsburg into a permanent backwater, but the city fathers were determined to meet this modern dilemma head-on. The township got together and decided to pledge $20,000 in stock to the Omaha and Chillicothe railroad with the stipulation that the tracks would run through the center of Pattonsburg and the town would become a stop on the railroad line. Railroad building and town building don't always proceed according to the same principles. The O & C Railroad searched out the flattest route it could find, which meant it bypassed Pattonsburg by about a mile and a half. It ran instead through a low area dotted with elm trees. Naturally, the leaders of Pattonsburg refused to pay, and a lawsuit was settled in their favor.

But the $20,000 pledge was one thing, the future of the town quite another. The train station was named Elm Flat, and over time the merchants of Pattonsburg began moving to be near the railroad. Never mind that this bottomland was considered intrinsically undesirable for anything but farming. The growing signs of commerce outweighed any geographical argument. And besides, it wasn't as though they were settling right on the water-soaked banks of the Grand, or of the Big or Sampson Creeks. The Grand River flowed a whole mile and a half to the south, Big Creek a full mile north, and Sampson Creek almost a mile west.

Soon hotels were springing up downtown—the Cottonwood House, the Valley House, the Cottage House. Also, there was a booming railroad tie business, which employed some one hundred men. But it wasn't long before the old problem resurfaced. Henry Hatch, one of the operators of the railroad, noted in his memoirs, "We made money all the time until the June freshets of that year [1876], then we had washouts galore. . . ."

By 1877, an article in a nearby newspaper indicated that the old town of Pattonsburg was no longer. That November 15, the post office at Elm Flat became the post office of the new town of Pattonsburg. The little burg that had nestled itself into a low spot between three bodies of water now had two dry-goods stores, two drugstores, one saw mill, a blacksmith shop, two hotels, and fifty-five homes. The blacksmith John Casebolt was the town's first mayor.

In 1881, a locally owned newspaper, *The Pattonsburg Call,* began trumpeting the town's progress to the wider world. The paper made the case that Pattonsburg was second only to St. Joseph as a shipping point in northwest Missouri, with sixteen trains stopping at the Pattonsburg depot in any twenty-four-hour period. One article told of the time the railroad couldn't keep pace with area production, which resulted in "small mountains of wheat" piled on Main Street waiting for boxcars to become available. By 1898, a second railroad, the Quincy, Omaha, and Kansas City, began coming through town. In 1896, Pattonsburg boasted a chair factory, the John Mead flour mill, the Killough cigar factory, several attorneys, a handful of surgeons, butchers, shoemakers, druggists, milliners, barbers, and bankers. There were Baptist, Methodist, and Christian churches, and several lodges where the town's powerful could gather after the business day had ended.

But even the power brokers couldn't change the nature of the course they had embarked on. "The first flood of any note after the town moved to the new location occurred in 1882," declared a 1977 centennial edition newspaper story. "A ferry used on Grand River at Groomer's mill was able to run through the main street of the town."

SMALL AMERICAN TOWNS inevitably seem to breed a boosterish can-do spirit that keeps eyes trained on the future instead of the past. It's a wonderful thing to be part of. When I was county judge of Yell County, Arkansas, in the town of Dardanelle, our enthusiasm spilled out in any number of ways, from hog competition at the county fair to Friday night football and Saturday afternoon baseball games.

I can just imagine how exciting it felt to live in Pattonsburg at the beginning of the twentieth century. It was a town on the move, one whose prosperity by 1906 had even caught the eye of the hatchet-wielding anti-alcohol crusader Carry Nation. Where business is good, there's likely to be the clinking of glasses and the lighting of cigars. They were strivers, and if they were intemperate in their pursuit of the American dream, who can blame them? They didn't set out to build a flawed future in the flats, but that's where progress led them. What's the old saying? "Life is what happens while you're making other plans."

By 1909, though, life was catching up to those plans. The following is from the Gallatin (Missouri) Democrat, July 15, 1909: "The receding flood waters in Daviess county show a scene of desolation and wreckage that is appalling. . . . The flood came, a seething, boiling, roaring mountain of water that swept fertile fields and devastated growing crops and happy homes."

Pattonsburg suffered the greatest damage of any community in the county.

On July 6, word came that the Big and Sampson Creeks, and the Grand River, were rising at an alarming rate. The town's mayor, R. E. Maupin, called together some thirty men, and they set about to riprapping, or stacking stones, on the town's dike, which was essentially a stretch of ground packed high to accommodate one of the early railroad tracks. But the water was rising too fast, approximately fourteen inches in a twenty-minute period. When the rate hit an inch a minute, the men gave up and ran for safety.

That night many people slept in trees. When they opened their eyes in the morning, their world was awash with logs and parts of houses and decaying animals. The water was said to be as high as a horse's back.

THERE IS NO disaster more devastating than a flood. With a tornado, an earthquake, or a fire, you know pretty quickly what you've lost, what you have left, and what you need to do to get back to normal. A flood fills a house—or a town—in no time, but it takes days or weeks to empty out. In the meantime, you cling to hope that you might preserve some of your useful goods or treasured memories. But as you wait, and wait, the hope inevitably fades. A flood saps your spirit in dribs and drabs.

The flood of 1909 was the worst Pattonsburg had ever lived through. But once again, the community pulled itself together, organizing committees for cleanup, disinfectant, provisions, manual labor, and so on. But major flood waters ravaged Pattonsburg again in 1947, 1951, and 1973.

Each time, the town reinvented itself into a thriving example of wholesome, small-town America. In the early 1920s, the population reached some one thousand citizens. In 1928, Pattonsburg was selected to be the site of an emergency landing field for the first airmail route between Chicago and Kansas City. In 1930, U.S. Highway 69 was built through the town, bringing with it bus routes and increased trade. In 1936 a tomato cannery opened, producing a brand known as Pattonsburg's Best. During the Depression, roads were graveled and a post office was built by the WPA. In 1947, the town premiered its first lighted baseball field, celebrating the occasion by beating neighboring Hamilton 4–1. In that same year, the Pattonsburg Manufacturing Company opened for business, making this scrappy town in northwest Missouri the baseball-cap capital of America.

◆ ◆ ◆

FLASH FORWARD NOW to the summer of 1993. For four unbelievable months the American Midwest had been inundated by heavy rains, causing swollen rivers to first creep and then storm over their banks. The ground was soaked to capacity, and there was nowhere for the water to go but up. As the newly confirmed director of FEMA, I had visited all nine of the affected states—Minnesota, Wisconsin, Iowa, Illinois, Missouri, Nebraska, North Dakota, South Dakota, and Kansas—but my most indelible memory of that time is of viewing the entire Midwest from the air. What I saw was the sixth and greatest of all the Great Lakes. Millions of acres were underwater, seventy-six hundred houses had been damaged or destroyed, five hundred counties declared disaster areas, tens of thousands of people evacuated from their homes in the floodplains. Most of the affected had no flood insurance. It was a disaster of monumental proportions, and I remember thinking that somehow we had gotten off track in this country. From the Atlantic to the Pacific, and in all the great sprawling land in between, we had insisted on overdeveloping our floodplains and our coastlines, paving over so much of our country that excess water had nowhere to go. And now the government had to bail us out. I was certainly concerned, and maybe somewhere inside me I was a little angry, too. When a reporter asked me about the wisdom of building homes in a floodplain, I said, "Well, a river's gonna go where a river's gonna go." I also said that when considering new development, we'd do well to develop considerably more respect for nature.

At that point, I had never heard of Pattonsburg, Missouri, one little town among thousands that were suffering mightily that summer. By then the town's population had dwindled to around five hundred. "We started really losing people during the 1970s," says Richard Mooney, a longtime Pattonsburg resident and member of the city council. "It started when I-35 came in and bypassed us by a mile and a half." There had been a time when Pattonsburg boasted four service stations. In the summer of 1993 there was but one, and it was short for this world.

Richard Mooney and his family lived in a forty-six-year-old house opposite the Christian Church, a half block off Main Street. The Mooneys had been lucky, considering that Pattonsburg had been flooded more than thirty times in the twentieth century. "I had never even had water inside my house,"

Mooney says. But he had never seen a spring and summer like 1993. On that July 6—eighty-four years to the day after the monumental 1909 washout— the surrounding river and creek waters swamped their banks, topped the eight-foot dike, and invaded the town. "That day three feet of floodwater was standing in my living room."

Like Pattonsburgers from time immemorial, the Mooneys and their neighbors began the all-too-familiar task of cleaning up, drying out, starting over. Then, less than a month later, it happened again. "The second flood," says Mooney, "the water in my house reached *four* feet."

And this time, the flooding apparently hit some emotional high-water mark in the community. After 160 years, the citizens of Pattonsburg had had enough.

David Warford, then thirty-two years old, had been mayor for about six months when the summer floods came. As in many small towns, Pattons- burg's mayorship is a part-time job that everybody in the business commu- nity is expected to take his or her turn doing. It usually doesn't require much more than presiding over a monthly council meeting, and then you go on with your life. But it's an honor, and in David Warford's case, there was a certain family pride attached to it. His grandfather, Walter, had been an especially prominent mayor back in the mid-1930s. Owner of a hardware store, two service stations, and the local Skelly distributorship, Walter War- ford is pictured in the town's 1937 centennial commemorative newspaper next to an article headlined "Pattonsburg Is a Great Trading Center." Wal- ter's grandson, owner of a motorcycle and ATV business at the time he assumed the title of mayor, bears a striking resemblance to him.

"The first flood was bad," David Warford says, "but it wasn't devastating. The water came up, the water went down. As mayor, and city council, we looked at the situation and just tried to help people get back in their houses. We wanted to get back to normal. At that point, there wasn't talk of 'other alternatives.'

"But when the second flood hit, that was devastating. To have spent the last month trying to clean up and then getting hit twice as hard. Ninety per- cent of all the houses in the community had water inside them."

After the second flood, Missouri's then-governor, Mel Carnahan, called a meeting in Jefferson City. "It was just a flood relief meeting to discuss possi- bilities," Warford says. "Anybody in the state that wanted to come was welcome." Warford and a couple of the city councilmen went to Jefferson City and were pleased to find that the meeting was more about brainstorming than laying down parameters. "It wasn't, Here's what we can do for you, work within these limits. Instead, it was, Come back to us with ideas on what we can do to help you. We don't *know* what to do."

Shortly after that, Warford got together with Phil Tate, his local state representative, and Denise Stottlemeyer, a member of the Green Hills Resource Conservation & Development Council, a group that provides technical and financial aid to help rural communities solve problems. They sat around for the better part of a morning, tossing out ideas. Nothing was too wild to be considered. "Our options seemed to come down to this," says Warford. "One, try to get money to rebuild Pattonsburg. Two, come up with money to buy everybody out and let them go wherever they wanted. And three, let's talk about moving the town."

Option one wasn't particularly appealing—after all, it was what had been done over and over for a century and a half. Option two would've been the easiest in terms of labor and logistics, but you couldn't very well ignore the emotional component: Pattonsburg was these people's *home.* They were rooted in that place, even if their roots were a bit waterlogged. "Everything kept coming back to the third option," says Warford, "even though at that point we didn't know if it was a real possibility."

The first order of business was to call a town meeting. "It wasn't my job to make this decision," says Warford. "It was the people's decision. It was my job to make their decision happen." In mid-September they met at the old schoolhouse, the mayor and city council sitting up front facing the citizens. By then the city council included Richard Mooney, Gene Walker, Mike Hartley, and Greg Teal. Representative Phil Tate explained the options. "Everything was presented as a *possibility*," says Warford. "We didn't want to get anybody's hopes up. These people had been through so much. When we asked for a show of hands on moving the town, it was overwhelming. They were ready to try something new."

ACTUALLY, SAYS RICHARD Mooney, this was the third time Pattonsburg had discussed moving. The first was back in the 1870s, when they gravitated to Elm Flat to be near the railroad. The second was in the 1970s. "The idea was to move the town, build a dam, and flood the whole area as a reservoir. My dad was on the city council then and the idea even got to the point of a vote. The citizens of Pattonsburg voted to move the town and go with the dam. But at that time farmland was very high and crop prices were good, and the farmers didn't want to sell out. You can't really blame them. But they voted it down, and there were enough of them to kill it." The result had been twenty more years of floods, hardship, and dwindling population. Now, in 1993, the time seemed ripe.

But the mayor and city council couldn't simply go back to Governor Carnahan and announce their decision; they had to say how they wanted to go about implementing it and how much it would cost. At this point, recalls David Warford, he began to find the job of mayor all-consuming. "I had spent from 1982 until 1993 building my business up," he says. "It didn't have a lot of cash, but it had a good client base, a good inventory—and a lot of debt. All of a sudden I lost more than a quarter of a million dollars in three days, and then was shut down for two months while I tried to repair the building. My income stopped, but the interest charges kept on going. I rebuilt, but that was about it. I couldn't concentrate on it. When you're gone on city business four days a week, and when you're at work but talking city business on the phone twenty or thirty times a day, it's tough."

To prepare the proposal for the governor, the mayor and city council had to organize, prioritize, itemize. The first question they needed to answer was where they might move. "We started looking around," says Warford. "Two main factors came into play. One was the interstate. The other was a large parcel of land owned by a single individual."

The landowner was Woodrow Morris, who, with his wife, Maxine, had run a gas station on U.S. 69 for many years. In 1955, the Morrises had bought 218 acres of farmland from Maxine's great uncle. "We'd had several offers over the years," says Morris. "Max never would agree to sell. We didn't have any children to leave it to, but, still, we weren't particularly interested in selling."

Interstate 35 runs along the east border of the Morris property about three miles north of the flats where Pattonsburg was located. David Warford went to see Woodrow Morris. "He had lived in Pattonsburg all his life," Warford says, "and he had made a good living here. But in our society, everybody's after the buck. That wasn't the case here."

"I went to Max, and she didn't want to sell," Morris says. "It'd been in her family a long time. I said, Max, I'm gonna tell you, we came here with nothing, we made a little money, and we made a lot of friends. The people of this community have been good to us. Let's sell it to 'em. And she said okay." Morris told Warford to get estimates of the market value of comparable farmland, and that's what he would sell it for. To his wife, Morris confided that he didn't think it would ever really happen.

"I think we ended up giving $600 an acre," says Warford. They also contracted for a parcel of land that FHA was selling. With the land problem solved, Warford and the city council went back to the state. At this point, things got very complicated for everybody. Consider the ramifications: Even if a community has all the money in the world, they can't simply decide to move their town. Towns are platted, and those plats are filed in county courthouses and in state archives. They're laid out on maps. Changing a location, even to just three miles away, creates a major domino effect. "The state told us to go back and recheck our numbers," Warford says. "And Governor Carnahan said he had to have proof the Pattonsburg citizens were committed to this move."

At this stage, FEMA and other federal agencies were involved in the discussions, but only on a what-if basis. The federal government's matching funds were dependent on the state government's okay. "We went back to Jefferson City and sat around with the governor's people, people from SEMA (State Emergency Management Agency) and FEMA, Denise Stottlemeyer from Green Hills, Representative Phil Tate," remembers Warford. "They said, how do you plan to pull this off, and I said I didn't know. But I told them I knew one thing—without their help, this community was going to die."

Councilman Gene Walker recalls that "someone" in Missouri state government said he thought that would be a desirable outcome. "He said we should be bought out and scatter to the winds, like leaves," Walker says.

That someone was Buford (Buck) Katt, now assistant director of SEMA, who ended up working with the Pattonsburg council on their relocation but was never convinced that it was the thing to do. Katt, a thirty-year military man who retired with the rank of colonel, says, "If you're spending government money, you have to ask the hard questions. The first one is, Do we really need this community? When we announced the Pattonsburg funding in July 1994, my phone rang and it was an alderman from Bethany, Missouri, just fifteen miles up the road from Pattonsburg. She asked me, 'Why are you guys spending all that money building an infrastructure for the city of Pattonsburg when we could absorb that community into our community?' It's a damn good question."

Unless you're from Pattonsburg.

Not surprisingly, the day after that first meeting, an offer was made to buy out the town instead of move it. "That's not what our people told us they wanted to do," said Warford. More huddling, more brainstorming. Finally the Pattonsburg contingent heard the words they had been waiting for. "I'm guessing phone calls were made to Washington," Warford says.

"The politicians," says Katt, "started making commitments before they had all the facts, out of the emotion of the moment."

"Anyway," recalls David Warford, "it was soon back to, 'Now we need some *real* numbers.' This was never presented as a situation where there would be endless funds. We got bids for new road construction, bids for building the new town, bids for the houses. Then we started matching those numbers up with different grant programs—through the state, through the locals, through different government programs, through FEMA and SEMA, through the Department of Energy, through the Department of This and That. It was a nightmare.

"And all this time, people's lives were on hold. They didn't know exactly how much they were going to get for their houses. They didn't know how much it was going to cost to move. Businesspeople didn't know what was going to happen to their old buildings or what they would go into. There were just so many ifs. My wife always said she could stand anything, as long as she knew it was going to end. She probably said that [for] fifteen years, and I didn't get it until we got into this."

GENE WALKER, UNTIL recently superintendent of Pattonsburg's schools, was in his mid-forties when he joined the city council in early 1994. That made him the oldest person at the table, which meant he had a certain amount of perspective, as well as some experience with budgets. He soon found himself very impressed with his younger colleagues, none of whom had ever had to wrestle with the kinds of issues before them. "I had been on the council in the late 1970s," Walker says, "and in those days I was the youngest member. Everything we suggested, somebody would say, 'Oh, we tried that and it didn't work.' But *these* guys would sit here and say, 'Let's try so and so.' I mean, they freewheeled!"

They spent a lot of time in Jefferson City and in Washington, D.C. In the nation's capital, more often than not they were shunted from one agency's middle manager to another department's undersecretary. Recalls Gene Walker: "One day when we were trying to get people in Washington to see us, one of the guys said, 'This is sort of like trying to get a date in a convent.'"

As the relocation process stretched on, covering four years, Mayor Warford and his city council held many, many meetings, trying to keep community enthusiasm up. A lot of the decisions they had to make boiled down to what all of them could live with, not what a few of them wanted. But one thing they all agreed on was the need to conduct their business in the open. "These citizens of Pattonsburg were about as independent and hardheaded a bunch of folks as you could find," says Walker. "Some saw a boogyman behind every tree, and others assumed the government was out to screw them. Many of them were here in the big flood of 1973, four feet of water, when all we got for government aid was a mop bucket, a mop, and a trial-size box of Spic and Span. So when we talked about getting government help, they said, 'Yeah, *right*.' But from the first meeting to discuss moving the town to today, we never had a closed session of council except when we talked about city personnel. Whether there were three people or forty here, we talked about it. If somebody had a question, we stopped and answered it. Because the way this whole thing could've gone off track was if a decision had come down that people didn't know anything about."

Walker actually ran for the council this time so he could represent the needs of the school district—and then it turned out the school wouldn't be moved. In fact, none of the public buildings or businesses would. Buck Katt was the man who convinced Governor Carnahan that that was the way to go. "We knew," Katt says, "that we had more people—not just in Pattonsburg, but around the state—who wanted to be bought out than we had money for. That being the case, we made a policy to spend no money for businesses and only limited money for people to elevate existing houses."

To avoid the lengthy process of conducting an environmental impact study, Katt decreed that no FEMA or SEMA money could be spent on buying or building any of the new town. Instead, the state agency Community Development Block Grant (CDBG) set up what Katt calls "a blind company" to buy the Morris farm property, which was then divided into parcels. At that point, Katt came in with FEMA/SEMA funds and bought property in the old town. "For example," he says, "say we bought Mr. and Mrs. Joneses' house and lot. Houses and lots had been appraised separately, for a very good reason. Suppose their lot in the old town appraised for $5,000. Mr. and Mrs. Jones would then have to surrender that $5,000 to this corporation that was formed by CDBG in order to gain a lot in the new town."

The plan also allowed homeowners to pick up and move their old houses to the new lots, if that's what they preferred. "The amount for jacking up and moving a house was $11,500," says Gene Walker, "whether it was a $5,000 house or a $70,000 house. We set up a sliding scale for valuation of houses. If it assessed for under $50,000, you got $12,000 plus 25 percent of the appraised valuation. If it assessed for more than $50,000, you got $15,000 plus 25 percent of the appraised value. I guarantee you, people in this town had their pencils and paper out. That made a lot of difference on what was moved, and what was sold."

"In many cases, the houses weren't worth moving," says Katt, "but people made that decision based on a variety of things. They might say, 'My daddy was born in this house and I was born in this house and I've got to move it.' The individual homeowners, using other funds from CDBG, had to put in their own foundation in the new town."

Government rules and funding are one thing, but deciding what's best for your friends and neighbors is another. After all, Buck Katt doesn't have to live in Pattonsburg. "The question," says David Warford, "was how we were going to be fair and equal to everybody, and at the same time keep it realistic and within budget."

"We did a lot of talking about the size of lots," says Gene Walker. "At first, we planned to make the ones closer to the business district smaller, because—or so we thought—older folks would want to be nearer town and wouldn't want to keep up big yards. But when it came down to it, they didn't want that. 'I like my big yard,' they said, 'and I don't want to feel like I'm in my neighbor's.' So in the end, all the lots were the same size."

And, too, there were the intangible aspects of community that had to be considered. If some people wanted to keep living next to the people they'd lived by for thirty years, and if others wanted to get *away* from the busybody next door, how could anybody short of Solomon sort that out?

The brilliant answer they came up with was a lottery. First, they threw all the names into a hat, then held a drawing to determine the order in which people would get to choose their lots. "I even had a preacher do the drawing," laughs Warford. Around town, the joke was that it was best to draw very early or very late: Draw first and you get to choose your location. Draw last, you get to choose your neighbors.

After the numbers were drawn, each person, in numerical order, was assigned a fifteen-minute time slot for picking his lot. If you had more than one lot in the old town, each individual lot required a separate time slot. That way, somebody with three lots couldn't simply block out most of a neighborhood for himself.

Richard Mooney says he drew number thirty and got the lot he wanted. Gene Walker, who owned two nonadjacent lots in the old town, was fortunate enough to get two lots next to each other in the new town. The last person to choose was Mayor David Warford. "It was the luck of the draw," Gene Walker says.

TODAY, IF YOU drive north on I-35, you may see two signs for Pattonsburg. The southernmost one isn't marked as an official exit to the town, but there is a sign that you can see from the highway. That's the old exit, the one that takes you in on U.S. 69, across the new Grand River bridge that was built, without sides, so houses could be moved across it.

Pattonsburgers prefer that you keep going north to the big exit sign. After exiting right and turning back across the interstate, you'll see a service station on the right. There are some other buildings, large and tan, behind and beyond it. A couple are auto garages. One is a lumber company.

Across the road from the service station is a kind of Quonset hut–like building. That's city hall. On past that is Pattonburg's new business district, two short rows of storefronts that are a mirror image of each other. The street between them is wide, with a boulevard island in the middle where young trees have been planted as future shade for a park bench. There's angle parking in front of all the businesses, which include a bank, a real estate office, a gift shop, a hair salon. But the most prominent storefront on

Main Street is the Old Memories Café, whose sign proclaims: A PROUD HERITAGE . . . A NEW BEGINNING.

If you continue on through the business district, you'll quickly enter the residential area. The first thing you notice about it is the absence of trees, reflecting the fact that this ground was a hayfield not all that long ago. "We miss the old-growth trees," says Gene Walker. "I had about fifteen or twenty in my yard before, and that was one of the things people said they wanted in the new town." During the planning process, a design team from the Department of Energy came and asked the people what parts of the old town they wanted to make sure were in the new. Besides trees, one of the things people mentioned was the old mill whistle, which sounded three times a day. It still does.

The residential area sprawls across rolling land, and the streets have been laid out in a traditional square grid. New houses sit next to old houses that sit next to mobile homes. On the western edge of town, four dome-shaped buildings make a visitor think a squadron of spaceships has landed. This is Pattonsburg's new monolithic dome school, serving kindergarten through grade twelve and designed to provide security against natural disasters. The domes have no windows but are lit by skylights. The largest of the domes serves as the gymnasium, stage, music, and art areas. The smaller domes hold classrooms, a library, a cafeteria, and offices.

In a valley next to the school, a bulldozer scoops out land for a playground. Woodrow Morris sits watching the dozer's progress from the shade of his west-facing garage. He's still amazed that his former farmland has been so transformed in so short a time. "I kept telling Max, it'll never happen," he says. "But then they started building that lumber company across the street, and people started coming."

Woodrow says that Maxine made a couple of demands in exchange for letting go of this property. "One, she got to pick her lot without going into the lottery. And two, she wanted a street named after her." Today the Morris house sits on Meadow Street, which honors Maxine's family.

Nobody in Pattonsburg pretends that everything about this relocation was, or is, perfect. Gene Walker still smarts when he thinks about the old school down in the flats. Richard Mooney, who before moving his house owed only $800 on it, now has a $40,000 mortgage. The population has dropped even more since the 1993 floods, though a few people who left have now come back. There was a flap of some kind, and the cap factory picked up and left town. Gene Walker says there were a few people who quickly went "from needy to greedy."

But perhaps nobody views the events of the past near decade with the same complex combination of pride and wistfulness as David Warford. Today he refers to the new downtown area as "the strip mall." "There were so many things I wanted us to do," he says. "As long as we were redoing it, I wanted us to look at new approaches instead of just building a cookie-cutter little town. In the new town, in the middle between the two strips of buildings, I wanted brick patios on either side so people could come out in the evenings and sit. And down below, on a low spot, I wanted to have gazebos. We talked about facing the houses to get the best use of sunlight, for energy conservation. Over by the school, I wanted to have nature paths. Some of those things just didn't take off like I wanted them to."

Ironically, David Warford today seems to be something of a ghost presence in the new town. Mention his name and you get funny looks from folks. There are the predictable references to "publicity seeking," and his being "in it for personal gain." Buck Katt says that Warford "tried to leverage me to buy his motorcycle dealership, but I wouldn't do it."

As to the charges of being a publicity hound, Warford laughs. "For an old farmboy, I sure got thrown into the spotlight," he says. "The first time I was on TV—and I knew everything about this project from the first inkpen to the last road built—when they started interviewing me, I couldn't even remember my name. I even gave a speech at the National Press Club. My message was that it's sad we can't address these disasters until after the disaster happens. Then we step in and say, 'What can we do to help?' But why can't we pinpoint the places it's likely to happen and address it before disaster strikes?"

Gene Walker recalls one of many early council meetings that went on late into the night. "I told them then, when we get finished with this, 50 percent of the town will think everything's fine, 20 percent will think they made out like a fat rat, and 30 percent will think somebody screwed them." He stands in solid support of Warford. "David spent endless hours on this," Walker says. "For a guy with no more experience than he had with any kind of business, he did a superb job. But he's been bad-mouthed a lot. It's not so much David. You got to understand, his family was reasonably well off. For a lot of the old-timers, it has more to do with his father and grandfather. David's grandfather, and this is all hearsay, was one of those guys during the Depression that would sell a farm and, well, the payments would get to the point that—sometimes he would sell the same farm two or three times. So he controlled a lot of ground. A lot of the old folks, there was just a kind of bad taste in their mouths. David actually spent so much time on this that it hurt his business."

Woodrow Morris says the same thing. "After I retired, I worked part time at David's Honda store," says Morris. "He was always on the phone dealing with city problems. David lost his own business taking care of them."

In the end, Warford and his family chose not to move to the new town, remaining instead in the flats, in the circa 1900 house his grandfather Walter once owned. "Bottom line," says Warford, "it was financial. This house had about $30,000 worth of damage that needed to be fixed. My business, I thought I had flood insurance for it, but I lost about $350,000. My mother-in-law had about $20,000 worth of damage to her house—which she ended up selling, but there was a period when we were helping her fix it back up. My dad had two businesses that were flooded. His house had about $80,000 worth of damage. Dad and I had about forty thousand bushels of corn in the bin that exploded and went down the river. All together, we're talking about nearly a million dollars. So at the point that I finally got around to looking at what *we* were going to do, I had lost all my money in the shop and had spent what money I did have trying to fix it all back up."

He insists that he doesn't feel sorry for himself. "I don't regret anything I did," he says, "though I might have tried to look after myself a little more. But, you know, we're all called for something at some point. Anyway, if it floods tomorrow, it's not up to FEMA to come help me out. You'll never hear me say that. I was given an opportunity to move, and I didn't do it."

He laughs. "I do have flood insurance now, because my wife says if it comes one more time, that's it for her. That's why I have insurance. So next time we *can* go someplace else."

IT'S BEEN MY experience, both personally and professionally, that the hardest part of taking responsibility is deciding to do it. Of all the powerful natural forces I've confronted in my work—tornadoes, hurricanes, earth-quakes, floods—I put inertia right up there with them. No, inertia doesn't cause those natural acts, but it can certainly cause them to be more deadly and costly. If you live in an earthquake zone, you have to *decide* to spend a few hundred dollars now to prepare your house in order to save thousands later. If you live in a hurricane area, you have to *decide* to give up a little ocean view for more natural protection. If you live in a floodplain, you have to *decide* to take flood insurance. And then, if the hassle of yearly flooding still outweighs the joys of living there, you have to do what the good citizens of Pattonsburg, Missouri, finally did after 160 years: you have to *decide* to take responsibility for your own life. Whether you're an individual or a cor-porate CEO, if your resources are being threatened, your first course of action has to be accepting responsibility for dealing with the situation.

Those examples are the obvious ones. Not all crises strike with the sud-den drama of a tornado or an earthquake. Especially in our business and personal lives, crises often build slowly, insidiously, almost imperceptibly. As I said in the introduction, sometimes a situation becomes a crisis because nobody's managing it. If your finances are getting away from you, if your relationship with your spouse is drifting, if the life you're living feels some-how inauthentic, you need to *decide* to be present in your own life.

In a corporation, that's not always easy. Just recall the case of Enron whistle-blower Sherron Watkins, who sent Chairman Ken Lay the now-famous memo urging that the company get a grip on its practices before it "implodes in a financial scandal." Another case that comes to mind is that of Odwalla, the California juice maker that marketed social consciousness as energetically as it peddled apple juice. "It was run by executives who were not shy about noting their commitment to a more just society," wrote jour-nalist Jon Entine. "Founder Greg Steltenpohl, who described himself as a former artist, would say that he was 'learning to respect the fruit' squeezed to make his juices. Such New Age brand positioning helped propel Odwalla to a 30 percent annual growth." Apparently, heightened market demand put impossible stress on the company's safety controls. In the fall of 1996, a sixteen-month-old girl drank some of the company's apple juice and soon died. The juice was found to be contaminated with E. coli bacteria.

There are any number of crisis management lessons you could apply to this story, but to me the essential one is that of taking responsibility—

"walking the walk" as well as "talking the talk." Odwalla expressed shock at what it called a freak occurrence and promptly removed its juice from the market. But evidence soon surfaced proving that, just months before this fatal poisoning, a U.S. Army inspector had rejected Odwalla's efforts to sell its products on military bases because of unacceptably high bacteria counts in a juice sample. It wasn't a freak occurrence. Unless Odwalla took decisive action, the company could, and most often in these situations would, be facing the same crisis again and again.

First, they had to prevent as many E. coli infections, and most importantly deaths, as possible. Before the first day had closed, Odwalla had not only recalled the juice from stores, they'd set up a Web site and gotten as much information as they could to the media. They had a doctor write up a FAQ (frequently asked questions) page about E. coli bacteria, covering the early warning signs of an infection, and shared the Food and Drug Administration's information on handling an emergency situation. Experts were available to answer questions by e-mail and phone. The Web site also pointed out that a team of experts was on-line to calm down frightened consumers. Odwalla knew that taking the juice off the shelves was crisis response, and it wanted to try to stop the crisis in its tracks if it could.

Despite their aggressive efforts in the eye of the storm, sixty-five more people became infected with the bacteria during the outbreak. It wasn't a crisis Odwalla could afford to repeat. One child had died, and several others were seriously injured. The company pleaded guilty to criminal responsibility for the poisonings. Even though 90 percent of its customers reported that they'd still buy its products, Odwalla had to take steps to prevent another E. coli contamination. Just as Odwalla was one of the pioneers in mass producing fresh juices, they decided to become a pioneer in how to make those fresh juices safe. The company developed a process it calls flash pasteurization, in which the juice is rapidly heated to a temperature high enough to kill off harmful bacteria like E. coli. The juice is then quickly cooled to keep it as close to its original fresh-squeezed flavor and nutritional value. Their company's goal now isn't just to meet FDA standards—it's to exceed them. "As Odwalla learned the hard way," wrote Entine, "corporate social responsibility is evidenced by actions taken before a crisis breaks out, not when scrambling to contain a brand-crushing screw-up." I couldn't have said it better.

The U.S. Postal Service, whose eight hundred thousand employees make it second in size among government agencies only to the Department of Defense and in the private sector only to Wal-Mart, had been burdened for years with crippling—and very expensive—labor disputes. The watchdog Equal Employment Opportunity Commission (EEOC) was receiving thirty thousand filings a year from the Postal Service alone. Disgruntled employees alleged racial discrimination, sexual harassment, and any number of other abuses committed by autocratic managers (one complainant reported that his supervisor addressed all the letter carriers under him only by number, which the employee found demeaning). With so many complaints, and because of the Postal Service's antiquated system of dealing with them, grievances dragged on for years—and some found their way to litigation— while management-labor relations continued to deteriorate.

Then in 1994, the Postal Service's V.P. of human resources, Mary Elcano, instituted a plan designed to open communication and sidestep formal proceedings. Called REDRESS (Resolve Employment Disputes Reach Equitable Solutions), the program allows for employee and manager to come together with an impartial mediator to work out their differences. The REDRESS program has solved some 85 percent of disputes without their going to arbitration, improving both morale and the bottom line. They've set up a huge effort to collect information about their successes, and their failures, so they'll be able to tell if the system is breaking down before they get to crisis levels again. Of course, the agency still has a long way to go, but REDRESS—which is now being adopted by other organizations, such as the World Bank—shows the Postal Service ready and willing to take responsibility for getting its house in order.

Lots of companies have mediation programs set up to keep those low-level management problems from blowing up into big disasters. What makes REDRESS different? Instead of placing the power in the hands of the manager or, better still, in the hands of the mediator, the REDRESS program is set up to give the supervisee—the person who is most likely making the complaint—an equal say in how the mediation goes. The Postal Service is using the mediation process to handle the conflict and to train both employees on how to communicate constructively, not destructively, with one another. The mediator isn't just the translator anymore. And, hopefully, the next time there's a conflict, those employees will be able to handle it themselves without going through mediation, or a lawsuit.

When I joined the federal government, I knew that one of my biggest challenges was to change what I call "the Washington mentality." There's a lot of buck passing in government—you know, "Not my job, man." If FEMA were ever to rise to the occasion in the next crisis (unlike the abominable way it performed during Hurricane Andrew), the common mind-set needed to be, "We as an agency are responsible, and I as a person who works here am responsible."

In order to instill this new thinking, we first had to dismantle the framework for the old thinking. The agency was too compartmentalized, like a bunch of neighborhoods that kept to themselves. Not only that, they marked their boundaries. Outsiders weren't welcome on any other neighborhood's turf. There was a lot of information hoarding, because information is power, and nobody wanted to give away their strength. What this setup accomplished, besides creating turf wars, was to provide a built-in "not-my-job" attitude.

My chief of staff, Jane Bullock, headed our reorganization group. For three days, they took both career and political employees off-site, broke them into teams, and then gave them assignments. They worked on establishing the agency's priorities and goals, rewrote the mission statement, developed a management plan. I didn't stay with them, and that was very important. I pointed the direction, but what they produced was theirs—which is to say, the agency's. They had a stake in it, a feeling of responsibility for it.

Of course, there were some subtle efforts at fief building in the process. But once they'd done their work, I gathered the senior managers together and said, "Now, then, I'm going to rotate all of you to head different programs." That was clearly a shock to them. Some of these people had spent years—*years*—in the same area of the agency, and they were afraid to make a change. I told them that if anybody had problems with it, to come see me and I would work with them.

One senior executive, a woman, was visibly upset. "I just don't want to do this," she said.

"Look, give me six months in this new position," I told her. "If after that time you still don't want to do it, let me know and I'll work with you."

She agreed. And after six months, she had become one of our best managers. Not only that, she felt energized by the change. The best part was, she wasn't alone. In transforming the agency into a flatter, more functional organization with lots of interdepartmental interaction, we had accomplished our bigger goal of getting everyone at FEMA to feel responsible for the agency's success.

In summary, then, here are some steps for taking responsibility and short-circuiting crises:

• **LAUNCH A PROBE.** The same crisis, or at least one that feels like it's the same, keeps hitting you again and again. The beauty of mitigation is that it's all about finding the patterns in crises and working them to your advantage. But is it the same problem or not? Are you facing the same flooding river or a slightly different (and slightly unpredictable) hurricane, whose landfalls shift up and down the coast? Your probe's goal is to find out. Create a list of crisis attributes, things like the timing of onset, the source, the duration, the impact. Is it the same factory or same division or department that keeps reporting problems? Is cash flow precariously tight every month, or just at certain times of the year? Is the problem specific to that unit, or does it come from a companywide way of doing business? You should plug every crisis you have into that "grid," and look for useful patterns that you can use to launch a prevention plan.

• **MEASURE THE GAP AND MAKE THE LEAP.** It took 160 years before the citizens of Pattonsburg decided to pull up their town and settle on higher ground. Even though you can see a crisis pattern doesn't mean you or others aren't going to be resistant to making a change. Adopting a prevention plan is one of the biggest decisions a person can make. All that responsibility taking puts a lot of weight on someone's shoulders. That's why measuring is so important. At some point, those cumulative numbers—sales lost, clients defected, employees turned over, crises recovered from—will reach a breaking point. Use the attributes you found in your probe to write a prevention plan, quantifying the problems as negatives and finding positives to counterbalance them permanently.

• **MAP OUT THE RIPPLE EFFECTS.** Once you've decided to change directions—to set up a preventive program to bypass problems, or to get out altogether from an area that keeps rocking your boat—the first thing you should do is identify the potential crises that will pop up in the repercussions. Will you have to train employees in new skills or new job responsibilities, and how will that expenditure of time affect other projects? Will you have to lay off staff, and how will that affect client relations or employee morale? As you consider different scenarios, ask for input from the people who could be affected, if it's possible. They'll know how much of a dent the change will make, and how the change could be rolled out to minimize that all-too-familiar anxiety—and they might even have good news. Whole new towns *can* be platted, after all.

• **MAP OUT THE NEW TERRAIN.** After you've made accommodations for the possible ripple effects, it'll be time to put the prevention plan in place. Everyone should know about the plan, and it makes sense to walk people through how it might affect their own work, or how they personally could help prevent a crisis. If you're keeping no more than 70 percent of a crucial part of your supply chain with a single vendor, your accounts payable department should know since they could notice that the POs are actually coming in way off target because of contracts that were signed long before the new plan was put in place. As we'll see again in the next chapter, it's your employees who will make it a reality.

• **PREVENT NOW, PREVENT LATER.** Some portion of responding to a crisis is preventing it from spreading. Your long-term prevention plans give you an opportunity to look at the big picture. Your short-term prevention plans should fall back on your preparations—your values and your plans of action. Don't get the two mixed up. Preventing now doesn't automatically help you prevent the same crisis from happening again. It can be a wake-up call if the crisis is bad enough, but it isn't the same as taking real responsibility for the future.

Taking responsibility is one path to preventing crisis. The other is what you do with that responsibility.

4

RECONSIDER THE THREE PIGS

In an earthquake, twigs trump bricks

It came at that hour of the morning when most of us have lapsed into our deepest, most drool-inducing slumber. Once again we've gotten past the oh-no hour, three A.M., when we wake with a start and lie in darkness silently enumerating undone tasks or insufficient dollars; then, finally, we wind down into sleep again, and by four-thirty-one A.M., we're so far inside ourselves that we need jackhammers for wake-up calls.

Like thousands of other Californians nestled in bed that January morning throughout the swath of valley between the San Gabriel and the Santa Monica Mountains, Lucile Jones was sound asleep. Her husband was in Boston on business, her two young sons had crawled in with her sometime during the night, and Lucy, as everyone seems to call her, was finally lost in her own dreams.

Meanwhile, many miles down inside the earth, a simmering, millions-year-old process was about to play itself out. Let me explain it to you the way a nongeologist like myself is able to understand it best: Picture yourself driving behind a lumbering SUV when suddenly it kicks a rock toward your face. Where that rock hit your windshield there's now a tiny crater. You say a curse word or two, then forget it. But the next morning, or a morning in the next week or month or year, you go out to your car and there's a crack across the whole width of your windshield—a crack that started from that weakened spot where the rock smacked your glass. That weakened spot was the "epicenter." Contrary to popular belief, earthquakes don't happen at epicenters. They *begin* at an epicenter but happen over a surface.

The other thing to know is that as that crack shot across your windshield, each inch of it was giving off energy. And because the energy was aimed and focused in the direction of the crack itself, it was most intense at the opposite end of the crack from the epicenter.

That's basically what happened below the San Fernando Valley at four-thirty-one A.M. on January 17, 1994. The earth's crust was like your windshield, and as the crack ran from southeast to northwest, the energy it released was enough to rudely jolt thousands of Californians out of their deep slumber—among them U.S. Geological Survey seismologist Lucy Jones.

"It was strong enough to wake me up and wake me up quickly," Jones says. "I immediately started counting, because the duration of the earthquake will tell you how big it is." She gauged the shock at five seconds but figured she must've missed the first second or two waking up. "I said, okay, it's about a magnitude six. Later, when I heard 6.7, I said no way—it didn't last long enough!" For the sake of perspective, consider this: The energy of a 6.7 earthquake is some thirty times greater than that of the atomic bomb dropped on Hiroshima.

In West Pasadena, where Jones lived, the shaking was minimal compared to communities farther north and west, including the Los Angeles suburb of Northridge, whose devastation soon gave this earthquake its name. "It was clear, though, that it was a big earthquake," says Jones, "so I jumped up and started putting on my clothes. I was grateful that my three-year-old and seven-year-old were both with me. Right away my aunt, who was helping me with the boys, came upstairs and got in bed with the three-year-old, Niels, who slept through the whole thing."

Not so her older son, Sven, who had begun to equate earthquakes with something resembling abandonment. "When he was five, we had a 7.3 right by the San Andreas Fault, and both my husband—a seismologist at Cal Tech—and I had been really busy. We were worried that it was going to set off something on the San Andreas, so we basically disappeared for days. Well, our son freaked out. *This* time, with papa out of town and mama running off to work, he's like panicking. So I offered to take him with me. 'You're going to be really bored,' I said, but he wanted to go."

The USGS offices are in a former single-family house on the edge of the Cal Tech campus. Today Jones is scientist-in-charge for Southern California (the northern headquarters is in Menlo Park), but at the time of the Northridge quake she was one of eight or so scientists working either in the USGS headquarters or at the newly built Operations Center across the street at Cal Tech. "There we had set up a wall between the scientists and reporters," Jones explains. "Smartest thing we ever did!" It's a glass wall, and the press can sit on their side, called the Media Center, and watch the scientists checking computers and maps and seismometers on the other side. There's always someone from USGS with the media to answer their questions.

On the day of the Northridge Earthquake, Jones rushed to the office, where she left Sven with the task of cataloging the plaster cracks in all the rooms. Meanwhile, she went across the street to the Operations Center, which was in chaos. "We really did fail at getting out the information," she says. "Our computer was so old and slow and so busy collecting data that it wouldn't talk to us for about two hours. So we were screaming at each other, and the whole thing sort of went to gridlock."

Jones's husband—Egill Hauksson—was then and still is head of the Operations Center. "He was beside himself that morning," Jones says. "He'd gone back to his hotel room to brush his teeth after breakfast, to get ready for his daylong meeting, and the TV was saying, 'Earthquake destroys Los Angeles!' He rushed to Logan airport and said, 'I'm a Cal Tech seismologist. I gotta get to L.A.!' Of course, LAX was closed, but United was great. They flew him first class to Ontario, California, about forty miles away. He was the only one that day who had time to think. For hours he was sitting on this plane, and he would call me and say, 'Hey, did you think about doing so-and-so?'"

One of the first things Jones did was to phone the state Office of Emergency Services to give them a probability of further damaging aftershocks. "It was essentially certain, given that size of earthquake, that there would be a big aftershock that day. But that was about all I could do for the moment, since I didn't have any data." In fact, within nine minutes of the quake, there had been two aftershocks measuring 4.5 and 4.8.

While the scientists at the Op Center coaxed and cajoled their sluggish computer, Jones took Sven to Starbucks to get him some food. "By the time the sun came up, he admitted that he was in fact bored, and wanted to go home to be with his friends. So I arranged for someone to pick him up." As they were leaving, Jones ran into one of the field geologists, who told her they had just gotten their helicopter and were about to lift off in search of faults. "Of course they didn't find any," she says, "because this earthquake didn't come to the surface."

But what they did find, as they swooped low over the densely populated San Fernando Valley, were thousands of collapsed homes, stores, and apartment buildings; buckled and caved-in freeways; derailed freight trains; ruptured gas lines spewing fire along entire streets; and rows of parked cars exploding like so many strings of July firecrackers.

ACROSS THE CONTINENT in Washington, D.C., Mother Nature was pummeling us with a dense and weighty snowfall. The arteries from the suburbs into the city were jammed with slip-sliding vehicles, which was the only reason I was still at home.

I got the call about Northridge just minutes after the event, and my first thought was that I was glad we hadn't yet shut down the disaster relief office we'd operated since the Malibu fires in October 1993. That happened to be the same office we'd opened during the Rodney King riots in summer 1992. L.A. was on a bad-luck streak. One of the papers called it a "string of perils."

My second thought was to get ready to fly out there, so I switched from my suit to my field clothes and headed into the office to direct the emergency response. By the time I got to my desk, high-flying U-2 spy planes were feeding us information about new fires and signs of further movement, and urban search-and-rescue (USAR) teams were on the ground helping local officials remove the dead and wounded. In Northridge, one apartment building had collapsed in on itself, and the probability of multiple casualties was very high. Even before California governor Pete Wilson had submitted his formal request for disaster assistance—which would make grants available to low-income residents—we dispatched a dozen USAR and four medical disaster teams from Utah, Nevada, and Arizona. By early Monday, fifty truckloads of generators, communications equipment, and other relief supplies had left Denver bound for L.A. In addition, the Forest Service sent in extra firefighting equipment.

Meanwhile, Housing and Urban Development secretary Henry Cisneros, Transportation secretary Federico Pena, and I were in constant discussions with President Clinton. Clearly, housing was going to be a major problem and expense, and the president was keenly aware of the urgency of fixing L.A.'s highways and getting that car-dependent culture and economy back on track. At one P.M. Pacific Time, the president dispatched Cisneros, Pena, and me to California. We were sitting on the runway at Andrews Air Force Base when, at two o'clock Pacific Time, he signed the formal disaster declaration, officially releasing federal relief funds.

All day long it had snowed, and by late afternoon a nasty mixture of snow, sleet, and ice was coming down. Cisneros, Pena, and I waited a seeming eternity to take off for California. The problem was that the base crew couldn't get ahead of the ice; it fell faster than they could clear it from the wings and runway. All other flights in the area had been canceled.

But we had to get out, so finally the crew came up with a bold plan. They revved the engines while we sat in the hangar. Then, like a slingshot, the plane roared through the open door, careered along the airstrip, and lifted, miraculously, into the icy night. I know at least one person aboard that plane was praying mightily.

"RECOGNIZING THAT MAJOR engineering issues were coming up, one of the most important things we had to do was figure out where the fault was." Lucy Jones is explaining that it doesn't really matter where an earthquake starts, it's the length of the rupture and its closeness to the earth's surface that counts. "Santa Clarita and Simi Valley had worse shaking, in general, than Northridge. On Rinaldi Boulevard," she says, referring to a northern thoroughfare, "the ground velocity got up to two meters a second. That means the piece of ground you're standing on moves six feet away and back again *in one second.*"

In the case of Santa Clarita and Simi Valley, the earthquake was closer to the surface there—about three miles down, compared to twelve miles at Northridge. And far northwestern Simi Valley had, in Jones's words, "the rupture propagating toward it. All those areas had much worse shaking than farther south. But newer buildings."

The morning of the earthquake, Jones and her colleagues began deploying extra seismometers to record the aftershocks. "An aftershock *is* an earthquake," she says, "but it's an earthquake we know where and when is going to happen. A lot of things we want to look at, having an instrument nearby makes a huge difference." At some point that morning, Jones got a call from her husband, who was in the air over a patch of crazy-quilt midwestern farmland. "He had an idea," Jones says, laughing. "FEMA had given us some money to buy these new kinds of instruments—broadband digital seismic stations—that, compared to our old ones, give us *so* much more information about an earthquake. Think of it as a modern CD player compared to an AM transistor radio. These are like sixty-thousand-dollar laboratory instruments, and we had bought seven of them and were starting to experiment. Four had already been installed—one in Pasadena, one in Palm Springs, one in Santa Barbara, one up in the Owens Valley. But we had a few more sitting in the lab.

"Well, this was the subject of Egill's call. My father had just gotten remarried. My mother had died, and my stepmother had a house in Calabasas, very near the earthquake. She'd moved in with my dad but couldn't *bear* to give up her old house. So we had this empty house sitting in Calabasas. 'Why,' he said, 'don't you call Lucy up'—her name's also Lucy, just to make things easy—'and ask if we can put one of the broadband stations in her house?' Here's this observatory-type instrument that takes six months to install, and he was suggesting we use it as a *portable!* It was an amazingly novel idea, because in this case, we didn't need all the self-contained batteries and radios and whatever. There was still power and a phone line on at Lucy's house. Lucy loved the idea, of course, so we took it over and installed it in her garage. It stayed there four years."

As Lucy Jones and her fellow scientists consulted their instruments and took their measurements, the Santa Monica Freeway—a stretch of I-10 that's said to be the world's busiest expressway—was closed because a huge section of concrete had buckled near L.A.'s La Cienega Boulevard. And up near Santa Clarita, the body of a Los Angeles motorcycle policeman lay bloody and broken on a segment of Interstate 5, California's main north-south artery. Officer Clarence Dean had headed to work that morning unaware that the cloverleaf connecting Highway 14 and I-5 had collapsed. He drove his motorcycle off the seventy-five-foot-high overpass and sailed through the dark to his death.

In Sylmar, a row of elderly men and women in nightclothes sat in their wheelchairs on a sidewalk in the harsh light of morning, nervously waiting for chartered buses to take them away from their flooded retirement home. Its pipes had burst. "These people are scared to death," the home's activities director told a reporter. "One's already had a heart attack."

Up in the heavily Hispanic farm community of Fillmore, which because of its old-fashioned small-town ambience was used as backdrop for such Hollywood features as *La Bamba* and *Chaplain,* residents surveyed the rubble of their landmarks—the theater, barbershop, hardware store, and produce market.

But it was the suburb of Northridge, in the central valley, that death and destruction visited with the most ferocity. At the Northridge Fashion Center mall, the roof of a Bullocks Department Store collapsed. So did a large part of the mall's parking deck, trapping maintenance worker Salvadore Pena beneath tons of cracked concrete and twisted steel. Pena's legs were crushed, and his spine was dislocated, and it took search-and-rescue teams eight long hours to free him. "Come down and pray with me," Pena said over and over to firefighters, "come pray with me." Rescuers had to blast through huge slabs of concrete, and when enough weight had been removed they slid flattened air bags into the crevices, then pumped in air to lift the debris an inch at a time.

A few blocks away, search-and-rescue teams faced an even grimmer task. When the quake hit, it lifted the three-story Northridge Meadows Apartments completely off the ground. As the stucco building came back to earth, the top two floors pancaked onto the ground floor. "This wasn't an earthquake, this was a bomb," resident and nursing student Erik Pearson told an AP reporter. "It felt like we were thrown a foot in the air and four feet over to the side. It lifted this place up and disintegrated it." Almost instantly, Northridge Meadows became the poster child for the Northridge Earthquake. The human stories were horrendous. "All you heard was screaming and crying," a resident named Daniel Gelman told *USA Today*. "None of us knew our building was the worst. We thought everyone was experiencing the same thing."

But in those predawn hours of January 17, several blocks of neat Reseda Boulevard were bathed in ominous red and blue flashing lights as emergency workers rescued survivors and removed the dead. I saw two newspaper photos that pretty much captured the tragedy with no need for words: In one, a Los Angeles County fireman searches through debris next to a wall with the letters "DB" spray-painted on it, rescue code indicating a dead body had been found in that room. By midday on that Monday, some fifteen such pieces of graffiti were painted on the walls of the Northridge Meadows.

The other photo depicts the inevitable result of the first: a hysterical woman is barely contained by a firefighter, who has just told her that both her husband and son have perished in the apartment collapse.

"WITHIN A FEW hours, we had a pretty good handle on what had happened," Lucy Jones says. "I can remember a press conference at noon when we could say what the fault was, we had the preliminary engineering report, we knew there wasn't a fault trace showing up at the surface, and I was giving aftershock rates. Northridge was a particularly robust aftershock sequence— about three times higher than the average. Nowadays, we would probably have all that information in five minutes. The reason is, FEMA paid for an upgrade to the seismic network. You know those sixty-thousand-dollar broadband digital instruments I told you about? Because we had such problems with our data at Northridge, FEMA gave us money to buy one hundred fifty of them. Nothing succeeds like failure in the government!"

At about two P.M., Jones went home to check on her kids and to see her husband, who had driven in from Ontario in a rental car. Because she was so busy, she has a hard time remembering the exact sequence of events on that day. In the midst of crisis, there tend to be very few indelible benchmarks. The ones that stick are usually matters of the heart, such as Jones's concern for her sons, or further acts of nature. "Oh!" Jones says. "I *know* I was home at three-thirty, because there was a huge aftershock then!" In fact, that was the most powerful aftershock of the whole Northridge event—a magnitude 5.3. And just a couple of hours before, two magnitude 5.1s were recorded two minutes apart.

In an era when we can clone life and encapsulate an entire law library in a few pieces of plastic, scientists still don't understand why aftershocks happen. They also can't predict earthquakes. "We don't recognize any patterns," Jones says. "As far as we can tell, it's random."

She thinks about that for a second. "Well, that's not completely true. There are . . . cycles is a bit too strong a word, but there are changes in the rate of activity. There are more active times and less active times. And so, and I love this, we go, 'Well, when you have a lot of earthquakes, you tend to have a lot of earthquakes. And when you're not having earthquakes, you tend *not* to have earthquakes.' This," she says, laughing, "is a basic principle we get."

They do have good enough data now to see that the "cycles" are real. "They're not cycles in the sense of being periodic, but they do change from time to time. And we're pretty sure that they go down after big earthquakes. If you get a really big earthquake, you take enough energy out of the system that the overall rate will calm down. When they come back up is still very, very uncertain."

By the afternoon of that first day, what Jones and her associates knew for certain about the Northridge Earthquake were the following: It had occurred along a previously unknown fault; the origin of the quake was on a shallow "thrust fault," where one piece of earth feels enough pressure to shift vertically and violently over another piece of earth (this is different from a "strike-slip fault," in which two pieces of earth move past each other horizontally); and finally, the quake compacted the San Fernando Valley while it pushed up the Northridge Hills by as much as six feet.

"It's like snapping your fingers," Lucy Jones explains. "The fault is like your fingers, two surfaces in frictional contact. If they could open up—if California could fall into the ocean—you wouldn't have earthquakes. Your fingers would slip without producing any sound. But because there's friction, and your fingers are pushed together, you push hard enough that it slips *suddenly!* And it makes the air vibrate. That's what a sound is, vibration of the air traveling from your fingers to your ear.

"Now, in an earthquake, a fault moves and it produces shaking that travels out, and it's like the sound coming into your ear and making the air vibrate there. But you aren't feeling the movement of the fault. We talk all this stuff about faults, but when it slips it releases shaking. That's what I mean by saying every point releases energy. That energy then travels out and causes shaking at great distances. Around the world, in fact. Northridge was recorded in New Zealand. The high frequencies die off more quickly than low frequencies, just like you can hear a low-pitched noise farther away than a high-pitched noise. And so, when you're on the other side of the world, you just get these very long frequency things left.

"If you're a couple hundred miles away, you feel a rolling motion. But if you're right on top of the earthquake, it feels jerky. And so when people ask why was this one a roller and that one was a jerky, all they're saying is how far away they were from the event."

By nightfall, many of the unfortunate souls who'd been closest to the event had no place to live. The Salvation Army had opened five shelters and the Red Cross twenty-six shelters throughout the Los Angeles area. "They're coming in from Glendale, Burbank, and throughout the San Fernando Valley," Red Cross spokesperson Barbara Wilkes told the press. "There are so many people out of their homes, we don't know what all their problems are yet."

Others tried to stay close to their damaged apartments and houses, pitching tents or wrapping themselves in blankets and sleeping under the stars in yards and parks. One man, fearing falling structures, put his family in the car and drove to the Northridge Park baseball field, where they spent the night in center field.

WE ARRIVED IN Los Angeles at seven o'clock Monday night, just as the Disaster Field Office for Northridge was being opened. The next morning, Secretaries Cisneros and Pena and I toured the earthquake area. I'll never forget the faces of the people we passed in our motorcade. Their eyes were hollow, and I felt as if we were in some third-world country.

On Wednesday afternoon we opened the first eleven Disaster Application Centers. Late that day I took a break from coordination meetings and went out to one of the centers to talk with some of the survivors. As my driver rounded the corner, I was horrified at what I was seeing: There before me were six thousand people standing in line waiting to submit their applications.

I went back to the field office and told my staff we had to do better. Half an hour later, they came back with a bold plan. We would put the application form in the *Los Angeles Times*. In addition, we overlaid Zip codes over the seismic shaking indices we had from Cal Tech, and if someone from one of the three Zip codes with the most shaking made an application, we awarded checks—$3,450 for homeowners, $2,350 for renters—without inspecting their homes. Ironically, given that FEMA had been criticized for taking so *long* to aid victims of Hurricane Andrew, this time we were criticized for rushing to "give away money." We did what we had to do. Later, we conducted post inspections of the homes of those awardees and came up with a 91 percent eligibility rate.

Over the next days and weeks, the cruel toll gradually revealed itself. According to the Office of Management and Budget, the body count—which continued to rise thanks to quake-related heart attacks—topped out at sixty-one. Sixteen of those victims died at the Northridge Meadows Apartments. Nearly nine thousand people were injured. Some sixteen thousand "dwelling units" were rendered uninhabitable, forcing twenty-two thousand people into Red Cross shelters and another eighteen thousand into makeshift camps in city parks. Freeways were damaged in two hundred locations, closing thirty-eight miles of roadway in all directions. Seventy-eight bridges were damaged, and six collapsed.

All told, the Northridge Earthquake affected the lives of some 670,000 people, more than three times the number affected by Hurricane Andrew. Within six months after Northridge, FEMA had approved more than 350,000 applications for disaster housing assistance, for a total of $1 billion. Another $750 million had been earmarked for infrastructure projects and $80 million for human services, including disaster unemployment assistance and crisis counseling. At the same time, HUD had assisted some six thousand families in their search for housing and social services. The SBA had accepted some two hundred thousand disaster-assistance loan applications—more than in the Midwest floods, Hurricane Andrew, Hurricane Hugo, and the Loma Prieta Earthquake combined.

Before very long, it was clear that the Northridge Earthquake would surpass Hurricane Andrew as this country's costliest natural disaster. As I write this, in the winter of 2002, that statistic still stands. The total tab for Northridge was some $40 billion.

◆ ◆ ◆

AND YET. "THIS was far from our worse-case scenario," says Lucy Jones. "Take exactly the same earthquake and put it under the L.A. basin. That would be *so much* worse. That would be a $200-billion earthquake."

If there's one thing I've learned in my career, it's that no place is completely safe. You live near a beautiful river, you're going to have flooding. You live in balmy Florida, you'll get hit by hurricanes. In the majestic mountains, wildfires will rage. The risk in sunny California is earthquakes. We can't run away from life; we just have to learn to live smarter.

I believe Californians need to take a page out of Dr. Lucy Jones's book on living with earthquakes. "Here in southern California we have hundreds of faults on which energy is accumulating," she says, "so that managing your earthquake risk by staying away from faults doesn't work—unless you want to evacuate all of southern California. But why? More people die of hurricanes—more people died in an *ice storm* on the East Coast the week of Northridge than died in the earthquake. I think if anything people are too scared of the personal injury risks and not scared enough of the financial risks."

It's fascinating to me that Jones comes from a family of both missionaries and scientists. "My grandparents went to China in 1915," she says. "My grandfather was a professor of New Testament theology at the University of Nanking. My dad was born and brought up there. Both my uncles were China analysts for the government. My aunt was a missionary in Hong Kong. My dad studied civil engineering and was going to go back and work on the Yangtze Dam project, but he got his degree three months after the Korean War broke out. So he became an aerospace engineer. My father was the only one who didn't stay involved with China. My uncle worked with the CIA and was stationed over there during the Vietnam War. He was in Vietnam, and his family was in Taiwan. So when I was in high school, I lived with them for a year."

Lucy Jones got her B.A. in Chinese language and literature from Brown University in 1976, and in 1981 received her Ph.D. in geophysics from M.I.T. While her scientific specialty is research into aftershocks and foreshocks, she has divined from that study an optimistic message of life and living that she conveys with the zeal of her missionary forebears. "Earthquakes are inevitable," she says, "but damage from earthquakes is not. We can construct buildings that will not fall down and bridges that will sway, not break."

There must be days, though, when Jones feels she's preaching to a race of engineering heathens. "Building codes have done a great good," she says, "but we're not all the way there. Our biggest problem is that building codes aren't retroactive. Santa Clarita did great in Northridge, even though it had really strong shaking. Hollywood had much less shaking and had much more damage, because the buildings there were built a long time ago. And the huge issue for L.A.—*huge* issue—is retrofitting. We could force retrofitting, but politically that's incredibly difficult to tell a homeowner he's got to spend $50,000 or $20,000 preparing for an earthquake that may not happen. I mean, the amount of money to do it—and you're only going to need it if you're right on top of the fault. But which fault's gonna go in the next hundred years? We don't know. We'll never know that one, probably."

The only mitigation law in California is for unreinforced masonry, or URMs. "A friend of mine calls them PPRs—potential piles of rubble," Jones says. "We're talking about an unreinforced brick building—no steel, no wood, just brick. That's been illegal since 1935." This means, she says, that the self-satisfied porker of Disney's *The Three Little Pigs* cartoon had it all wrong when he built his house with bricks. "The right answer was Twigs. Flexible, wood-frame construction. You got to tie them together, though."

Despite the banning of unreinforced masonry, Jones says many such structures have been allowed to stand for years. "It wasn't until the late '80s that California finally passed a mitigation law in which local jurisdictions were required to catalog their URMs and to develop a mitigation plan. But it didn't specify what the mitigation plan was. Some communities were— San Bernardino, for example, was very, very aggressive. Their URMs are gone. Pasadena is marginal. L.A. is okay. San Francisco? Their mitigation plan is doing the cataloging. 'We don't have any money for this,' they say, and they've been trying to get the federal government to pay for it. Or the state. So the state requires the local jurisdictions to catalog their URMs and do a mitigation plan. But it's up to the locals to decide what that mitigation plan is going to be."

The main goal of mitigation or retrofitting, Jones says, is to provide some lateral resistance to being pushed over and to make sure the roof is held up by something besides the brick walls. "Buildings are built to withstand the downward pull of gravity. Earthquakes push on a building in all directions—up and down, but most of all sideways. A safe building is one that can withstand the sideways push."

She gives the example of her own church, a beautiful copy of a fourteenth-century English church, complete with traditional English construction—brick and sandstone. Not exactly the ideal combination for southern California. "They don't have earthquakes in England," Jones says, rolling her eyes. "What we did was, we drilled holes through the walls, put steel beams into the foundation, then tied the roof to those steel beams. The roof is no longer resting on the brick walls. All the walls can come down, and the roof will stay up. The other thing we did was rebuild the tower out of steel and then tied the rock to it. That was pretty major—I think we spent $300,000."

More manageable to the average homeowner would be a house similar to the little yellow two-story the USGS uses for its headquarters. "This is wood-frame construction," Jones says. "It's great, very flexible. It moves around like mad up here when we have an earthquake." During a recent renovation, the 1921 house was retrofitted for earthquakes. "The main thing we did was go into the basement and bolt the house to the foundation. And then as we added on, the new law requires larger expanses of sheer walls—in other words, fewer windows, and no windows butted up against each other in a corner. More continuous wall space. This house is pretty good, because it's wood, and it's not that heavy. In fact, single-family homes are one of the best places to be during an earthquake. Most of us in California, if we undertake these mitigation measures, or have a newer house, the house is going to be okay. The really big issue is going to be the contents of that house. One-third of the costs of the Northridge Earthquake were nonstructural. I'm talking about damage to contents of buildings—computers being thrown around the room, television sets flying through the air. If we had an earthquake at this moment, all of these"—she pats her bookcases—"are bolted to the wall. I would get my books on me, and I would just have to pick them back up."

And how rare, she's asked, is this kind of setup in southern California? "Very rare," she says.

It's a quandary, getting people to take responsibility for their lives. But after hearing Lucy Jones talk at length, you get the feeling she doesn't blame the earthquakes. In fact, it's probably safe to say she *loves* her earthquakes.

She doesn't love what we let them do to us, but she loves their mystery, their power, their almost religious reflection of the timeless struggles of the planet—or at least of her little corner of the planet. An important thing to know about Lucy Jones is that she grew up in Santa Monica. California and earthquakes are in her blood. "My mother was from L.A.," she says. "She was in the big Long Beach earthquake in 1933. And my earliest memory is of an earthquake. I was two years old. I remember Mom getting us, her three children, from the living room into the hallway. I have this whole image of the house—we moved every year because my dad was an aerospace engineer, but it's very clear which house this was. We lived in Ventura then. And the image is of Mom taking us into the hallway and covering up our heads and her sort of on top of us. And the cats screaming—we had a pair of Siamese cats, and they yowled."

There's a lively USGS publication Lucy Jones wrote called *Putting Down Roots in Earthquake Country.* In it, she says, "Earthquakes are as Californian as the snows of Mount Baldy and the sands of Malibu." Yet it took her some years to understand just how much that meant to her. In college, she intended to become a physics major and follow in her father's footsteps. Then she met a geophysicist at a party who told her, basically, "Why not go play in the mountains and get paid for it?"

"He got me interested enough so that when I came back for my senior year, I took a geology class. I was *hooked.* I actually sat down and read the thousand-page textbook the first week. My favorite part of physics was wave theory, so seismology was obvious. And then I got interested in earth sciences.

"After that, earthquakes became my history of California."

AS A FORMER builder, I think we often get our priorities wrong in this country. When construction is begun on any new public project, there's a "groundbreaking" ceremony, complete with blow-dried politicians flashing hundred-watt smiles and wielding gold-plated shovels. Behind them, on an easel, will stand an architect's rendering of the finished building, which inevitably gleams in soaring glory against a cloudless sky. Then, once the steel work is completed, there's another high-profile event—a "topping-out" ceremony, in which the same politicians return (this time in custom-designed hard hats) to scribble their names on the uppermost beams.

In other words, all the focus is on reaching for the heavens. But if I had my way, the big celebration would be the "foundation pouring." And for those who live in California and other areas beset by earthquakes, we would invite the politicians back later to flash their smiles at the "wall bolting" ceremony. Gold-plated wrenches would replace the shovels as the sides of the future skyscraper were secured and tightened to the foundation itself. Unfortunately, foundation pourings and wall boltings don't have the attraction of topping outs. But anyone who's ever built anything lasting knows the infinite value of a proper foundation and the right support.

When I'm at home in Wildcat Hollow, I like to spend my evenings reading the novels of Louis L'Amour. By now, I must've read most of his books, some of them several times, and what I especially like about them is their reality. L'Amour grew up in North Dakota in the early part of the twentieth century, but his knowledge of the West reached back to the glory days of the American frontier. His grandfather told him personal stories of both the Civil and Indian wars, and his uncles regaled him with their experiences as cowboys. But the author L'Amour literally grounded his western tales in the geology of the land, the varieties of the plant life, the natural behavior of the animals, and the true artifacts of day-to-day living. He built his novels on a firm foundation of truth, much as the contemporary author Tom Clancy does his.

It's not such a broad leap from books to business. As readers, we *trust* L'Amour and Clancy precisely because of the way they bind their tales to the integrity of their research. One of the dictionary definitions of integrity is "the state of being unimpaired; soundness." Think of a "proper foundation" that way. If you were a CEO, or that CEO's customer, wouldn't you want that company's product to spring from, and be tied to, a foundation of impeccable integrity?

ALL WE HAVE to do is utter the relatively new word *dot-com* to summon up images of companies whose weak foundations crumbled in a crisis. And yet one of the great success stories of the past decade came from that very dot-com world.

I just called up AOL Time Warner on the Internet, and the AOL summary for 2001 is astonishing. By the end of that year the web service had "crossed the 33 million member worldwide milestone." Following the September 11 terrorist attacks, AOL and other groups joined together to raise more than $30 million for those in need. On-line shopping was up 67 percent in 2001 (to more than $33 *billion*), with the holiday season accounting for $7.2 billion.

Clearly, the little company that began business in 1985 as Quantum Computer Services, Inc., and became America Online has done something very right. Judging from what I've read, the management team that blueprinted this phenomenal success followed these basic steps: They identified their market (and therefore their mission); spelled it out for all to see; delivered the system they promised; promoted their product relentlessly; and built on that base to add increasing value to their core product.

"The commercial market then consisted of barely 500,000 bodies, divided largely between technical and business users on CompuServe and Dow Jones News/Retrieval," wrote Mark Nollinger in a 1995 piece for *Wired*. "So [Steve] Case and his partners figured a service for home users might be just the ticket." For home users, they wanted to make the Internet everything it then wasn't—fun, accessible, inexpensive. "Critics who dismiss the service for emphasizing breadth over depth miss the point," wrote Nollinger. "AOL is about pop culture, not pocket protectors. Shrewd alliances with partners ranging from the American Association of Retired Persons to MTV have made AOL the service for Everyman. You want 'information'? Fine, check out CompuServe. But if you want to swap opinions on Medicare cuts or hang out with Courtney Love online, AOL's the place to go."

Not that it hasn't had some growing pains. In late 1996, when AOL infamously changed its pricing system and a deluge of customers were "put on hold," they had their share of crisis response. They'd succeeded all right, and now people wanted their product, connecting to other AOL members, far beyond their high-end projections. The experience sobered the company, which rushed to upgrade its infrastructure. You can see its mark on every new partnership the company strikes up.

The general idea of establishing a proper foundation encompasses many of the other subjects of this book—knowing what you believe in, creating personal support systems, team building. These are important bases for success in all walks of life, not just in business. The AOL accomplishment I most admire is their laserlike focus on their mission even as the company was growing beyond its founders' wildest dreams. I suppose you could conduct a whole Harvard Business School course on the fine line between diversifying and losing your way, but it seems to me that so many companies start out building on their foundations and then, the higher they go, they either get greedy or scared and decide to branch out. So instead of building the foundation first, they start adding on floors well above the ground, forgetting to add in support beams along the way, and eventually they topple over from their imbalance. AOL has done anything but.

My latest favorite story about dot-coms in crisis involves a company called Logical Net Corp., which I read about in a recent issue of the magazine *Inc.* At the time—the winter of 2001—this $8 million Internet Service Provider (ISP) was headed toward bankruptcy fast. In six months it had flip-flopped from turning a profit to losing $130,000 a month. This was a result of getting caught up in too-quick growth, the inexperience of its CEO, and the wave of dot-com bankruptcies that evaporated Logical Net's accounts receivable. So what happened? The CEO, Tush Nikollaj, leveled with the employees. "He drew one stark, startling graph on a blackboard," writes *Inc.* staffer Ilan Mochari. "His presentation took ten minutes."

The CEO's managers were stunned by the news, of course, but also by Nikollaj's candor. Shrewd candor, it turned out to be. "After crunching the numbers, he realized that the only way he could avoid bankruptcy would be if all his employees moved to cut costs and raise revenues—drastically. To motivate swift action, Nikollaj knew he'd need buy-in." That's precisely what he got. Once the numbers were laid on the table, even the employees destined for pink slips understood. And the other ones suddenly realized it was *their* job, too, to trim expenses and maximize profits—which they did, saving the company. "I've never been more excited than when I heard an engineer talk about return on investment," Nikollaj told *Inc.* "Except when my children were born."

I have no idea what the condition of Logical Net Corp. will be when this book comes out, but I wish them well. What I like about this story, however, is what it teaches us about another aspect of proper foundations. A manager can and must guide the design and construction of a sound base to build on, but it's his employees—through their attitudes and aptitudes—that determine the level of success that foundation will support.

And what binds and strengthens the manager/employee relationship, like the wire mesh at the heart of poured concrete, is constant two-way communication.

Since the big United Parcel Service (UPS) strike of 1996, management professionals have had a field day analyzing how such a thing could've happened. UPS was this much-admired corporate giant, a homey brand whose brown-clad drivers know and are known in the offices and on the front porches of America. That 185,000 of these employees would go on strike against the company was unthinkable—not just by outside observers, but by UPS management itself.

"That spectacular misjudgment reflects just how insulated the employee-owned company's managers are (its corporate culture is described variously as 'cultlike,' 'militaristic,' and 'unimaginative')," wrote Linda Grant in a Reputation Management case study. "UPS was an ideal union target. When the lights came on, CEO James Kelly was without a strategy, outmaneuvered at every turn. . . ."

"Every company in America should pay attention to what happened to UPS," New York PR expert Gershon Kekst told Reputation Management. "Corporate loyalty is dead, but managements don't know it."

If corporate loyalty is dead, it's because management has come unbolted from the integral—as in *integrity*—foundation of the corporation. When I became director of FEMA, I turned immediately to the agency's career employees as my partners in rebuilding. Under a series of political appointees—which I was, too, of course—those people had been devalued, diminished, and depressed. For years, they'd received threats and intimidation as their reward for imagination and ingenuity. So naturally they didn't feel comfortable opening up to me when I started having a series of conference room meetings debating our new mission and strategy. "Let's talk it out," I would say. "If I'm wrong, tell me."

In time they learned—sometimes too well, I thought!—that I was serious. And that led to more openness, and more good ideas, and more teamwork in implementing them. We had gotten about halfway through our reorganization when the Midwest floods hit. Suddenly this energized new staff—so used to being referred to as "bureaucratic jackasses" and the like—got high marks from the media on their handling of this major disaster. "FEMA's Response to Flood Changes Bureau's Image," was a headline from the *Tulsa World*. "Agency Rises Above Reputation," said the *Atlanta*

Constitution. For these good people, this was a major turnaround—not just in their performance, but in their view of themselves. From then on, they pitched in with everything they had to help us help people in crisis. I can honestly say that if FEMA had been a corporation instead of a government agency, I don't believe I would've had to worry about a strike.

In his study of the agency's results-based management, George Mason University's Jerry Ellig wrote: "Overall, the financial rewards for superior performance at FEMA appear fairly small—but the intrinsic rewards are substantial. The agency tends to attract 'fixers and scrappers who want to get something done,' in the words of one employee. . . . Employees who transferred to other federal agencies have often sought to return to FEMA, both because of the excitement and because the agency's small size fosters a sense of belonging. This situation represents a significant change from 1993, when half of FEMA employees surveyed said they would take a job elsewhere if offered one."

In summary, then, here's the blueprint for building—and tending—the kind of foundation and support beams that'll help prevent a disaster:

• **LAY A GROUNDWORK FOR YOUR STRATEGIES, NOT YOUR TASKS AND TACTICS.** Let's assume you've got to stay in a crisis-prone area. How will you weather it? Will you earthquake-proof your business for the big one or decide that insurance and the current building code are enough to pull you through the smaller, somewhat powerful quakes? Figure out what your infrastructure should include. Just as you create a list of crisis attributes to come up with a prevention plan for a recurring crisis, you should create a list of project attributes to come up with a prevention plan for riding the less predictable disasters. Identify the patterns in what you need to deliver to and get from suppliers, customers, employees, vendors, clients, and the media on a regular basis. Some of these things will have already emerged when you focus on your values; others might surprise you, especially if you're starting a new product or service strategy that requires an attribute that you don't already have in place. (Like enough bandwidth to let your entire customer base access their accounts at the same time.) Looking for patterns helps you see the real-world commonalities in your strategies, just in case they don't match up with the ones you're *supposed* to be pursuing.

• **TEST AND STABILIZE YOUR INFRASTRUCTURE.** When your last crisis is still fresh in people's minds, it's often harder to make ambitious decisions. But you can't let a recent crisis hold you back from launching new ventures or new products, and you can't let it hold your partners back from being your partner. You definitely don't want it to keep your clients or customers from buying from you. Those moments of hesitation have a lasting legacy. Keep an eye on how your project attribute list changes after a crisis. Have you changed what or when or how your business delivers its products or services? How does that affect your current business, and how could it affect your new projects? Revise your plans, focusing on those whats, whens, and hows. You don't want to trigger a new crisis simply because you've just been through one.

• **REMEMBER THAT YOUR EMPLOYEES ARE YOUR BUILDING BLOCKS.** Don't taper down your concept of infrastructure so it just includes phone lines, factories, storage facilities, computers, credit lines, insurance, and the like. Without people, those resources are useless.

• **AIM HIGH—BUT NEVER TAKE YOUR EYE OFF YOUR FOUNDATION.** As I said before, when you start to overreach your foundation, you're at risk of toppling yourself. Every time you expand, acquire, or merge, make sure your crisis-prevention infrastructure extends to your new employees, offices, and projects immediately, before a crisis hits.

Sometimes, however, all your work to prepare or prevent a crisis won't be enough. So let's see what lessons you need by your side when it's time to respond.

III

RESPONDING TO
CRISIS

5

TWINE IS STRONGER THAN STRING

The Power of a Personal Support System

Mark Ghilarducci and Kim Zagaris were in a San Jose, California, hotel watching CNN and getting ready to give talks at a Western States fire conference. Rick Martinez was attending a seven A.M. English class in Sacramento. I was in my Washington office talking on the phone.

Like the JFK assassination before it, like the World Trade Center attacks after, the Oklahoma City bombing was a demarcation point that forever changed the way you look at the world. At nine-oh-one on April 19, 1995, life was one way. By nine-oh-three, that old life had vanished and a new, harsher one was now a reality. Consequently, we all—especially those of us who went there—remember exactly where we were when we heard the news.

With CNN's special report still breaking, Ghilarducci, head of the Sacramento USAR task force, picked up the phone and called FEMA headquarters, where we were just getting our first sketchy intelligence on the disaster. We said we'd get back to him. For several minutes after the blast, the facts were as foggy as the smoke cloaking the remains of the Murrah Federal Building. I've seen a picture of the first fire truck on the scene. Flames rage behind it, and the air is so thick you'd think the photo was taken at night. In those early moments a couple of theories emerged: One, that this was the result of a gas line explosion. Two, that a jetliner had crashed into the building. When the smoke lifted and the Oklahoma City firefighters could begin to see the full extent of the damage, they were stunned by the sight. They had arrived in Beirut.

Still uncertain as to exactly what had happened, but knowing that it was bad, we were back on the line to Ghilarducci within twenty minutes, telling him to get his group ready to go. We told him we were deploying two search-and-rescue teams. Phoenix, because it was closer to Oklahoma City, would arrive first. Sacramento would arrive not long after.

The Sacramento task force is one of twenty-eight elite urban search-and-rescue teams positioned throughout the United States. Each one is comprised of sixty-two people representing several disciplines, including a search component made up of seismic and canine specialists; a rescue group equipped to cut and break up debris; a medical team staffed by physicians, nurses, and paramedics trained to perform surgery and give life support on the scene; and a technical staff made up of structural engineers, map compilers, hazardous materials specialists, plus communications, logistical, and documents staff.

California, because of its size and its wide variety of disasters, led the nation in developing these teams, starting with eight in the late 1980s. Each is based out of a local fire department, with the non-fire personnel attached from the same locality. In state emergencies, these teams can be mobilized as needed. In the early 1990s, the system was taken to the national level. Today California's eight original teams are part of the national system, with twenty other task forces spread out across the country.

Ghilarducci and Zagaris delivered their talks as planned, then hurried back to Sacramento. They didn't have to go home and pack. Each search-and-rescue member always has with him a suitcase containing enough clothes and supplies for seven days. "Every morning you kiss your wife and kids and say good-bye," Zagaris says, "and you don't know if it's just for today, for a week, or . . ." He doesn't complete the thought. Each team also has prepacked and preweighed pallets of material—some fifteen thousand pounds made up of everything from buckets to backhoes, shovels to sonar cameras—lined up and ready to go at whatever airport they fly from. In Sacramento's case, that's Travis Air Force Base. By late morning, Pacific time—some five hours after the bombing—Ghilarducci and Zagaris's team, including search dogs, hunkered down in the belly of a huge cargo plane, their pallets stored in the hold below, and the plane lifted off for a mission that would change their lives.

They landed at Oklahoma's Tinker Air Force Base just before midnight. Before being bused to the bomb site, they received a briefing from the Oklahoma City fire officers. "They had been going hot and heavy for fifteen hours," Ghilarducci recalls. "They were thrashed." Most of the Oklahoma firemen knew somebody buried in rubble.

An hour later the Sacramento task force arrived at the Murrah Federal Building, its shattered shell eerily lit from below. One of the task force members, Ed Vasquez, remembers how quiet everyone on the bus was when they approached the scene. "We're trained to focus on the job and not to take in the big picture," Vasquez says. "But when we rolled up to the Murrah Building that night, you couldn't help thinking about the big picture. The damage was just so immense."

I HAD FLOWN to Oklahoma City the afternoon of the bombing, arriving about one P.M. All day long, the media had been focusing its attention solely on the Murrah Federal Building. So I was astounded to see the damage surrounding ground zero. When the blast occurred, it literally suctioned all the air around it to fill the vacuum created by the bomb. Across the street a building was leveled, killing seven people. Beyond that, a concrete roof was sucked up, as if by a tornado, and dropped whole onto a busy parking lot. In all, 365 downtown buildings sustained some amount of damage, ranging from totally destroyed to partially damaged.

The Murrah Building itself was like nothing I had ever seen in my life. The whole back of the building was blown away, like one of those cutaway pictures in textbooks. All nine floors were opened up for everyone to see. From the street you could make out desks, filing cabinets, the potted plants that used to add life to an office. Haunting details stood out, like the smiley-face coffee cup on a table and the abandoned tricycle with its handlebar

streamers still as death. Every one of Oklahoma City's thirty-seven fire stations was dispatched to the scene, along with some twelve hundred police
officers. In those first hours before the search-and-rescue teams arrived,
firemen managed to clear the site for hazardous materials, create a floor-by-
floor manifest of who might've been in the building (first estimates put as
many as nine hundred people there), and begin the excruciating task of contacting relatives, friends, and business associates of the Murrah workers to
pare the list to some five hundred most likelys. At our makeshift base of
operations, we updated these constantly shifting estimates on crude
sketches of the bombed-out building pushpinned to the wall.

The Oklahoma City bombing was the first presidentially declared disaster
that was also a crime scene, which meant that in addition to the firefighters,
policemen, search-and-rescue teams, and a task force of funeral directors,
we also had some two hundred FBI agents, forty-five U.S. Marshals, and
seventy-five ATF officers on hand. As FEMA director, besides being the
administration's voice on the scene, I was charged with keeping all these
people moving in the same direction. By late afternoon of that first day, when
we knew positively that this disaster was man-made, I was glad to have the
distractions that these competing agencies brought me. The idea that someone would deliberately commit such an act made me sick at my stomach.
When I could find a minute to think about myself, I phoned my wife, Lea
Ellen. "I need you to come be with me," I said.

OVER THE NEXT seventeen days, eleven USAR teams would be deployed
to Oklahoma City—the most, at that time, for any disaster in U.S. history.

In federal search-and-rescue efforts, local authorities retain control of
responding to the disaster. But as a buffer between the locals and the people
who've been deployed to help, a core group of experts called the Incident
Support Team (IST) takes charge to integrate the operations of the search-
and-rescue forces into the general plan of the local command. Mark Ghilarducci would be handed overall leadership of the IST; Kim Zagaris was chief
of the planning section, charged with devising a general strategy for dealing
with this incident. Ray Downey, battalion chief and head of rescue operations for the New York City fire department, became chief of operations, the
guy who made sure the action plan was carried out. Jim Hone, assistant

chief of the Santa Monica fire department, was put in charge of "interior operations," which meant he oversaw daytime work inside the bombed-out Murrah Building. Other top officials from around the country, with expertise in everything from finance to communications, rounded out the IST group.

When this elite team arrived in Oklahoma City that night, they walked into what Ghilarducci calls "controlled chaos." For the first half hour Ghilarducci and Zagaris just stood and looked at the Murrah Federal Building. "We really were in awe at the complexity of what we were up against," Ghilarducci says today. "We still didn't have a good handle on how many people we were looking for. People were wandering in and out of the area. And while the Oklahoma City firefighters had done a good job of clearing most of the upper floors of the Murrah Building, they hadn't had time to deal with any of the other buildings. Any plan we came up with had to incorporate all of those aspects."

In my experience, no job in any disaster is more difficult—both physically and emotionally—than that of search and rescue. These teams are the infantry of the disaster world. They are hands-on, up close and personal. They don't deal in abstracts; they deal in concrete and steel, wood and glass, water and mud, and, all too often, flesh and blood. It takes a certain kind of person to do this work. Ask how they cope and they look at you like you're speaking Martian. Because one way they cope is not to think about coping. Instead, they focus on the job at hand.

And yet I don't believe you can go into a crisis like the Oklahoma City bombing without some coping strategy, spoken or not. You've got to connect yourself to something bigger than you are. Some search-and-rescue people carry lucky charms. "For thirty years I've carried a Mexican coin in my pocket," says Rick Martinez, fire chief at Sacramento and one of the task force team leaders at Oklahoma City. "I've rubbed it so much that it's almost smooth. I also wear the same cap at every disaster. It's just something I do."

But this job takes more than superstition. These people have to have unswerving belief not only in the importance of what they do but in their absolute ability to do it, no matter how long the odds. "These are the ultimate macho guys," says Dan Gibson, a minister who works as a chaplain with fire departments and search-and-rescue teams. "They're taught from day one that they have to maintain control of everything. Now, you and I know that's impossible. But when they come onto the scene, they put on that big badge and they hide behind it. The way they do what they do is through an abiding belief in two things: one, their own training and skill; and, two, the team itself. They always work in groups."

And when they arrive at a disaster site, they expect to perform the tasks that give their team their name: not just search, but rescue, too.

"From the get-go, we approached this as a full rescue—not a recovery," says Ghilarducci. "We believed that there could be void spaces where people could still be alive." After suggesting to the Oklahoma operations team that they tighten the perimeter, set up an outside staging area, and define specific procedures and routes for workers entering and leaving the disaster site, Ghilarducci and Zagaris made their first foray into the Murrah Federal Building.

By now it was two or three in the morning, a time when anyone with a normal life would've been safely in bed. The floodlights cast jagged shadows in the rubble, and the dark spaces were dark beyond belief. All of this was enclosed in a spooky silence. Then, suddenly, a creaking would sound from somewhere in the darkness and soon a sliver of loose concrete would slip off an upper floor, ricocheting into the void. Other pieces would then shift, slide, and go quiet again. "I gotta tell you, it was a house of cards in there," says Ghilarducci. "The whole infrastructure had been ripped away. The building was literally trying to resettle itself."

For search-and-rescue workers, this is the most treacherous environment imaginable. Most of nine floors had caved into a tight heap in the basement, but huge chunks of concrete and steel, not to mention desks, file cabinets, and refrigerators, still teetered on the craggy edges of the upper floors. The challenge was first to clear away as much of that debris as possible and to replace or shore up infrastructure where needed—all this while the rescue workers began the dangerous task of searching for survivors in the pile at the bottom.

Before the first sun had risen on this unspeakable scene, interior operations chief Jim Hone began directing his force of some three hundred people, including structural engineers, Oklahoma City fire and police officers, military troops, and two search-and-rescue forces, in the delicate balancing act that resembled nothing so much as a deadly game of pick-up sticks.

✦ ✦ ✦

THERE WASN'T MUCH sleep to be had over the next few days. My wife, Lea Ellen, flew to Oklahoma City the morning after I called her, and even though I didn't see her much, just knowing she was there made me feel better. She worked in the command center answering phones or doing whatever else needed doing. I seemed always to be in meetings, usually late into the night. We stayed in a motel about a mile from downtown, and she always waited for me to get finished, no matter what the time. We would talk some on the way back to the motel, but mostly we would just be together. For me, that was enough. In the mornings we would pray and read Scripture, and that helped me deal with the challenges I had to face. One day a man came up and thanked me for all we were doing to help the victims. "It's our job," I said—and then I asked if he had lost anyone in the bombing. "My sister is still in the building," he said, and he broke down and hugged me and wouldn't let go.

Ghilarducci and Zagaris didn't sleep at all for the first forty hours they were on the scene. There was just too much to do, and time was of the essence. They still didn't know exactly how many people they were looking for, but they had learned pretty quickly that their initial theory about void spaces where people could still be alive was wrong. "An earthquake will break concrete into pieces that can hold up debris," Ghilarducci says. "This bomb pulverized the concrete." Consequently, the search-and-rescue teams weren't finding survivors.

Ghilarducci and Zagaris tried their best to bring some reason to the proceedings. "In third-world countries, the rescue teams just go up to a pile of rubble and start digging," says Zagaris. At Oklahoma City, once a search dog sniffed out something beneath the debris, other search-and-rescue members with tiny probing cameras containing microphones would insert them into the tiny spaces, looking and listening for signs of life. But Zagaris thought that was still too hit-and-miss. From the beginning, Chuck Smith and his Disaster-Mortuary, or D-Mort, team had worked hard to provide searchers with a road map to work from. Instead of the crude drawing we used at the beginning, Smith got hold of the Murrah Building blueprint. Then he talked with the building manager and especially the maintenance crews, who were able to draw in office layouts. This more detailed map was constantly updated according to what the IST members knew about who was, or wasn't, in the building when the bomb exploded.

That annotated blueprint was the searchers' bible for the crucial first few days. Eventually, though, Zagaris came up with an idea for an even better tool. All USAR teams have a Geographic Information Specialist (GIS) component, or map unit. In disasters such as forest fires, this group can produce maps of the area, showing the land consumed by blaze and the terrain immediately threatened, so that firefighters can focus their efforts where they're needed most. Zagaris wondered if his GIS unit could make a map showing the areas of the Murrah Building that might contain the most victims, living or dead.

Over the next few days, the team worked at creating three-dimensional models of the Murrah Building. What they produced was nothing short of miraculous: 3-D maps of the building, shown from every angle, with different-colored triangle symbols for every known worker on every floor in the building—and then their trajectories as a result of the massive blast. The maps told them that the search should be concentrated generally in the bottom left portion of the building.

As the search-and-rescue operation intensified, the Murrah Federal Building took on a life force of its own. Parts of the structure earned nicknames. A huge piece of concrete hanging by twisted rebar from the roof was dubbed "The Mother Slab." Should it break completely loose, this massive chunk was heavy enough to destabilize the entire building. The team couldn't risk that, so they strapped it into place with steel cable. Below the Mother Slab was a scooped-out area called "The Bowl." "The Christmas Tree" was an area where floors had collapsed on either side of a column, resulting in a precarious A-frame of wreckage. Down on the first floor was "The Forest," so named because there was so much vertical wood shoring wedged in between columns sixteen and eighteen. "The Cave" was a low place where several bodies were pinned. But most of the victims were found where the GIS team had projected—in a hellhole known as "The Pit." "This was where the child daycare center collapsed into itself, from floor two to floor one," says Hone. "It's the area that required the most challenging shoring, because we had to secure it in two directions. We had to shore the columns in compression, so that they didn't push *into* the building from the weight of the debris pile outside; then we had to tie one-inch cables around the columns and put them in tension, so that if they moved debris on the *outside* they wouldn't push the building in that direction."

But even with all their high-tech expertise, the searchers weren't finding anyone to rescue. In short order the hopelessness began taking its toll on everybody. Even the search dogs became depressed. One team member had a colleague lie in the rubble so the dog could finally find someone alive. At first, the teams ran on pure adrenaline, but then the adrenaline began to fail them. Psychiatrists will tell you that usually happens at about the three-day mark, unless there's good news to keep you going. At Oklahoma City, there was no good news. Almost immediately the weather turned cold and rainy, chilling the rescuers and making every bucketload of debris heavier. We had to get them rain gear, and then heavier boots. People working inside the Murrah Building would wear out a pair of steel-toed and steel-shanked boots every couple of days. Among the workers, a subtle shift in mission occurred: Maybe they couldn't *rescue* these people—but they sure as hell could see that their bodies were treated with the utmost respect.

I had gone inside the Murrah Building every day since I'd been there, and it got harder instead of easier. No one could keep the tears from flowing.

DESPITE THE SHORING of the Murrah Building, the precarious give-and-take turned out to be felt most acutely among the on-site agencies themselves.

Every evening, I went to the staff meetings for the search-and-rescue effort and then to the staff meetings of the FBI. The experience was surreal. Here were two earnest, dedicated, well-trained groups working as hard as they could—and yet there was an inherent conflict between them. In clearing out the debris, the search-and-rescue people needed to proceed slowly, carefully. The FBI wanted to pick up the pace, to get their hands on crime evidence immediately—and they wanted that evidence not to be contaminated. Each group was under tremendous pressure. The search-and-rescue people couldn't quit while there was even the slightest hope of finding someone alive (and as Ray Downey pointed out, in a store collapse in Seoul, Korea, a young woman was found alive after *sixteen days* of entrapment). The FBI, on the other hand, was under unprecedented pressure to build an airtight case against those who had committed this horrendous deed. In those nightly meetings, FBI deputy director Weldon Kennedy was completely candid with me: He wanted the Bureau to take over the operation.

The increasing pressure to switch from rescue mode to recovery rested heaviest upon the shoulders of Mark Ghilarducci, who coordinated the overall efforts. "I was torn by the decision," says Ghilarducci. "I sought advice from everyone—the engineers, FEMA, Oklahoma City fire chief Gary Marrs. I wanted to make sure that there was no slim possibility that someone was alive in there, so that Governor Frank Keating and the fire chief could go to the family members and say, 'We've done everything humanly possible. We're now going to recovery mode.' We could've probably gone to recovery a day or two sooner than we did. Even a lot of the rescuers were saying, 'Why are we in rescue mode? There's nobody alive in here.' But given all the pressures, and the way the world was watching us, I had to make sure. Ultimately, the final decision had to be made by Chief Marrs, but I had to make the recommendation."

So the grueling process continued, with its attendant strains, stresses, and animosities. I don't know who felt it most, but nobody felt it least. The poor families stood outside the perimeter begging any worker who walked by to save their loved ones. The criminal investigators, pressed by an outraged nation to nail Timothy McVeigh, could hardly keep from mutiny. Even the Oklahoma City rescuers, exhausted in every way possible, sometimes snapped at the very people who had flown in to help them. "Chief Marrs and I were joined at the hip," says Ghilarducci. "And just when we thought we had things under control, we'd have a flare-up. One of the search-and-rescue guys would say to one of the Oklahoma City guys, 'Hey, could you guys pick up those extension cords,' and the Oklahoma guys would go, 'Bullshit! I'm not carrying stuff for you!' We spent a lot of late nights trying to smooth over hurt feelings."

In the process, each "family" began falling back on their unswerving belief in, and absolute loyalty to, their own. Whenever Ghilarducci would show signs of stress, Kim Zagaris would step in and tell him it was time for them to go get a cup of coffee. When Jim Hone, lifting a piece of debris and uncovering the body of a little boy, began beating his hands on the wall, a pal came up and put his hand on his shoulder. "Go ahead," he told Hone, "let it out." Rick Martinez says that late at night, after showers were taken and all the tools were cleaned and ready for the next shift, and there was no more busywork to help keep minds off the situation at hand, "Sometimes a guy would just burst out crying. One of us would just go over and put our arm around him."

TODAY IT'S KNOWN pretty much by all involved as "the come-to-Jesus meeting." It took place late at night on day seven, April 26, and in many ways it was the beginning of the beginning. "After that meeting, we were all working together," says Ghilarducci. But for a while there, cooperation didn't look like the most predictable outcome.

Sometime earlier in that evening, I was asked by Weldon Kennedy to call a meeting of the FBI, the search-and-rescue team management, and my FEMA staff. I was glad to do it. I knew that there would be fireworks, but that ultimately we had to get through this moment in order to come out the other side.

When he got word of the impending summit, Mark Ghilarducci had just finished a long meeting with Fire Chief Marrs. "We'd been reviewing the progress that had been made and talking about the work that was coming up. A lot of cleanup had been done on the inside of the Murrah Building. Because every action has to have an equal-and-opposite reaction, we were having to shore up the infrastructure before we started removing much debris from the *outside* of the building."

What Ghilarducci didn't know was that the FBI had been filming the outside every day, and every night they would get together and look at that video and talk about the progress—or lack of it—that they saw being made.

When everyone assembled, some wearing three-piece suits, some tired and dirty from the day's work, I felt as if I had slipped into one of those old B westerns where the ranch hands were facing off against the prosperous landowners. The search-and-rescue teams sat on one side of the table and the FBI sat on the other. Right away, Weldon Kennedy started talking. He said the FBI was "very concerned" because they didn't believe progress was being made, and they were "very concerned" about wrapping this thing up, and they were "really concerned" that search-and-rescue management didn't know how to handle the job at hand. I watched Mark Ghilarducci while this was going on. I hadn't seen him lose his temper once since we'd been at Oklahoma City. Now his face was turning red.

Kennedy didn't notice. Before Ghilarducci could get a word out, Kennedy pressed his indictment further. "In fact," he said, looking across the table, "we submit to you that you're *dragging this out* and using it as a training mission for your people. We think you don't really want this to come to an end."

I fully expected to see Ghilarducci leap across the table. His men were steaming, their jaws clinched tight. Ghilarducci said to Kennedy, "Have you actually been inside the building?"

Then one of the other FBI guys piped up: "Hey, look," he said, "I was in Buenos Aires"—or maybe he said Chile—"when there was a bombing in a building, and I was sent down there to handle it. We took control of that operation. I brought in a clamshell. . . ." That's a crane with a big scoop on it. It's a technique that can be used in recovery, but not in rescue. "We can expedite this whole process," the agent went on. "We can cut the time in half. We can be out of here and turn this operation back over."

"Yeah," said Kennedy. "And the Fire Chief is very unhappy." Ghilarducci, who had just finished a perfectly cordial meeting with Chief Marrs, was so angry he was shaking. There's a whole lot of ego involved in these highly trained teams, and it often rears its head when agencies have to work together. But usually it doesn't stand up and wave a red flag at the opposition.

Ghilarducci wasn't going to listen to any more of it. "Wait just a minute," he said to the FBI. "This is the United States of America. In this country it isn't *acceptable* to use a clamshell in a rescue operation, and we're not going to do it. Unless I'm *forced* to turn this operation over to you, that's just not going to happen."

Frankly, even though I had found Weldon Kennedy to be a good man, I felt that this meeting had taken an unnecessarily accusatory tone. It was time I got involved. It was time to find some common ground among all these players, and the way to do that was to pull more people in instead of pushing people out. "You know, Weldon," I said, "I thought things were going well, and I've talked to Gary Marrs and I thought *he* thought things were going well. I think the best way to settle this is to talk to Gary right now."

"We've already talked with him," Kennedy said. "We all think it's time to make some changes. . . ."

"Well," I said, "I want to hear that from the Fire Chief. I think we need to get him in here."

Kennedy was clearly becoming uncomfortable. I like to think that he was starting to see that he was pushing his agenda without weighing what other people were doing and what they needed in order to get their job done. The search-and-rescue teams were tapping into an essential need. The people of Oklahoma City, of the whole United States, needed them to be looking for survivors until it didn't make any more sense. They needed those teams to treat the victims with respect and diligence. And, most important to the FBI's criminal investigation, the search-and-rescue teams were shoring up the walls of the building from the inside, keeping the area safe and the site clear. It was deliberate work, but in a few days the search-and-rescue teams would be finished up.

Kennedy backed down. Four days later, on April 30, 1995, the Oklahoma City operation switched from rescue to recovery mode.

TO MY SURPRISE, going home was hard for me. Like the USAR teams when all the work was done, I suddenly had too much time to think. I felt alone, isolated. At work, my staff says I was very distant for a long time after my return. In my head I was questioning: How could somebody, an *American*, do such a thing? And what could I have done differently to help the people of Oklahoma City?

"Their sleep patterns were *so* altered," Chaplain Dan recalls, talking about some of the search-and-rescue members, though he could just as well be describing me, "and they had a hard time getting themselves up to work again at peak efficiency. Firemen critique themselves to death, so that had a big effect on them. And finally, those that had children—they transferred their pent-up anger against the perpetrators of the Oklahoma City bombing. 'How could they do that to children?' they kept asking. 'I have kids. And Sacramento is a lot like Oklahoma City. . . .'"

Gibson says that the vast majority of the USAR task force handled re-entry adequately, if slowly, dealing with their memories in their own way. Mark Ghilarducci was able to discuss those seventeen grueling days with his wife, because she's worked in search-and-rescue. Ed Vasquez, on the other hand, only wanted to talk with people who'd actually been there. Rick

Martinez went to a counselor a few times, then got on with his life. When he went back to English class the following week, somebody said, "Hey, I saw you on TV! You were at Oklahoma City!" Martinez said, "Yeah," and let the matter drop.

My own reemergence came as a result of a request by my pastor, Reverend Don Bowen. He wondered if I would talk about my experiences at Oklahoma City at a prayer breakfast the church was having. Reluctantly, I did. Then he asked if I would share my experience with the entire congregation at the next Sunday's church service. I didn't make any notes. I just talked from my heart about what everyone had gone through, and I thanked the people for their prayers, which were a huge support. It was while standing in that sanctuary, in front of all those caring people, that I suddenly felt a weight lifting from my shoulders.

My problem in coming home was trying to carry the burden of Oklahoma City all by myself. There's no need for that, with the Murrah Building bombing or any other disaster. Remember, you owe it to yourself, your family, your neighbors, your employees—whomever—to manage your own management of a crisis. Don't start thinking you're in it alone. That's arrogance, and totally nonproductive.

I know that all of us who were at Oklahoma City will forever feel the weight of those trying days. But instead of a burden, it's a bond we have. Now, whenever our paths cross, we inevitably touch on that indelible time. And the strange thing is, Oklahoma City continues to live, evolve, and take on new meaning in our lives. Rick Martinez tells the story of a simple artifact he picked up from inside the Murrah Building as his USAR team was about to leave. "It was just this thick piece of glass from one of the front windows," he says. "I chose it because it was small enough to put in my pocket. Now, almost seven years later, it's the most precious thing I own."

At first, it was only a piece of window glass. But in time, he began to see something more in it. He holds it up. The broken glass, green in tint, is shaped uncannily like the state of Oklahoma.

WE LOVE THE IDEA of the lone cowboy, the rugged individualist who goes his own way with only his horse for a friend. But the truth about cowboys is that they don't work alone. Even well-known "corporate cowboys" like Lee Iacocca and Jack Welch are successful because they've been able to surround themselves with a network of devoted supporters.

I find "networking" a very descriptive buzzword. The word itself implies how one person draws a line to another and another and another, and how each of those people draws lines to still other people, and before you know it, you've woven something much stronger than any of the individual parts. In times of crisis—business or personal—you want and need that net. I told you in the introduction how a flood once washed out thirty-three bridges in the county where I served as judge. Something like that, being cut off from neighbors, from work, from the next town, makes you appreciate your connections to the rest of the world. Much of life is about building bridges—and keeping them in good repair.

In the narrowest business sense, that's the way a personal support system works. It helps you connect to others and build bridges. It helps you get jobs. It helps you succeed in jobs. And it helps you survive the inevitable bumps along the way.

It's easy to talk about the importance of a personal support system, but building and maintaining one is something else again. People equals conflict, *especially* during times of high stress. Anybody who's ever lived or worked with at least one other person has at some point heard that interior voice hollering for time alone. After all, life's a lot easier when there's nobody around to tell you things you don't want to hear.

Time alone is fine—most of us wouldn't be particularly good company without it. But blocking people out can become an insidious thing, in both life and work. It's easy to couch it in positive terms: "I've got a report to write." "I've got a campaign to think out." "I've got to get away from this mess in order to meet my deadline." "I've got to put my priority on *my* people." "I've got to *focus!*" Well, sure, but doing so puts up walls between what you need to accomplish and what others need to accomplish. When a crisis comes, it's hard to pull those walls down. And if you've been building walls for a long time, it's hard to break the instinct at short notice.

In my experience, the difference between success and something less is the difference between reaching out and digging in. I've known people who handle the everyday pressures of life and work by burying themselves in the task at hand, cutting themselves off from the people around them. The truly successful people I know see their task at hand in a wider context. They don't just fulfill an assignment, they fulfill themselves as human beings.

Through trial and error, I've learned that the best way to lead is to reach out to others. Before I got to FEMA, there were walls between the managers and the employees. I'm speaking both figuratively and literally—they built private bathrooms, private elevators, anything to keep from having to mingle with the people who worked for them. On my first morning at FEMA, I stood at the entrance to the building and greeted every single employee as he or she came through the door. Later I instituted an open-door policy and even invited employees to write evaluations of me. Those small gestures went a long way toward getting those people in my corner in times of crisis.

Another thing I've learned is that once you're able to see your world as a conglomeration of customers, you've made the first step toward placing yourself at the center of a perennial personal support system. In government, people have traditionally taken a back seat to "programs." Agencies are organized to run programs, every program has an office, and in every office employees come to work in the morning and say to themselves, "What does my program need today?"

At FEMA, we defined our customers as people either preparing for or recovering from disasters. The moment we decided to measure our success based on how those people were served, instead of how our programs were run, we were on the road to beating crisis. But we didn't stop there. We broadened the idea of the customer to include everyone, both inside and outside the agency—the people in the next office, the congressmen on Capitol Hill, the FEMA staffers in the field, our counterparts at the state and local levels. If you accept that your job is to serve your customer, then there's no place for the primacy of programs or the fostering of fiefdoms.

In the business world, executives often pay lip service to such notions—and then they go right back to focusing only on the bottom line, the corporate equivalent of that program mind-set. When times are bad, executives' first thought might be to jettison thousands of employees since the costs of keeping them on the payroll are so high.

Not all are that way, though. Probably one of the best known examples of business leadership in the all-the-world's-a-customer sense has to be the story of Malden Mills, maker of Polartec and Polarfleece, following a devastating fire that destroyed the Boston-area company's offices and plant on December 11, 1995. Nearly three thousand workers were facing the bleakest of futures. Malden Mills was family-owned, and most employees figured that fire was the end of the company.

"This is *not* the end," said CEO Aaron Feuerstein that night as he watched his plant burn to the ground. He didn't just mean for himself and his family—Feuerstein next announced that he was keeping all of his employees on the payroll, with full benefits, for the next month while the plant was rebuilt on a minimal level, and was giving everyone an end-of-year bonus on top of it. Feuerstein thought it might take one month. It turned out to take three. But Feuerstein didn't back down from his promise.

"The fundamental difference," Feuerstein said, pointedly comparing himself to his shortsighted critics in the business world, "is that I consider our workers an asset, not an expense." Furthermore, he added, he had a responsibility to his workers and to his community. "It would have been unconscionable to put three thousand people on the streets and deliver a death blow to the cities of Lawrence and Methuen."

That part of the Malden Mills story became business legend in the late 1990s, at a time when downsizing was the most beloved strategy for cutting costs and holding profits steady. (There was even a lively exchange in the press between Feuerstein and Al "Chainsaw" Dunlap about the business sense of keeping workers on—or letting them go.) But the real power of developing a personal support network comes home when you take a close look at how Malden Mills was able to get its business rolling after the factory reopened in 1997 and how the company has faced a new crisis: the plunge in garment retail sales during the 2001 recession.

Back in 1995, Aaron Feuerstein looked around him and took inventory at all that was lost. Not just to him and his family-owned company. Malden Mills was the town's largest employer, and nearly every family in Lawrence would be facing hard times. The clothing mills were a way of living, a way of life and a legacy.

He paid nearly $25 million in salaries to workers without jobs. He redesigned the mills in keeping with the local historical board but with amenities that suited his twenty-first century workforce. He set up emergency manufacturing to fulfill contracts with clothing companies for the spring, the busiest season for retailers. The retailers stayed with him, but Malden Mills's upholstery customers—half the company's business before the fire—turned to other manufacturers. Feuerstein then promised to retrain the workers in those units for new jobs.

The literal rebuilding took time. In 1997, when the factory reopened, he rehired most of the original employees and had retrained many of those who had worked in the upholstery division. Feuerstein's bold move rippled around the country—he had politicians praising his decisions and more media attention than time for interviews. The newspaper, magazine, radio, and television features reaped a bounty of sales as well for Malden Mills's top clients, including L.L. Bean, Lands' End, North Face, and Patagonia, who proudly displayed Authentic Polartec and Polarfleece tags on their products, estimating—correctly—that Feuerstein's compassionate management appealed to their best consumers. It was a phoenix's rebirth from the ashes.

The warning signs of a new crisis came in early 2001, when the British market for Polartec goods started to weaken. By the fall of 2001, the recession was hitting Malden Mills hard. Retail sales were down across the board. Like so many others, the company was in financial distress after several years of bounding growth. But the support network that Feuerstein had built in the wake of the 1995 fire rallied around the company—from employees and the community to the company's creditors and national politicians.

Soon after word hit the media that Malden Mills was facing Chapter 11 bankruptcy—the sort that allows you to rebuild a company because there's more value in its future than debt on its books—the surrounding Massachusetts towns began the "Buy Fleece" campaign. Although the company had seen clothing sales climb in the years immediately following the fire and the factories' full reopening, media attention had died down. But the community remembered Feuerstein's promise to his employees, and they knew that one way to recharge sales would be to remind the public about the real meaning of a Polartec label: quality and compassion. For too long, their thinking went, consumers had simply looked at the price tag. The campaign got attention in the *New York Times*, the *Wall Street Journal*, and elsewhere, giving the company some free, favorable, and ongoing advertising. Feuerstein received hundreds of letters of support. People even sent in checks for the company. The company gave Feuerstein a standing ovation when he kicked off an official "Polartec Promise" campaign on Christmas Eve, 2001.

At the end of 2001, Feuerstein saw yet another benefit of the support system he had built back in 1995. In renegotiating their three-year contract, Malden's unionized workers voluntarily took a pay freeze and cut their paid days off in order to help the company meet its obligations and its latest challenge—sacrificing over $2 million from their own pockets for the company's bottom line. Ginette Gauvin, who worked at the mill for twenty-four years, summed up their feelings when she said, "We're ready to make sacrifices for a little while. Whatever [Feuerstein] asks us to do to keep the place going."

A personal support system isn't always limited to the pact between an employer and its employees. I was particularly struck by the way Lehman Brothers and their client Sheraton Hotels interacted following the bombing of the World Trade Center and the destruction of Lehman's offices, a story that inspired other businesses to turn to the suffering tourist industry in the fall of 2001 to find synergies for support.

It's good to know how your friends are faring in a crisis. Just days after the September 11 terrorist attacks, Lehman Brothers and the Sheraton Hotel had found a happy synergy that would pull them both through challenging times. Lehman, based at 2 World Financial Center, needed space desperately. Their offices, connected to the demolished World Trade Center, could not be occupied for the time being, and managers knew that even when the infrastructure in their building was back up and working it would be impossible to get workers overlooking the devastation of the attacks to work at anything near their best.

Sheraton Hotel, on the other hand, was facing a drop in bookings that didn't just rival their worst months in their worst years; it defined a new level of financial crisis. As Barry S. Sternlicht, the CEO and chairman of the Sheraton's parent company, said, "It was like the thousand-year flood." After a few days of sustained bookings when travelers were stranded in New York, the situation looked dire. The hotels, grasping for a way to help out and keep employees motivated, opened rooms to rescue workers and donated hotel supplies. But the Sheraton needed a strategy. It needed a partner. Within a day of the attacks, Sternlicht was contacting executives at displaced companies to see if they needed to make short-term arrangements.

The synergy came naturally. Sheraton and Lehman Brothers had built a strong relationship when Lehman had raised money for Starwood Hotels and Resorts Worldwide, the parent company of two New York City Sheraton hotels as well as several others in the area. In the days after the attacks, an investment banker who had worked with Starwood came up with the idea as he inventoried his clients, who might be displaced, and who might be concerned that their deals were on hold as Lehman floundered without offices. He presented the idea to executives, who had also heard from Sternlicht directly, and the agreement to convert all 665 guest rooms at the midtown Sheraton into offices for bankers and analysts was finalized on Friday, September 14.

Nothing's quite that simple, of course. Sheraton had to upgrade guests to another hotel in the area order to give Lehman contiguous office space and rented the rooms at a fraction of their usual rate. But with hotel vacancies so high, and cancellations rather than bookings coming in, the managers knew that the arrangement was a win-win situation. The offices were ready for the Lehman staff when Wall Street reopened on Monday, September 17.

The web of connections extended even further. A few weeks down the road, Lehman's competitor Morgan Stanley decided that its plan to centralize its staff in several buildings in midtown Manhattan didn't make good sense after the attacks—they had seen what would happen when an entire company's employees were stranded, or worse. A heavy concentration of employees, all using the same telecommunications and power infrastructure, many commuting side by side, could turn out to be a terrible risk, whether the company faced a disaster or a smaller crisis such as rolling brownouts. In a move that surprised a lot of people, the two competitors realized that they could help each other out; Lehman needed permanent office space, and Morgan Stanley needed to find a buyer for a breathtaking skyscraper that failed to meet its new risk strategy, especially during an economic downturn that meant they could only partially fill the building with their own staff.

Synergies of support aren't panaceas, but they go a long way. And the newspaper coverage of the Lehman-Sheraton arrangement inspired other financial district businesses—even small ones like the personal injury law firm run by Robyn Brilliant—to contact New York hotels for temporary office space. At a time of crisis, each business becomes stronger when it relies not just on the talents of its employees, but on its wider support network.

You reap what you sow, as my sharecropper dad used to say. But there's a lot more to sowing that burying a few seeds in the dirt. In this mobile, fast-paced world, it's easy to let relationships wither. You don't have to wait until a crisis hits to keep them going strong. In organizations, as in marriage, steady and clear communication is the key to contentment. Just as Lea Ellen and I talk several times a day, at FEMA I made sure to establish clear internal and external lines of communication. Two internal publications—the *Director's Weekly Report* and *The Rumor Mill*—provided a direct link between my office and every employee's desk. They knew exactly what we were doing and what I expected. Small things leave an indelible mark on the people and networks around you.

External dialogues are harder, of course. An executive I know makes it a point to spend at least an hour a week jotting notes to old friends and far-flung colleagues, clipping and sending newspaper articles that reminded him of them, maybe enclosing a cartoon he knew they'd enjoy. The thing about maintenance is, a short note is enough. The job doesn't become oner-ous unless you've let it slide too long. How many of us have avoided getting in touch with someone because we've let so much time go by that anything less than a ten-page letter seems inadequate?

Twine is stronger than string. Anyone who's tied up a package, or a deal, can testify to the difference. You can harness the power of a personal sup-port system by:

• **BUILDING SOME TWINE.** Create an "incident support team" that draws on experts from different areas of your company or department and who can coordinate responses even when it seems as though they're trying to meet competing goals. Charge two different members of the team with planning the responses on the fly and making the plans a reality, since ideas and action can sometimes feel like competing goals, too.

• **REACHING OUT TO PEOPLE.** Take an immediate and literal inventory of how a crisis is affecting your company as well as the people and busi-nesses around you—your suppliers, clients, partners, neighbors, the media, even your competitors—and identify where their needs and your needs can serve one another or where serving their needs is essential to beating the crisis at hand. Go to those people—at least the ones you have strong relationships with—and ask them to do the same when they're facing a crisis, since you won't always be able to see the synergies yourself. Then, work together. (Make that twine into a rope.)

• **VIEWING EVERYONE AS YOUR CUSTOMER.** Evaluate the short-term costs and effectiveness of a response in the light of long-term benefits. If you were trying to win a new customer, you'd try to win them for life, since it costs you less when customers return time and time again. Everyone, including your employees, should be viewed the same way. In addition to knowing how much it costs and how long it takes to recruit and train a new employee in different fundamental roles at your company, and comparing it to the savings of taking a job off payroll, you should create short-term/long-term costs analyses for all your major cost centers. Don't under- or overestimate.

• **REMEMBERING THE WEEDING AND THE FEEDING.** Strong relationships don't blossom overnight, and they usually can't be planted in the middle of a crisis. Require open communication with employees, clients, and partners, and open your own door as the first step. Create "tickler lists" for maintaining contact with colleagues you may not work with on a regular basis. To assess how well you're remembering to weed and feed, try drawing up a map of your support network—all those dots and lines should combine into an enormous web—but don't allow yourself to keep a contact on as an active part of your network if you haven't been in touch with him or her in over six months. Share your contacts generously.

Developing a personal support system might not come naturally. The next chapter shows you how to build them—and keep them working in a crisis.

6

TREAT THE HEART WITHOUT LOSING YOUR HEAD

The Importance of Empathy in the Midst of Action

GRAND FORKS, NORTH DAKOTA, AND
EAST GRAND FORKS, MINNESOTA
APRIL 1997

On Valentine's Day, the National Weather Service posted its first missive of the annual flood watch season, and considering the mounds of snow that had piled up on the Northern Plains that winter, no one was the least bit surprised:

2/14/97   SNOWMELT OUTLOOK:
Severe potential for Grand Forks (record or exceed flood of record)

For Pat Owens, the new (seven months) mayor of Grand Forks, North Dakota, it was beginning to look like some kind of cosmic plot against her. "After thirty-three years as assistant to the city's mayors, I had decided to run for the office myself," she recalls. She won by a landslide. "I was elected in June of '96—at the ripe old age of fifty-five—and starting that fall it seemed like there was just one blizzard after another. I was forever closing the city. I remember thinking, *I'm going to be impeached!*"

A blizzard is defined as a storm with wind speeds of at least thirty-five miles per hour, considerable falling and/or drifting snow, and visibility near zero. Folks in Grand Forks know their blizzards on a first-name basis. Andy debuted the 1996–97 season, dumping a foot of snow on the ground in November. A month later Betty arrived, carrying another 8.7 inches. Two days after that, Christopher showed up. He brought only 4.2 inches, but by the end of December the accumulated snowfall had built to 42.4 inches.

In this vast flat slab of American heartland some hundred miles south of Canada, New Year's always comes as a suspicious stranger. The locals on either side of the Red River of the North slant their eyes warily and brace for spring surprises hidden up winter sleeves. "Usually in January, we review all the weather service information we can get," says Jim Campbell of the Grand Forks, North Dakota, emergency management office. When Campbell says "we," he refers to his interaction with the two cities' chief engineers, the front-line officials in any flood fight. In 1997 on the North Dakota side, the city engineer and director of Public Works was Ken Vein, a tall boyish-looking man who rides Harleys to let off steam. On the Minnesota side, Gary Sanders of the firm Floan-Sanders, Inc., was retained—as he had been since 1966—as consulting engineer to the city. For both Vein and Sanders, the events of spring 1997 would be especially, and personally, excruciating—to the point that they still can't discuss it without obvious emotion.

January 1997 brought three more blizzards—Doris, with 8.8 inches; Elmo, with 0.4 inches; and Franzi, with 8.6 inches. Accumulated snowfall at the end of January was 67.4 inches. "In January, we reviewed everything," recalls Jim Campbell. "We go back and look at what the moisture content was in the soil, what the water table was at freeze-up, and then, of course, we monitor the amount of snow we've received all winter long.

"Then in February and March we had numerous meetings, going over our emergency response plan. We opened our Emergency Operations Center (EOC) at the police station around the first of March, because we knew we were going to have quite a flood. The Weather Service at that time was talking about near-record flooding. But near-record flooding didn't bother us so much. We knew we could handle that."

The emergency response meetings, held around long conference tables on either side of the river, are just one of the rites of what passes for spring in this harsh climate, a part of the world where one of the great winter pastimes is racing automobiles on frozen lakes. What makes this climate brutal isn't just the snow but the wind. I'll never forget the first time I saw this part of the country. Coming from my part of Arkansas, which is nestled between the Ouachita Mountains and the Boston Mountains in the Ozark National Forest, I was stunned by the long, black-dirt vistas of these Northern Plains. That's why the wind cuts so—there's just not much here to impede the progress of a strong and determined current of air. Once it tops the Rocky Mountains in western Montana, a wind is pretty much home free, able to pick up power at will all across North Dakota, a state that grows ever flatter the farther east you travel. Then, just west of the Grand Forks, the gathering gust reaches the Red River Valley, a section of the state described by the Grand Forks *Herald* as "Flat. Flat-top haircut flat. Flat as a bad singer. Flat like a ruined soufflé. In the spring, when the small grains are small and green, it looks like an infinite pool table. Flat, flat, flat, flat."

The creation of this incredible flatness occurred some fourteen thousand years ago when glacial ice covered what is now Canada and parts of the northern United States. Apparently, the weight of these glaciers caused the ice to ooze along on a lumbering course, flattening the earth's crust as it went. But geology aside, the effect is what matters to those North Dakotans and Minnesotans gathered around their conference tables every winter while, outside, the snow blows crossways. Lots of blizzards, a gash of river, and flat, flat land: It adds up to what is conservatively called a "flood problem."

In early March, blizzard Gus blew into town. He didn't carry much snow—only 0.2 inches. But by now, with the help of regular old everyday snowfalls, the accumulated total was 83.3 inches.

3/14/97   SNOWMELT OUTLOOK:
Numeric crest potential with normal precipitation 49.0 ft.

When you grow up in this area of the country, harsh weather and its fall-out are part of your sense of place—part, even, of your cultural heritage. Pick up the Grand Forks phone book and scan the names at random: Hoff, Boonstra, Gehrke, Olson, Lauf, Schumacher, Menke, Hylden. They're Germanic, Scandinavian, cold-country names right out of Garrison Keillor's Lake Wobegon tales. But although their accents and vocabularies are similar

(They all say "Oof-da!" the way Jewish people say "Oy!"), the people on either side of the bridge connecting Grand Forks, North Dakota (population 52,000), with Grand Forks, Minnesota (population 8,500), are apparently very different in the ways they view their world. "It's quite possible," says Grand Forks *Herald* editor Mike Jacobs, himself a born-and-bred North Dakotan, "that there aren't two neighboring states that have a greater difference in political climate than these two. Minnesota's is classic liberalism; North Dakota's is populism—not unlike that of Mississippi or Louisiana, minus the racial connotations. But still an entitlement culture with the same sorts of economic grievance." Those political differences, says Jacobs, spring from the states' cultural differences. "Minnesota is a self-confident, self-actualizing kind of place. North Dakota is ill at ease, not quite sure of itself."

In the spring of 1997, those very cultural and political differences would come into play along the Red River of the North. And in many ways they would help determine how the two cities of Grand Forks would respond to—and recover from—the disaster the winter blizzards were sending their way.

LEA ELLEN AND I got to know Pat Owens well only after the crisis of 1997. It was at a U.S. Conference of Mayors in New Orleans, where the three of us sat in a park eating hot dogs and talking about the aftermath of the Grand Forks flood. This was probably in the year 2000—I say that because Pat was going through some troubling times, and I remember telling her that the third year after a major disaster is the beginning of the worst period. It goes on through year six. By this time, survivors have progressed through all the postdisaster stages—shock, disbelief, feeling sorry for themselves, acceptance, and depression. There was, and still is, a lot of depression showing itself on both sides of the Red River of the North.

Mayor Owens had felt very confident that her city was prepared for the forty-nine-foot forecast. After all, Grand Forks' record crest had been just slightly higher—49.09 feet—all the way back in the legendarily blizzardous year of 1979. And because of the area's history, they had in place an extensive flood-fight plan that was updated annually. "The plan," says Owens, "was to build a wall of sandbags atop the dikes along a several-mile stretch of the river." City officials were worried, as they always are this time of year, but they weren't panicked. "The corps of engineers requires that you go three feet—what's called the 'freeboard'—above the predicted crest. Our engineers and emergency management people were certain that we could handle forty-nine feet."

"We were ready for fifty-two feet," recalls Ken Vein. "We knew every elevation of every outlet of every low area of town adjacent to the Red River, and also of the English Coulee to the west, which was another issue we had to manage. Traditionally, we in the city were primarily responsible for the public infrastructure—the public property and public levee systems—and the private landowners were responsible for their own property. But considering the severity of what we saw coming up, we figured way back in January that the private sector was probably going to need some help. So we went in and designed a flood-protection system for every homeowner adjacent to the river. Plus we designed our own system, which involved moving, in the lower areas, thousands and thousands of yards of clay. We had a good plan set up. But we were relying on the National Weather Service."

Across the river in East Grand Forks, Gary Sanders was similarly occupied. "Our usual snow accumulation is about twenty-five or thirty inches, so we knew we were going to have a significant event," Sanders recalls. His eyes look sad when he tells the story. "We were planning for a little higher than Grand Forks. The hundred-year flood record was fifty and a half feet back in 1897, so I told the corps of engineers I was using that number plus two feet. We were going for fifty-two and a half."

All during March, Vein and Sanders had their respective bulldozers and backhoes busy digging clay for levees. The two cities also pitched in together to handle the onerous job of filling sandbags. Fortunately, the Minnesota side had access to four sandbag machines and the North Dakota side had a National Guard armory—in Bismarck—in which to store the bags so they wouldn't freeze. Late that month, Mayor Owens led a Washington delegation of senators and congressmen from both states on a tour of the flood preparations. I was part of that delegation, along with several of my FEMA people. In the snow and the mud, we took a bus out to the lowest-lying areas, notably the Lincoln Drive section. Looking out the window at this old, established neighborhood, with its stone churches and its neat rows of Craftsman, Victorian, and American Foursquare houses, I thought about how it could be anywhere in this vast country. It wasn't just North Dakota, it was America. The river snaked through a park, skirting a golf course. The flood plans seemed adequate, at least at that stage of the game. "They thought we were pretty well prepared," Owens recalls.

After we all boarded our planes and flew back to Washington, there wasn't much more that Owens or Mayor Lynn Stauss of East Grand Forks could do except trust their engineers and try to keep up the semblance of a city government. "We briefed Mayor Owens regularly," says Ken Vein, "but this was work that we had to do." On April 3—a Thursday—crews began actually building and shoring up dikes and stacking sandbags. That same day, the National Weather Service posted the first of its daily flood forecasts:

4/3/97   FIRST DAILY FORECAST:
12:20 pm—Stage 18.1 ft, continue to rise, referred to crest outlook value of 49.0 ft.

Then, one day later, Blizzard Hannah hit. Actually, she showed up first in the form of a steady rain, which soon froze, coating trees and power lines with heavy ice. In a couple of days, two thousand telephone and electrical poles had snapped or toppled. Then, once the ground was encased in ice, seven inches of snow came and spread a blanket across the plains. No one had heat or power. In dark homes all over the region, family members huddled together around fireplaces, wondering what could possibly be next. Knowing exactly what might be next, Jim Campbell put out an urgent call for sandbag volunteers. So did Gary Sanders. Meanwhile, Ken Vein, as director of Public Works, had to turn his attention from the flood fight to the ice storm.

By Monday, April 8, the temperature warmed up enough for crews to haul off a bit of snow and for flood-fight operations to continue. The North Dakota governor activated the National Guard to help. Jim Campbell estimated that in some places the earthen levees along the river needed to be raised as much as seven feet. "We built up the levees with clay at first, until it wasn't possible to get machinery up on top. Then we went to sandbags. We had a lot of help, not only from the Grand Forks area but from all over North Dakota and Minnesota. There were schools in Minnesota as far away as 150 miles that bused their students in to help us fill sandbags. With our four sandbag machines and a lot of manpower, we could do as many as nine thousand bags an hour. As near as we can tell, we filled approximately three million sandbags."

4/8/97   FORECAST:
4:30 pm—Stage 38.8 ft., outlook crest 49.0 ft mid to late April

"In 1979, we didn't have all that much snow and we crested at just over forty-nine feet," Gary Sanders is saying, "but when you convert the snow to water we had about four inches throughout the Red River basin. In 1997, we had over seven inches average throughout the basin. I guess the Weather Bureau thought 1979 was so extreme—warming up fast and coming at the same time—that they didn't anticipate the same thing happening. Typically, when you get a lot of snow, it doesn't warm up real quick. And the later the flood goes, the worse it gets. Because you've got so much snow and it takes a long time to melt it. And then when it starts to move out of the rivers and the ditches, it really comes fast."

OVER THE NEXT few days, engineers Vein and Sanders kept a close eye on the rising river level. "I had my 'pager,'" Vein says. "I could just hit a button and it would tell me that in this one particular place the water was 42.4, 42.7. . . . Everything was related to that gauge reading. So every hour I would take a look at what our reading was. And what was most alarming, the National Weather Service was telling us our projection was forty-nine feet, and I could see that the rate of rise was a tenth of a foot an hour. And I'm thinking, *This thing's gotta start slowing down.*"

4/11/97   FORECAST:
12:30 pm—Stage 42.0 ft, outlook crest 49.0 ft fourth week in April

Monitoring the situation from his East Grand Forks headquarters, Gary Sanders was thinking exactly what Ken Vein was thinking. Today Sanders rummages through a big flat drawer and digs out a huge graph labeled "Previous Flood Crest Patterns: Red River of the North." Across the bottom are the months from March to June, and up the side are the gauge readings from twenty-six feet to fifty-five feet. In the center, drawn in different colors and patterns, are the rises and falls of every flood for the past half century. It looks like a drawing of a mountain range. "See this?" he says, pointing to the trajectory of the 1979 flood, which had started to level off at about 48.8 feet, on its way to a crest of 49.09. "Now look at this." He calls attention to an adjacent line. This one, the 1997 trajectory, would go on to become the Mount Everest of this depicted mountain range, towering over all others. And even as it shot past the mid-forty-foot mark, it showed no inclination of slowing down.

4/13/97   FORECAST:
11:10 am—Stage 42.8 ft, outlook crest 49.0 ft broad crest occurring as early as 4/19 and as late as 4/21–22

"We were scrambling," says Ken Vein. "At that height, our problems expand almost exponentially, because we're just so flat. All of a sudden water's coming from here, coming from there, we've got overland flooding coming from behind us. Typically, if we can get the overland flooding from behind us through before the main stem crests, that's what we shoot for. We were fortunate that we didn't have rain during this time frame, or it would've been worse."

On that last week before the flood, starting Monday, April 14, Vein and his people were digging clay anywhere they could get it. "It was clear that we couldn't keep up under existing means, so I just started looking for parks, open spaces, wherever. And I said, 'Let them know, but we're going to go and start digging dirt.' We had no other choice. We soon went into people's front yards and backyards, digging and dumping, hoping that we could stay ahead of it." Gary Sanders lent them some dirt from his fill. "In hindsight, I probably should've kept it," Sanders laughs ruefully. "But neighbors are neighbors."

4/14/97   FORECAST:
4:30 pm—Stage 43.7 ft, first operational forecast crest 50.0 ft 4/19–22

"We had the Sandbag Central, but we couldn't even begin to keep up," says Ken Vein, "so individuals were all sandbagging. There was no school going on. Everybody was sandbagging. I worked out of the Operations Center downtown, but we were dispersing our people up and down the river as much as possible. At that point, the river started breaching parts of our levees, and we were just trying to patch it, just trying to stay ahead of it. It's probably one of the most tingling experiences I've ever had to stand on those dikes and look across and everything is being protected by those sandbags. And the water is flowing really, *really* fast."

On Tuesday, April 15, the Weather Service issued two separate forecasts, one at one-thirty P.M. and another that evening at nine-thirty. They were sticking with a crest of fifty feet, "We still felt like we were okay," Vein says. Then at nine-twenty on Wednesday morning came reports of a huge ice jam downstream, near Crookston, Minnesota. This was significant because the Red River of the North flows *northward,* toward lower-lying land. These chunks of ice—which at any minute could break loose, begin to melt, and increase the surge of water—were time bombs waiting to blow. Still, thirty minutes later, the Weather Service issued this projection:

4/16/97   FORECAST:
9:50 am—Stage 47.5 ft, forecast rise to 49.0–49.5 ft on the 17th, slow rise to 50.0 ft 4/22–23

In the evening of the same day, the NWS published a revision, now projecting a crest of 50.0 feet to 50.5 feet as early as Sunday, April 20.

That Wednesday night, Mayor Owens, Ken Vein, and Jim Campbell held an open meeting for residents who lived along the river. "Maybe a thousand, fifteen hundred attended," Owens recalls. "We couldn't seat them all in the Civic Auditorium. I had to tell them to start *thinking* of evacuating and moving their things, because we weren't sure of the level. Some did evacuate. Some did not."

Thursday the seventeenth was a critical day. One of the major considerations of those fighting floods is the velocity of the water flow, which is measured in cubic feet per second (cfs). In the 1979 flood, peak water flow was 82,000 cfs. On the morning of April 17, the United States Geological Survey was measuring the flow on the Red River at 82,700 cfs. By just after noon, the river was at 49.6 feet. By four P.M., the water control people in Grand

Forks were openly discussing a potential crest of up to 52.5 feet. East Grand Forks mayor Lynn Stauss urged his residents to raise their dikes "Two feet in two days! Two feet in two days!" It became no less than a battle cry.

Meanwhile, in Crookston the ice floes had damaged the automatic gauge that measures the river's height, so crews went out to take a manual reading. There was so much fluctuation in water level while they were there that their reading had a margin of error of plus or minus a half foot. By evening, word came that the ice jam had broken, resulting in an additional surge in flow.

4/17/97   FORECAST:
9:25 pm—Stage 50.9 ft., forecast crest 51.5–52 ft 4/18–4/19. Ice effects noted in forecast

At times like this, you try to keep finding a reason to believe. Gary Sanders met the fifty-two-foot projection by clinging desperately to his meager advantage. "Even then I didn't feel *too* uncomfortable," he says. "I had 52.5 for the top." The emergency operation continued around the clock in those frantic final days, and from time to time a siren would sound calling for more help at some weak place in the dike. That Thursday night Sanders was home for only a half hour before the sirens sounded and he was needed on site. He chokes up telling about it, touched to the core by the heroic effort of all his friends and neighbors and family members. "It still hurts, even after four years," he says.

Across the river, Ken Vein was living the same nightmare Sanders was. "At about ten o'clock on Thursday night, I told my crew that I just had to go home to get a couple hours' sleep," Vein recalls. A little after eleven, his phone rang. The water was starting to come through in the Lincoln Park area. "I had hoped we could just get through the night," Vein says, the exhaustion still evident in his tone. When he got back to the EOC, he was met with grim faces all around. For a couple of hours he and his staff studied and discussed the situation with Jim Campbell and representatives from the corps of engineers. Then Vein spoke the words everyone was thinking. "We've got to call Mayor Owens."

The mayor had left for home about nine P.M. "We had been working around the clock," she recalls, "trying to give confidence to people, giving guidance and direction, approving the various orders. It was about one-twenty A.M. on Friday when they called me to come back in. I just knew at that moment that we'd had some traumatic event. When I had gotten into my car to go home a few hours earlier, I had seen water coming up from the catch basins."

Owens drove back to the police station and went down to the basement command center. "I walked into this room and sat down at the head of a long table," she says. "All the engineers were there, plus the corps of engineers, Jim Campbell, and his emergency management people. Ken Vein is the one who told me. 'We've got people out on the dikes right now,' he said, 'and it looks like we're not going to be able to maintain them.' Then Jim Campbell said, 'The mayor has the authority in the city code to start evacuation.'"

Owens told Lea Ellen and me that as she sat staring at this table full of bleary-eyed people, the whole scene felt surreal. Here she was, the first female mayor of a major city in North Dakota, and all these men were waiting for her decision. Owens remembers thinking that calling for an evacuation seemed somehow presumptuous. But a split second later, this thought occurred to her: *The first rule in a disaster should be, If you can't handle it, get the people to safety.*

"In everything we do," she told them, "we're going to think of the people first." She told Vein to get those people off the dikes, and then she began signing orders for evacuation. By four-fifteen A.M., when boils appeared in the Lincoln Park dike, Mayor Owens had already ordered immediate evacuation of this section of town, which contained some six hundred homes. Also included were 106 residents of a retirement home. "It's one of the major disasters of our lifetime," the mayor later told CNN.

April 18, Friday, dawned ironically sunny and warm, though by eight A.M. water had overflowed the riverside Lincoln Park Golf Course and was coursing down Lincoln Avenue toward downtown Grand Forks. Across the Red River of the North, Gary Sanders felt strangely optimistic. "We moved our sandbag machine from Grand Forks to a parking lot over here," he says, "and we got out there early in the morning, set to make bags. Soon about four hundred National Guard troops that we hadn't asked for showed up. Obviously, people knew things that we didn't know, and that they didn't tell us."

4/18/97   FORECAST:

9:05 am—Stage 52.0 ft., forecast crest 53.0 ft. on 4/18–19

Just after noon the river started coming overland from the south side of East Grand Forks, giving it direct access to communities and eventually the downtown area. "When that started, we took scrapers and Cats and basically dug up a field and built a ring dike about two thousand feet long," Sanders says. In a while they had that water cut off. Then the dikes started to fail behind a residential community backing up to the Red Lake River, which joins the Red River just south of the city. "One of my guys was there, and he came to me and said, 'We're losing it.' I told him he had to go back in—that we'd just blocked off water from this other direction, so we couldn't walk away now. Sure enough, in a little while he called and said that dike was secure again, and they were building it higher. I think at this point the river was at 52.3."

At about two P.M., Sanders was escorting the Minnesota lieutenant governor and other state dignitaries on a tour of the flood-fight area. An hour or so later, he stopped by his engineering office for a few minutes. "As I got out into the parking lot about to leave, a policeman yelled at me," he recalls, his voice cracking in the telling. "The policeman said the dike had broken on the south end, in an area known as the Point. I knew that was major, because no matter what broke out there, it was going to flood eight hundred to a thousand homes. Including mine. And my wife and thirteen-year-old son were out there."

Sanders immediately called home and told his wife to get out, to go to her parents' house, which stood at a higher elevation. "My wife," Sanders says, shaking his head. "She had the presence of mind to shut off the power before they left. I hadn't thought of anything like that, because I had never conceived of losing this fight."

TODAY, HALF A decade later, those rushing floodwaters seem poignantly emblematic. Following that fierce, heartbreaking battle to maintain the integrity of a way of life, something elemental finally broke in the people of both Grand Forks. And time has shown that it will take more than high dikes to fix it.

Into the breach stepped Mayor Pat Owens. Later in the year she would be honored with a Phoenix Award, presented by the Small Business Administration (SBA), for the way she handled herself during the crisis. "I remember seeing her in Grand Forks," former SBA director Aida Alvarez says. "I really admired her. She was—you know, on the one hand she was very emotional. You could see she felt this very deeply, but she had such a clearheaded approach. She had a sense of humor, courage. She was just what was needed in a disaster situation—someone who really feels for what's going on but who doesn't get taken over by events."

The classic Pat Owens line is the one she still delivers in speeches: "The first time I realized what danger we were in," she says, "is when I went down to the police station and saw the Coast Guard there."

By four-thirty P.M. Friday, water in the Lincoln Drive area of Grand Forks had risen to the same level as the river, inundating hundreds of houses to the roof level. At just after eight P.M., the National Weather Service revised their crest projection—now it looked like fifty-four feet sometime on Saturday. As she signed orders for evacuation, Mayor Owens ministered to her staff. "That evening I had a couple of engineers who pulled me aside. 'We know you're so busy,' they said, but they needed to talk. One of them had a wife and little son on the Minnesota Point, and he was worried about their evacuation. I told him, 'Make sure your family's safe first.'" Owens understood the young man's concern, because her own ninety-three-year-old father lived in Minnesota, on the Point. He'd had no heat since the early-April ice storm, and she had been trying to get through to him while tending to her duties as mayor. "I think the young man made some phone calls, and then he continued to work," she says, reflecting her own actions. "So many people were worried about their loved ones, but they never stopped helping the public."

But the person Pat Owens says she'll never forget was a young engineer she talked with in a small room off the EOC. During that weekend in New Orleans, she told Lea Ellen and me the story: "He put his elbows on his knees and his hands over his eyes, and he said, 'Oh, Mayor, I feel like I've deserted the people. I feel like I've failed.' I said, 'You did not fail. You fought to the bitter end. You're my hero. All of you—you are my *hero*.'

"He went back to work that night, but eventually this young engineer would leave Grand Forks. He worked through the process, but it was very emotional on everybody involved. It took a toll on people, body and mind. That's one of the key things when you're going through a disaster—keeping watch on your own employees and how they respond." Considering the relationship between depression and alcohol, it's interesting to note that one of the orders Mayor Owens gave that Friday night was to ban the sale of alcohol in Grand Forks.

At nine-forty P.M., storm sewer backup began pouring into the Emergency Operations Center, so Vein and his team quickly abandoned that site and retreated a few miles west to a room at North Dakota State University. Within half an hour, the former EOC was full of water. Meanwhile, across the swollen river, Gary Sanders and his team were still trying to hold on. "We had lost the Point," he says, "but that was just one area." At eleven P.M., however, the dike near the Kennedy Bridge failed, cutting off the last link between the two cities. Sanders then turned his attention to downtown East Grand Forks. "The old railroad track bed was of relatively high elevation," he recalls. "The water was in the residential areas moving north, but the downtown was still dry."

Not for long. "What happened was, the Red Lake River broke out and came down our street system." That flooded an area called Griggs Park, which in turn caused flooding at the Valley Golf Course, which led to the topping of the dikes downtown. By four A.M. Saturday, April 19, the business district of East Grand Forks was lost. "At that point," Sanders says, "pretty much everything along the river was under water. It was just a question of how far under it would go."

Mayor Stauss described the situation this way: "I'm the first mayor to lose a town; that's how devastating it is."

On the other side, Grand Forks was four feet under. At eight A.M., the water treatment plant failed, meaning the city would have no fresh water for the next three weeks. At ten A.M., Mayor Owens ordered an evacuation of everyone within a mile of the river. By noon, half of Grand Forks was flooded. Meanwhile, the mayor's father was refusing to be evacuated without his dog and three cats. "Well," Owens says, "the National Guard had assigned a young captain to follow me around, and he arranged for the Coast Guard to send a helicopter to go pick up my dad and his animals. They took them back to the Grand Forks Air Force Base, where I was now staying with my husband, son, and nephew. Later my sister came and got the cats, but the dog, a little beagle named Nikki, stayed with Dad."

Eventually, 90 percent of Grand Forks was inundated. "We evacuated almost our entire population," Owens says, "and the emergency people said it was the largest evacuation of a city since Atlanta in the Civil War. We were also told this was the worst disaster per capita at that time ever in the nation. I don't know. We didn't really have a lot of time to think. We just had to react. And I'm proud of the fact that we lost no lives."

IN A DISASTER, don't ever make the mistake of saying things can't possibly get worse.

On Saturday afternoon, Gary Sanders was watching TV coverage of the flooding at his in-laws' house. "I was just sitting there looking at all that water, and suddenly they were showing pictures of a building on fire in Grand Forks. And it was the building a branch of my company's offices were in."

No one could believe it when fire sirens started sounding at four-fifteen P.M. The Security Building, a vintage five-story one block from city hall, was in flames. I've seen pictures of the fire crews who first responded—they're wading in waist-deep water while, behind them, a deep orange ball of fire churns from the old brick structure. Most fire trucks couldn't even get to the scene. One pump truck did manage to negotiate the flooded streets, only to give out after two minutes when the motor blew from taking on so much water. This wasn't placid water, either. One burly fireman, six-foot-six and 270 pounds, told the newspaper he had to use every bit of his strength to stand against the current, all the while dodging chunks of ice and fast-flowing file cabinets.

Before the fire crews could even try to fight the fire, they first had to rescue forty apartment dwellers who had ignored Mayor Owens's order to evacuate. Meanwhile, fire and emergency officials were trying to figure out how to get the fire engines to the fire itself. "Everything we do in fighting fires is dependent on your equipment and your water supply," said battalion chief Jerry Anderson, "and we couldn't use either one." The first thing they did was call in a fire-bombing airplane, the kind used in forest fires, to drop fire retardant on the blaze. That was at seven-fifteen P.M., three hours after the fire had broken out. By then the flames had spread from the Security Building to other structures on the same block. Forty-five minutes later, fires were burning in two other downtown blocks.

Fire engines eventually arrived riding piggyback on flatbed trucks, but there was very little the fire crews could do. When Sunday dawned, eleven of Grand Forks's buildings were either destroyed or heavily damaged. That afternoon, helicopters finally doused the flames by dropping two-thousand-gallon buckets of water on the buildings, sixty drops in all.

HOW DOES A city heal from a wound like this? Thousands of people are displaced and have lost their homes, and many have lost their spirit. Can leadership bring a city back? "The Red River is bringing us together to build our community," said Mayor Lynn Stauss. Mayor Owens promised her townspeople, "We will rebuild, and we will be stronger, and we will be in it together."

But that's not quite how it worked out.

In that first week following the 54.11-foot floodwaters and the fire that destroyed much of downtown, Grand Forks city government was pretty much wherever Pat Owens happened to be. "The mayor," says *Herald* editor Mike Jacobs, "performed magnificently during the crisis, and was a tremendous inspiration. The evacuation was orderly. There was no loss of life. And there was no lawlessness."

"Everyone was scattered," Owens recalls. "I couldn't find but two of my City Council for possibly a week or ten days." Working out of space at a bank and then at the Civic Auditorium, Owens formed a core operations group based on three of her twelve department heads. "One was Ken Vein, our city engineer and director of Public Works. Our water plant was down, and we had no infrastructure. He was going to be the one that would have to put all that together with his staff. Another was John O'Leary, our community development director. We were going to be lobbying for a $500 million disaster aid bill, and I knew he would have to deal with housing and getting businesses back on board. Finally there was John Smedick, our director of Finance. He would be dealing directly with the funding and what we could use it for, and also with contractors and making sure that what we were doing was all legal. I knew that these three department heads would be the ones I would need to meet with many times a day to get Grand Forks back up and running. I called them my 'Tri-Chairs.'"

On Tuesday after the disaster, Owens, Stauss, and others were on hand at Grand Forks AFB to welcome President Bill Clinton to town. Mayor Owens joked that, being an evacuee herself, she had a hard time deciding what to wear for the occasion. "But what I wear," she told the president, "is the heart and soul of my community." More than once she wiped tears from her cheeks.

"You look good," Clinton said, telling the mayor and her people that they should not be ashamed because they were heartbroken. "When I saw pictures of some of you stacking sandbags in a blizzard, I thought at first that I had a problem with the reception on my television," the president said, and he promised the full help of the U.S. government.

That same day, somebody handed Mayor Owens a letter. "I don't know why I received and read that one," she says, "because I had no office. People would just give me stacks of things wherever I was." This letter was from the man who had been mayor of Rapid City, South Dakota, back in the 1970s when a flood hit the town and 248 people were lost. "He was in his twenties back then," Owens says, "and he said he suffered pretty much close to a nervous breakdown. So did many of his department heads. He told me the ins and outs of what to look for so I could keep my sanity. He said to rest, which was impossible; he also said that as things progressed, the politicians would start to bicker."

It was good, and very prescient, advice.

As if on cue, an Associated Press story soon appeared with this headline: "Finger-pointing begins in Forks: Mayor says poor forecasting doomed city; weather service says it gave its best effort." The article outraged Owens, who called it "inaccurate." "I will not finger-point," she said. "That is not the way I do business. . . . It's past. We need to go into the future. The worst thing that we can ever do is go into the future by damning someone when we are not sure what happened."

In the meantime, Mayor Stauss told an audience of evacuees that the weather service "not only missed it, they blew it big." The mood in the room reflected the sentiments of whoever had penned a very popular piece of current graffiti around town: "Forty-nine feet my *ass!*" Stauss received thunderous applause.

These listeners were the same people who, at first, had just been grateful that the Civic Auditorium had been turned into a veritable department store of recovery, with the United Way, Red Cross, Salvation Army, FEMA, SBA, HUD, and so on all on hand for one-stop shopping. They were thankful when FEMA provided fully equipped trailers for evacuees to live in. They were appreciative when, on April 27, a Northwest Airlines 747 landed in Grand Forks bearing two hundred thousand pounds of flood-relief goods. They were beholden to the National Guard for manning a warehouse of food, clothing, furniture, and other supplies that were being trucked in from all over the country. They were grateful when nondrinkable water was restored in Grand Forks on May 2, and very grateful when potable tap water was restored in East Grand Forks on May 9 and in Grand Forks on May 12. Probably a lot of them were deliriously grateful when, on April 28, Mayor Owens rescinded the order banning the sale of alcohol.

The tide began to turn when the euphoria of disaster gave way to their new reality. "I think the largest challenge was when people first came back and saw their homes," Owens says. In Grand Forks, some 850 houses in the Lincoln Park area had to be destroyed and, because it was a floodplain, they couldn't be built back. "The other item that was very, very difficult was the buy-out of the homes. Some people had flood insurance; some did not. Of course, no one had expected a flood of this magnitude. And we had lost all of our records in our county assessing department—as far as taxable valuations and so forth—so a lot of that had to be reproduced. Some people were angry, feeling that their homes were worth more and that they should be able to keep their insurance in addition to getting the value of their home prior to the flood. FEMA and our city attorney handled that beautifully, but it was just one challenge after another."

The first City Council meeting after the disaster took place on April 28 in a bank conference room. Owens, lacking her traditional gavel, called the meeting to order by tapping a can of purified water. One of the major announcements in that first session was that the council would now get together weekly instead of twice a month. Thus began nearly two years of something resembling an inquisition. "Make a decision!" a man shouted to the council during one meeting, urging them to do something—*anything*— about a permanent flood protection plan. Any decision was inevitably wrong to somebody. "It seemed like everything we spent our money on was always challenged," Owens says. "Because people couldn't see immediate results."

"A lot of what Grand Forks did *isn't* visible," says Mike Jacobs. "For example, we have a completely new water system—but there's no sex in that!" In the meantime, the East Grand Forks leadership was spending that city's aid dollars on a showy new downtown, including an imposing city hall and a gigantic Cabella's outfitter's store. Jacobs laughs. "East Grand Forks built way more city hall than the town of East Grand Forks really needs. They were able to do it because they had a single source of financing. And they were very, very focused. The truth about East Grand Forks is, they got equally as much per capita as Grand Forks did, and they sank it all into very specific projects, all downtown. It made an enormous difference. Grand Forks just made some other choices.

"The essential thing is, it's a different political culture. Grand Forks has more people. And the Grand Forks city government has always been kind of plodding, asking everybody's opinion and then making up its own mind. So anybody whose opinion wasn't accepted is aggrieved."

In any case, says Owens, "It soon became very evident that the City Council couldn't focus. I think it was just that they were being torn at by fifty thousand citizens. You have to realize that people are not themselves when they go through disasters. There's togetherness at the beginning, and then after the bills start coming, they look for someone to blame."

And as the people try to pin blame, ambitious politicians begin to circle. "As time went on and everybody got more tired, the situation became more traumatic," says Owens. "Most of those people are no longer on the City Council." They were replaced by candidates who ran "because they disagreed with what was done or they thought things were not right."

Ironically, when it came to the subject of permanent flood protection, it was East Grand Forks that came up with the invisible plan. More specifically, it was Gary Sanders. "Oh, yes," he says, smiling, "I've taken a lot of razzing for my Invisible Wall." While Grand Forks decided to build a massive dike along the river, East Grand Forks adopted Sanders's idea for a wall whose panels could be slipped in during flood threats and slipped out for the view the rest of the year. "Seems to me," Sanders says, "either we live with the river and protect ourselves when we have to, or we might as well move the town fifteen miles away. The Red River of the North isn't a pretty river, but it's the activity center of the town. It's made our restaurant row really viable. People sit on the decks in the summer so they can look at the water and the bridges. It's the only place in the community that we have a view. Otherwise, all you see is flat ground."

Not everyone is convinced that the Invisible Wall will work when it has to, but they applaud the imagination involved. "East Grand Forks, because they were down so far, were able to think a little differently," says Jacobs. "Over here, there just wasn't that kind of creative thinking."

TODAY PAT OWENS lives in Ocala, Florida, half a continent away from Grand Forks. In the mayoral election of 2000—just weeks after she sat with Lea Ellen and me in New Orleans—she was voted out of office by three hundred votes. In time, the Grand Forks *Herald*—which had praised Owens so highly in the early part of the crisis—turned against her. "I think it was because I didn't take people out, like my department heads, and just publicly step on them," she says. "Like John O'Leary. He worked as hard as he could, but of course all the HUD money went through his community development department. We just all had to build boxes around ourselves and go on."

Editor Mike Jacobs casts the problem differently. "At the same time there was a lot of flood recovery going on, there was also a lot of rethinking going on about how the government ought to be behaving as a city. Pat failed to understand that that was happening."

The loss was devastating to her. "I am just finally over it, to some degree," she says, and this is a year and a half after the fact. "I did the very best I could. But sometimes you extend yourself a hundred percent to people, and they lash back at you. I just have to put it in perspective and say, 'I don't have anything to be ashamed of. I stood by the people, but the people wanted change. They wanted a new face that didn't represent flood.'"

All these years later, Pat Owens is justifiably proud of having gone to Washington to lobby Congress for disaster aid (and of snagging $171 million for Grand Forks); she's proud of the ingenuity that prompted her to form the Mayor's Business Redevelopment Committee, a group of top business leaders who "spun off into areas to try to get our community back on board, like day care." She's proud of the decisions—unpopular though some of them were—to spend that aid money on less glamorous infrastructure while her neighbors across the river were turning their downtown into a showplace.

But what she *prefers* to remember about those trying times are the human interest stories. All during the recovery period, she made it a point to sit and listen to the very young and the very old, those segments of the population least able to cope with such loss. "It was very hard on the senior citizens," she says. "Those of us who were younger, it was easier for us to pick up again. For some of them, it was final, where they had to leave their homes and go live with sons and daughters or go into nursing homes." She says that the death rate among seniors accelerated after the flood.

At the other extreme were the children, the segment we adults often look to for hope in a disaster. They're the future, and so on. But while they may be the future, some of them have an especially hard time dealing with the crisis of the moment. They can hold healing and hurt in the same small hands. "The children in Grand Forks have a Summer Performing Arts program," says Owens, "and that first year they staged a production called 'Keep the Faith.' They put in both seriousness and lightness, and I think that saved our community's sanity in some ways. But one of the things that we lost were three schools totally. One was an old-time school in the Lincoln Drive area. The governor and his wife came one evening for a ceremony, in which we were going to lower the school flag for the last time. The next day the school would be demolished.

"Well, that very week, the school custodian, a man in his sixties, took his own life. I had to give a talk, and it was very sad. So I talked about the school and the community and working together—the memories, in other words. I also told the audience that we don't really know how people are hurting, so if anyone out there was hurting they should let us know so we could guide them to someone who could help."

After that ceremony, as Owens was saying hello to a council member and his family, a little boy came up and hung there at the edge of the circle. When everybody left and Owens was walking away, the boy said, "Mayor, you said if you needed help that we should talk to you." She sat him down on a bench and asked what was the matter. "I'm really hurt," he said. "I lost my grandpa." He explained that his grandfather had been cleaning out his basement after the flood and had suffered a heart attack. "Our house is wet, and my grandma's devastated. And I was really close to my grandpa."

Over the next few months, Mayor Owens helped take care of the boy. "I couldn't adopt all," she says, "but I did adopt many. And he was one of them. His name was Matt, and his dad would call me and say, 'Matt's not doing well today. Can he come with you?' And I'd pick him up and take him with me. We'd go to various things where he would meet some of the dignitaries and listen to the people." In time, Mayor Owens recalled someone else who had come to her hurting right after the flood. "At the Civic Auditorium, our one-stop shop with all the rescue and recovery services, a lady had come up crying. Her husband had just died, she said, and she was overwhelmed with all the paperwork. So I took her to FEMA, and they guided her through everything." Eventually, after spending time with Matt, the mayor put two and two together: That lady was Matt's grandmother.

"There were just so many people who needed comforting and reassurance that things were going to be all right," Owens says. Early on, she got a call from the mayor of Winnipeg, who told her that the three things every evacuee needed to take with them were their "pets, pills, and pillows." On her rounds of the various temporary shelters, Owens had that lesson reinforced time and again—especially the part about the pets. "I remember running into a disabled couple who had left their cat in their apartment. They were just crying and crying, they were so distraught. I told them to give me their keys and if I had to I would go get their cat myself. I turned around and hadn't walked ten feet when I saw someone wearing a red jacket. He was from the National Humane Society. By gosh, I said, and I handed him the keys. And he went and got the cat."

The task of remaining emotionally invested while still making sound decisions was draining to Owens. "In my old jobs, I always wanted people to like me," she says, "but I knew I couldn't do that here. I had to do the leadership part, but many people expected me to do the emotional part, too."

In spite of the stress, the only time Owens really broke down was one morning as she drove out to her dad's house, after he had moved back home. "It was five-thirty A.M.," she recalls. "He lived about five miles in the country, and I would check on him first thing and then try to be at work by six-thirty. Well, this particular morning I drove through downtown Grand Forks, and everything was dark and the city was deserted. It was like you were all alone. I started crying.

"So what I did was slip a little tape in that I had gotten from some first-graders. They said, 'This is a tribute to Mayor Owens,' and they talked about 'This is my town' and 'It's a great big beautiful world.' And you know what? It's funny what gives you strength at times. But that did."

LONG BEFORE I knew who said it, Hemingway's phrase "grace under pressure" often came to mind when I was dealing with a crisis situation. Hemingway meant it as a definition of guts, but to me it defines the essence of humanity.

You never know how victims are going to react in the heat of the moment. Some wail and fall apart; others become catatonic; still others act imperious, as though the bad stuff were happening only to them. In this way, crises tend to reveal something about who we really are. Even disaster professionals are sometimes caught off guard by their emotions. At the Oklahoma City bombing, a fire chief described one of his men who had broken down crying: "He *became* the building," the chief said. In other words, the firefighter failed to maintain that safe sliver of distance between his head and his heart.

In my experience, the people who handle crisis best are the ones who, either naturally or through training, tend to think of others before they think of themselves. Do such people really exist? I believe they do. Certain kinds of personalities are drawn to working for the Red Cross, the Salvation Army, the Mennonites, and other relief organizations. I know for a fact that certain types are attracted to working for FEMA, the one government agency whose mission is to get out in the field and *help people.* Many FEMA workers even spend their vacations going to disaster sites and pitching in anywhere they're needed. Whether you're a victim or a recovery worker, focusing on the welfare of those around you is a key to negotiating the emotional undercurrents of a crisis situation.

For those in charge, there's usually plenty of work to keep the mind occupied. At Northridge, here are just a handful of the services we were responsible for coordinating: identifying and bringing in 263 linguists speaking eight different languages; arranging a mental health/stress management team to debrief relief workers; setting up distribution/storage systems and personnel to deliver water to ten sites; bringing in mobile homes and tractor trailers from Texas, since the ones we were going to fly in from an East Coast air force base wouldn't fit on a C-5 aircraft; constructing a parking lot; arranging to get health care to people living in parks; ordering office supplies from the General Services Administration (GSA); finding a thousand mylar blankets locally to augment the GSA stock. This doesn't even include taking applications from, and getting emergency checks to, earthquake victims.

But you can't be a totally successful crisis manager by simply crossing items off your to-do list. Good managers interact with their people, and so do good crisis managers. During the Grand Forks flood and fire, Mayor Pat Owens had plenty of crucial decisions to make, but she also found time to listen to her employees and townspeople as they opened up about their fears and loss. The worst kind of manager in a crisis is the "type-A" personality who believes he has to control everything in life. You can't control a crisis—all you can do is manage it. To my mind, that means going beyond handling the nuts-and-bolts issues of response and recovery; it also means instilling a sense of comfort and hope among those most hurt by the event. A physician can be the best technician in the world, but his patients still want him to have a good bedside manner.

THE TRICK IS balance. Years ago when I was head of the Arkansas Office of Emergency Services, a huge flood coursed through downtown Hot Springs, the town where then-governor Clinton had grown up. He was beside himself with worry. He phoned me repeatedly at the county Operations Center. "How bad is it, James Lee?" he would ask, and I would tell him how high the water was. Finally, he said, "You think I need to come over there?"

"Probably wouldn't hurt," I said.

In a couple of hours he showed up for a briefing, wading through ankle-deep water inside our office. When we had him up to speed on the situation, he asked what we wanted him to do. "Why don't you go over to Central Avenue, let the store and restaurant owners see that you're here, tell them we're doing everything we can and that they will recover."

"Good idea," he said, and he took my cell phone with him, a big mistake on my part. Soon he was calling about every five minutes: "James Lee, get some pumps over here. These people are hurting." "James Lee, we need some sandbags. . . ." "James Lee this, James Lee that." It was constant. One time I asked him, "Governor, when are you going back to Little Rock?" We both laughed.

At the end of the day we went out to one of the hardest-hit subdivisions. He allowed no media to go with him, and he walked into every single house and met with every family. He hugged them, talked to them, listened to their stories. He had mud up to his knees and tears running down his cheeks. It just broke his heart. When we got back in his car, he said, "James Lee, we've got to help those people. Give them all ten thousand dollars apiece!"

"Governor, we can't do that without changing state law," I said.

"Well, how much can we give them?"

"Twenty-five hundred dollars." Oh, it killed him.

I know it sounds like a caricature, but empathy is one of the most important roles for a leader helping others respond to crisis. Point is, there are things you can and can't do. You can't heal every wound. You can't make people completely whole. You can't pay every bill they'll incur. You can't let your caring cause you to make promises you can't keep.

But you can empathize with their pain and embarrassment at being helpless. You can make adjustments to the recovery process based on their need for dignity. You can make sure they have shelter and a hot meal. You can listen to their stories and acknowledge their concerns. You can hug them and let them cry on your shoulder. You can say to them, as I do, "We can't bring back your memories, but we can help you build new ones."

One of the best examples I know of corporate crisis management was Swissair's handling of the crash of one of its jumbo jets off the coast of Nova Scotia in 1998. The company had a thoroughly prepared crisis plan in place before the accident, no doubt having gone to school on TWA's mistakes in the summer of 1996. When TWA 800 went down off Long Island, the airline was slow to respond. "The first twenty-four hours are critical if an airline is to build a relationship of trust and communication with the crash families," Gary Abe of the National Transportation Safety Board (NTSB) told Reputation Management. "If you don't take advantage of the first twenty-four hours you can never really overcome that."

Swissair was on top of the situation from the get-go. Hours after the crash, the airline announced payments of some $20,000 to help the families of victims with immediate financial needs; it established a team of grief counselors; it arranged for families to visit the crash site; and it chartered jets so journalists could get to the scene. Furthermore, the company's public communications during this stressful time seemed open and genuine, which had the effect of calming victims' families, the media, and—not unimportant—Swissair's investors. It's now the industry standard.

The Swissair case goes to show that if you tell the truth—which often means saying, "I don't know" or "I can't do that"—you never have to "spin" the story. Spinning usually spins you out of control. But if you have a crisis plan in place, one that calls for the unbeatable combination of truth and compassion, you've already gone a long way toward effectively managing the situation.

To find the right balance between head and heart in a crisis:

• **CONTROL WHAT YOU CAN AND ROLL WITH THE REST.** Rolling with the rest isn't listed on most employees' job descriptions, though controlling their work is implicitly there. And it may sound as if I'm telling you to take on a split personality when you're dealing with a crisis. It's a question of attitude. If you can't control something, despite your plans, despite your improvisations, will you let it control you? Rolling with the rest is essential to managing stress, which can derail the best-laid plans. If you've got the right priorities and plans in place, you'll have a lot of skills and resources for controlling a crisis. Don't let the things that aren't your priorities—or aren't within your control—eat up time or energy from executing your plan, or remembering important details. As you work your plan, check off the things you've done as well as the things you can't control. As conditions change, start with a fresh list.

• **NEVER PROMISE WHAT YOU CAN'T DELIVER.** Know your limits. The biggest difference between the heart and the head is hope. Our heart begs for hope, and before we realize it we can be promising things that just can't happen, at least not first. Fall back on your values to help you make the decisions you hadn't anticipated, to do the triage, and don't let your heart lead you away from them.

• **THINK IN TERMS OF GOODWILL.** When you've sorted out what you can and cannot do in response to a crisis, let people know what you're going to do in terms of the heart as well as the head. Just as hope can cloud us to realities, it can be an incredible force when it's tied to action. Leverage the action with hope by tapping into the empathy of everyone you work with, including suppliers, vendors, the media.

• **TAILOR RESPONSES TO KEEP PEOPLE CONFIDENT AND PRODUCTIVE.** People need to be seen as individuals, even though they respond best to a crisis when they're working in teams. You can't check your personality, your past experiences, the other stuff that's going on in life, at the door when you enter crisis mode. Each department and division has its own personality, too. If you're prepared, you'll have built these relationships long before the crisis, and you will be able to tap into them.

• **FORGET BLAME.** Scapegoating creates fear and destroys trust. It's sure to trickle into any stressful, big-ticket crisis, but by being clear in how you interact with others, and what you're willing to accept from them in their behavior, you'll set a tone that can minimize the finger-pointing. If people are busy covering their backsides, they aren't going to be responding to the crisis.

Now let's see how to pull this together in highly functional, highly efficient teams that can respond to big or small crises as they unfold.

7

TEAR DOWN THE STOVEPIPES

Team Shouldn't Be Just Another Four-letter Word

LONG ISLAND, NEW YORK
JULY 17, 1996

Paula wanted Jay to know the city's gardens—the open serenity of the Tuileries, the quiet privacy of the Luxembourg, the pocket retreat in the Place des Vosges. And Jay, even though he had turned nine only six days before, was precocious enough to appreciate this gift from his mother. "Our nephew Jay had a voracious appetite for knowledge," his uncle Frank Carven would tell mourners at the double funeral in Bel Air, Maryland. "He read everything. He loved the environment. And he was bound for great things." Of his sister, Frank said, "Paula wanted Jay to enjoy all of life's wonders—the space shuttle taking off, skiing in the West, whale watching off New England, a birthday trip to France. She encouraged him to do everything."

The Carvens were traveling with Paula's old friend and former TWA flight-attendant colleague Pam Lychner and her daughters, Shannon and Katie. Earlier in the day, the Lychners, who lived in Texas, had flown into Washington's Dulles to meet up with Paula and Jay, and then all had shuttled to New York's Kennedy for the flight to Paris. It was TWA 800, leaving that night at 8:30.

Traveling was a Carven family theme. For thirty years, Paula's father had been an executive with General Motors, so Paula and her four brothers had grown up enjoying the luxury of a larger life. Then, in 1979, Paula became a flight attendant for TWA. Travel for the immediate family was one of the perks. "If I said I wanted to go to Germany," Frank told the mourners, "she would bring me over a subway map. If I said I wanted to go to Greece, she had the name of a TWA person who rented a house there. If I said I wanted to go skiing in Colorado, she had the maps of the ski resorts."

"Paula and I went to Puerto Rico when I was in law school," recalls youngest brother Sean. "We went on a family skiing trip to Utah. She arranged for my brother and me to go to New Orleans for Mardi Gras."

But it was her mother, Ann, who became Paula's most frequent travel companion. Especially after Mr. Carven died in the early 1980s, travel was a way for Ann to cope with the loss. "I regularly traveled with Paula and her flight-attendant friends," Ann says. "We went to Ireland, we went to Egypt, we went to Greece."

So it was exceedingly strange for Ann to feel the way she did that July day when Paula and Jay left to go meet the Lychners in Washington. "They had to leave Bel Air precisely at 1 P.M.," Ann recalls. "It couldn't be five of, or five after. Never before in my life had I felt like, 'It's going to be the last trip.' And I don't ever sleep in the afternoon. But as soon as they drove off and I closed that front door, I said to myself, *I've got to go to bed. I'm going to need my strength.* And I slept until 4 o'clock."

THE FILM WAS a forgettable trifle called *Multiplicity*, but at least it was something to do. For Jim Hall, in his third year as the Clinton Administration's appointee to head up the National Transportation Safety Board (NTSB), weeknights could be long and lonely. Not wanting to uproot two teenage daughters in high school, Hall and his wife had decided the three girls would stay home and Hall would commute back and forth between Tennessee and Washington. On this particular summer Wednesday—July 17, 1996—Hall and two NTSB colleagues had accepted an invitation to a screening from a friend who lobbied for the motion picture industry. With

Chairman Hall were Ken Jordan, still the board's managing director but looking for a different job, and Peter Goelz, who was to become managing director when Jordan left. Goelz had brought his wife to the event, which included a pre-movie buffet. After dinner, the guests had taken their seats, the lights had been dimmed, and the movie had begun.

"Sometime around 8:45, my pager went off," says Goelz. "It was from the Federal Aviation Administration." A few seconds later, Hall's pager sounded, then Jordan's. Goelz went out and phoned the FAA operations center. "I was told that it was likely that a 747 had gone down off Long Island. That there was fire in the water."

At the time, the NTSB had no sophisticated command center. If a plane crashed after hours, the usual drill was for the FAA to check the NTSB duty log to see who was on call, phone that employee at home, and then it was that employee's job to track down the NTSB team needed to answer the emergency. From the very beginning, then, this event was very, very different.

Some 240 miles up the eastern seaboard, a similar drama was already being acted out. "We were at the Friar's Club in New York City," Jim Kallstrom recalls. With twenty-four years of law enforcement service under his belt—twenty of those years in Manhattan—Kallstrom in the summer of 1996 was assistant director of the FBI in charge of the New York Division. "Most of the heads of law enforcement agencies in the city were at the Friar's that night. We were toasting the promotion of Ray Kelly, former police commissioner, to become the undersecretary of the Treasury in Washington, which meant he would have oversight over the Secret Service, ATF, U.S. Customs, and IRS criminal investigators."

Shortly after 8:30, as the party was breaking up, Kallstrom's beeper went off. "A few seconds later," he says, "*everybody's* beeper went off! I went out and got my car, and instead of heading north to my residence, I headed south to the FBI building. I didn't go home for over a month." At the state-of-the-art FBI Command Center, information was coming in fast. At about 8:30 P.M., a TWA jetliner had exploded in midair, just minutes after having taken off from Kennedy Airport. What on earth had caused such a blast? "It was very elementary," says Kallstrom. "Either it was criminal slash terrorism—perpetrated by bad guys, in one form or another—or it was caused by some catastrophic failure of the airplane."

At Ann Carven's in Maryland, the question was so much more basic. Ann and Sean had just gotten back to the house after going out for crab cakes. Sean, still living at home after law school, had been craving them, and even though his mother hadn't felt up to it, he had talked her into having dinner out. As they walked in the door, the phone was ringing. Sean answered. It was Frank, wanting to know how many daily TWA flights there were to Paris. Sean didn't know, but Ann did. "One," she said.

In Washington, Peter Goelz went back to the screening room and got Jim and Ken, and they left for NTSB headquarters. "Frankly," says Goelz, "we usually hear about air crashes first from CNN. So we switched on the TV and tried to figure out how we could get our team to Long Island."

The NTSB had a set procedure of who goes to events, and how they go. "The team was headed up by an IIC, or Investigator in Charge," Goelz says. "Then there would be various other senior investigators over disciplines like power plants, weather, operations, air traffic control, fire and explosion. Usually on a major crash, the Go Team would number ten or twelve people. And there's this cockeyed system over there that I tried to change, but couldn't: A member of the board also goes."

The National Transportation Safety Board is, in fact, a board of five presidential appointees who serve, following Senate confirmation, full-time five-year terms. After a president appoints a member to the board, he goes back and names a chairman and a vice chairman. The board members have pretty much equal powers, with this exception: The operational staff—the investigators and so on—report to the chairman.

And yet the way the NTSB was set up at the time of TWA 800, the board members rotated the duty of going to air crashes as the agency's spokesperson. "It's not very effective, and in this case it was really the last time we did it, because it caused the agency a great deal of agony," says Peter Goelz. "The guy on duty for TWA 800 was Bob Francis, who was the vice chairman. He was this very aloof, arrogant guy who really did not think Jim Hall should be chairman. Francis thought Bob *Francis* should be chairman. Francis was a career FAA guy who came over as a Clinton appointee. But there was always a coolness between Bob and Jim. And after TWA 800, there was no relationship at all."

"I was at home that night," says Bob Francis, "when I got a call from one of the senior investigators. By week and increments, each board member is basically on Go Team, and whatever happens during that week is . . . your accident. It has nothing to do with how many you've had before, or what kind you've had before. There was an enormous amount of resentment inside the NTSB for the fact that, on the 11th of May, I went to the ValuJet crash in Florida—probably the biggest accident in the history of the agency to that point. And two months later, I was on Long Island."

The night of the plane crash, nothing seemed to go right at NTSB head-quarters. "By 9:15, we knew there was a problem," says Goelz. "By 9:30, we knew we had to get up there. But all the commercial flights were done for the night. And though the FAA is mandated by statute to provide us a plane, no planes were available. It was very frustrating. We could not find a way to get up there. At one point, we even contacted a limo service to see if we could rent a series of limos and drive them all up. We figured we could get there in five hours—four if we had a police escort. We actually had the limos lined up, and at about 11 P.M. the FAA called us back and said they could have a plane ready at 5 A.M. So we decided to wait till morning. But the fact that we weren't there that night was a significant setback to the investigation. There was a vacuum. And a vacuum in New York is filled quickly."

At the FBI Command Center in lower Manhattan, a massive investigation was gearing up. "Within a day," says Jim Kallstrom, "I had a thousand agents assigned to the case." The FBI investigates two relevant federal statutes. "One is crime aboard a U.S. flag–carrying aircraft, and the other is destruction of a U.S. flag–carrying aircraft. NTSB is sort of the civilian agency that investigates plane *crashes* that are presumed to be mechanical. In this case, because of the circumstances—we had a 747 that blew up, in a huge fireball seen for forty miles, no mayday from the crew, everything was perfectly normal; we were in an extremely high state of alert in the United States from the standpoint of terrorist threats, the Olympics in Atlanta was a week away. Because of all that, no one knew—no one could *possibly* know—what had happened to that airplane.

"If it was criminal, under that heading you had a whole host of scenarios—somebody carried on a bomb, someone put a bomb in the luggage, someone put a bomb in the cargo. And the other scenario that was sort of new to America, although it had been talked about in law enforcement for a long time, was the possibility that somebody actually shot the plane down with a missile. That became part of the potential scenarios that evening, because in the first four or five hours, we had reports of people saying they saw things in the sky ascending toward the plane. Within a few days, the number of people giving those kinds of reports was over a hundred, and it grew to over two hundred.

"The other possibility was that this was caused by some catastrophic failure of the airplane not induced by a criminal. What could that be? Well, there's a whole bunch of stuff that could be, but none of them fit any pattern, and none of them were obvious to the NTSB people. Nobody had gotten on the radio saying the rudder doesn't work or my engine is acting funny. Just instantaneously, this plane blew up. So everyone—and I mean *everyone*—pretty much thought that although we don't know, and we don't have one shred of evidence that it's mechanical *or* criminal, more than likely it's criminal."

About midnight, Kallstrom had a twenty-minute phone conversation with Bob Francis. "I filled him in on what I knew, which wasn't much, and he told me he was coming up with a crew the next morning and I arranged to pick him up on Long Island in a Black Hawk helicopter. We would have to run two parallel investigations, and my initial impression was, this sounded like a good guy to work with."

HUMAN CHEMISTRY IS a curious science. The main thing I remember from high school chemistry in Dardanelle, Arkansas, is the term *catalyst*, which my dictionary defines as "a substance, usually used in small amounts relative to the reactants, that modifies and increases the rate of a reaction. . . ." In human chemistry, a catalyst could be something as simple as where you're from, what you did or didn't grow up with, the college you went to, how tall or short you are, even the kind of car you drive. Usually, it seems to me, some of those or a hundred other elements go together to create a sense of self, which either mixes with or reacts to another sense of self. I don't pretend to know the catalyst of Jim Hall's and Bob Francis's combustible relationship, but that human chemistry is critical to the effectiveness of any team, especially in a crisis.

Hall, a lawyer, longtime political manager, and friend of Al Gore's in Tennessee, reminds me of home. Comfortable in that Southern blue-button-down sort of way, he says things like, "We have a saying in Tennessee—today you're the rooster, tomorrow the feather duster." In his rooster days, Hall ran a successful gubernatorial campaign and then served on the governor's staff for both of his two terms in the Tennessee state house. He came to Washington in 1993 to take on the chairmanship of the NTSB.

"Trying to run a five-member board in Washington, D.C., is a difficult task," Hall says today, and his laugh tells you that's an extreme understatement. "You're having to work with, obviously, five different personalities. In terms of the board structure, each one of the five members has an equal vote when it comes to the board's 'products'—the safety reports and so on. However, the chairman is the CEO and COO of the board, and he or she is responsible for the day-to-day operations of the board—the direction of the staff, funding, that kind of thing. That is not, and should not be, a shared responsibility. However, when the ValuJet accident happened—which was the first major aviation disaster in several years—and the vice chairman went down, the board found that in the modern media society, whoever is the spokesperson sometimes becomes confused with who is running the investigation. The person running the investigation is a professional board employee, called an Investigator in Charge. But we're dealing with public perception. And with the media, public perception sometimes—unfortunately—becomes reality."

Speaking of perception, Bob Francis appears to be everything Jim Hall is not. Tall, tanned, and urbane, Francis, when he received his appointment to the NTSB, had been living in Paris, France, for nine years as the FAA's senior representative for Western Europe. His office was in the U.S. Embassy, Ambassador Pamela Harriman was a friend, and the city's high life appealed to him mightily. "In some ways it was not an easy decision to come back," Francis says. "On the other hand, I was sitting there in Paris as a G-15, which is the equivalent of a colonel in the army. And somebody says to you, 'Do you want to be a three-star general?' It was that kind of a promotion."

On the morning after TWA 800 went down, Jim Hall turned on the TV at seven o'clock sharp and saw his investigation going down the drain. "There was Bryant Gumbel reporting from Long Island, and our inspection team had not even arrived. All because the FAA hadn't had a plane available, and the Coast Guard had taken their plane but hadn't provided any seats for our investigators. So here we were, supposed to be in charge of the investigation, and yet the FBI, the Coast Guard, the New York mayor, governor, and media circus were already in full force."

Jim Kallstrom's Black Hawk helicopter had lifted off from Manhattan in the pitch dark that morning, and by first light he was over the crash site. "It was unbelievable," he recalls. "The debris field was enormous. There were still fires on the water, a little bit of smoke. It was a gruesome scene."

Kallstrom landed at the Coast Guard station in East Moriches, where the FBI would set up a command post. "My routine stayed about the same for the next three months. Basically, I would fly out to Long Island every morning, stay till about ten or eleven o'clock at night, fly back to the city, go into the office, have briefings in the command center. We had literally hundreds and hundreds of things going on simultaneously with this investigation, some of which were managed out of the command center, others out of the command post on Long Island."

Bob Francis and his NTSB Go Team arrived early Thursday morning at Long Island's MacArthur Airport. The meeting with Kallstrom was postponed, so Goelz soon found them accommodations at a Sheraton hotel. Besides Goelz and the investigative staff, Francis had brought a secretary and a lawyer, who reported directly to him. After checking into the Sheraton, the group drove to East Moriches to meet with Kallstrom. "The assumption early in TWA—not an unreasonable assumption—was that it was a criminal act," says Francis. "So there were *hundreds* of FBI guys out on Long Island doing all sorts of things. And now we arrived with our little dozen people, or whatever it was."

Kallstrom briefed Francis, who remembers "good chemistry" in that initial meeting. Kallstrom thought Francis was "a good guy." "Kallstrom ended up alienating a lot of people in the NTSB," says Francis, "but he and I got along fine. For one thing, we were both basically field people. And both of us, I think, had our egos more or less under control."

The whole situation made Peter Goelz a little sick. "The FBI had already set up shop. And they had all the accoutrements, the playthings, of power. They had helicopters, they had cars with lights, they had guns. They had everything, and we had nothing. We were lucky if we had cell phones." But it was the way Francis acted that really bothered Goelz, who soon found himself squeezed between the chairman and vice chairman. "Because of NTSB tradition—the member on scene was the member on scene—Hall stayed in Washington *in the dark,*" Goelz says. "He was calling me five times a day saying 'What the hell is going on?' Francis, quite frankly, was the kind of guy who was *never* going to admit to Jim Kallstrom that he wasn't in charge. I went to Francis within the first day or so and I said, 'Bob, you *must* call the chairman twice a day. There are decisions being made here that he must be informed of, and that you might want to seek his input on.' He refused."

For Francis's part, he says, "Peter was there, and Peter was Hall's guy. There was nothing that went on that Peter didn't know."

Goelz then tried another tack. "I had a drink with Kallstrom, and I said to him, 'Jim, do you understand that Bob Francis can't give anyone here a direct order?' He looked at me like I was from outer space. I said, 'He can make suggestions, but he has no line authority.' He didn't believe me. I said, 'Technically, and in reality, the chairman runs the agency on a day-to-day basis. When he's not there, the managing director does it. And I'm about to be the new managing director.'"

Kallstrom chuckles. "After the fact, some of these stories about how the FBI took over the investigation . . ." He shakes his head. "Look, the FBI had to *do* the investigation. The NTSB had no *people* to do an investigation. Nor are they *chartered* to do a criminal investigation. So basically, they could just sit there and wait for the pieces of the plane to wash ashore. The FBI, on the other hand, had literally thousands of interviews to do at that point. If we were going to treat this as a crime scene, we had forty square miles of the Atlantic Ocean and all of Long Island. If somebody had actually shot down the plane, then maybe they were still on Long Island. We had to do a neighborhood of all of Long Island. We had to do literally hundreds and hundreds of things—not only in Greece, where the plane had come in from, but at Kennedy Airport, which was a potential crime scene. Who touched the plane, who put food on the plane, who maintained the plane? What about the fuel, the videotapes, everything that went on the plane? What cargo was on the plane? Who were the passengers, and what was their possible role, if any, in this thing?"

THE CARVENS HAD spent an agonizing, frustrating, infuriating night trying to get information about Paula and Jay from TWA. "There was an 800 number," Sean says, but they called and called and couldn't get through. When they finally did, it seemed to serve the airline more than the families. "Instead of giving you information, you called and gave *them* information. Then they were supposed to phone you back. It's six years later, and my brother Frank is still waiting for that return call."

Everyone had gathered at Ann's that night—Frank and his wife, Liz, brothers Jay and Tom. The family was in shock, and in various stages of denial. Sean, the hotheaded one, wanted to drive to Long Island *immediately,* as though he could dive into that dark water himself and save his sister and nephew. "I had no idea where we would go, or where we would stay," Sean says. "I just wanted us to be there." Instead, they decided to leave about dawn. On the way up, Frank phoned the Maryland governor and asked him to contact Governor Pataki in New York and find out where the families were to gather. They were told to go to a Ramada Inn near Kennedy Airport.

When they arrived about 10:30 A.M., what they found there made them crazy. "There was absolutely zero organization," Sean says. "Totally ad hoc. No one told us if Paula and Jay were actually on or off the plane, or whether they were dead or not dead, or if there was any recovery or anything. There was a complete absence of information. It was just a huge room in this motel with people running around not knowing what they were doing. There were some FAA people, and maybe some Port Authority. I don't think the NTSB was on the scene. They didn't have a complete manifest from the plane yet. Or if they did, they weren't disclosing it for some reason."

Over the past year and a half, Peter Goelz, at Jim Hall's direction, had actually been conducting interviews with families of passengers on several air and other transportation accidents. This process had started when relatives of those killed in a 1994 U.S. Airways crash in Pittsburgh contacted the NTSB with complaints that the airline had been mistreating them. "Expecting to be sued, the airline was basically treating the families as litigants from day one," says Goelz. The families were kept in isolation, and rather than volunteering information about the passengers, the airline sought information. If it was discovered, for example, that a deceased passenger had been a smoker, the air carrier's lawyers could argue that his life wasn't worth the amount of damages the plaintiff's lawyers were seeking. "Also, it was the custom, in those days, of airlines to destroy everything—any baggage, all personal effects. A burnt teddy bear, or something like that, could be used against them in litigation. To give the airlines their due, some of them said they were destroying these things with the best interests of the families in mind."

The "family rights" issue had proven to be a very hot topic—even inside the NTSB, where many people (Bob Francis, to name one) initially felt that this was an inappropriate area for the agency to get into (Francis has since changed his mind). "They thought we were just tin kickers, engineers," says Goelz. Early on, Goelz and Hall had tried to get the Department of Transportation to take the lead in hammering out something on the families' behalf, but Secretary Federico Pena declined. "Too explosive," Goelz says. "But he agreed to do it with us, and he assigned a Coast Guard commander to become part of what we now thought of as our 'working group.'" Later, the group had a "very testy meeting with the Air Transport Association, in which they essentially said, Why don't you mind your own business."

And then ValuJet happened. "When that plane went down, I got on the phone and gave some advice to the ValuJet chief of operations. 'Treat the families decently,' I said. 'You're not mandated to, but you ought to. You ought to put them up in a hotel, get security, keep them protected, that kind of stuff.'" Later, on site, Goelz was asked by Secretary Pena to participate in a briefing to the families. "That was my first family briefing," Goelz says. "It was rugged. ValuJet was the first time DNA had been used to identify aviation victims, and I don't think they identified more than sixty of the hundred and some-odd passengers. There was just nothing left. But out of that came a more aggressive movement on family assistance."

When Goelz arrived at the TWA 800 crash site, then, this issue was like an electric undercurrent buzzing through the industry. Not that you could tell it from the situation at the Ramada Inn. "There was more information on TV than we were getting in that room," Sean Carven recalls. "First of all, at the Ramada there was no cable service for the first week or ten days. But you could just turn on the local news and see that the authorities were telling things to the news cameras before they were telling us. That made us livid."

On his first morning at East Moriches, Goelz could see that some thirty or forty bodies had recently been recovered, and another fifty or so were laid out in the boat house. About 8 A.M., Goelz met with the TWA station manager. "There was a debate about the manifest," Goelz recalls. "One of the complaints that the family members in our working group had had, and which was magnified at TWA, was that airlines really weren't sure of the passenger lists. I had some words with the TWA guy: *'Don't you know who was on your plane?'* I said. That was the beginning of the end for TWA. They just were unprepared for this event."

It wasn't until his second night on scene that Goelz was asked to go to the Ramada Inn to talk with the families. "First I met with Governor Pataki and Mayor Giuliani," Goelz recalls. "Things had already started to go south with the families at that point. The place was just *chaos.* There were hundreds of family members in a big ballroom, but you didn't know who was who. A number of them didn't speak English. There were people from France *and* Italy, because an Italian flight had been cancelled and they had been loaded onto this one. There were news people all around. Rumors were flying about bombs and missiles, and there was no real information coming out. Giuliani and Pataki had tried to talk to the families, but it was getting out of control. People shouting, things like that. So Giuliani said to me, 'We gotta get somebody to talk to them.'

"'Okay, set it up,' I said. 'I'll go do it.'

"'Are you sure?'

"'Who else you gonna get?' I said. "Bob Francis was against the whole family assistance stuff. He was on the 'it-interferes-with-our-mission' side. Besides, he was too busy fooling with Kallstrom, anyway."

BOB FRANCIS AND Jim Kallstrom had an understanding. "He acknowledged, initially and forever, that until it was proven to be a criminal act, we had the lead," says Francis. "So I chaired the press conferences. Sometimes he had more to say than I did. Sometimes he had nothing to say." For the first week or so, Francis and Kallstrom held press conferences three times a day.

Still, the perception in Washington was that Kallstrom's FBI was running roughshod over Francis's NTSB. One of the early flaps involved the photographing of victims. "I love to tell this story," Francis says. "Both of us realized that neither of us could be operating as we usually operated. They were law enforcement people, and we were doing an aircraft investigation.

At the same time, we had to understand that it was potentially a criminal act. Rules of evidence are different for the NTSB than they are for the FBI.

"Pretty quickly we ended up with a classic situation, in which some of our investigators came to me and said, 'Remains are being brought in from the ocean and the FBI is not letting us take pictures of them.' Their justification for wanting to photograph the remains was that that was the way we always operated. So I went to Jim and said, 'Apparently, your guys aren't letting our guys take pictures.' And he said, 'No, they're not. The reason they're not is that there's a custody-of-evidence issue. We can't have your people taking pictures and running off to Snappy Photo to have them developed, because then we don't have a chain of custody.'

"Then he said, 'Tell me how many photographers you want. I'll bring them in and they'll take whatever pictures your guys want. Then we'll develop them and give them to you.'

"'That's fine,' I said. There was a lot of grumbling within the NTSB on that issue. But this is what I mean about being a field person. It's a mentality, I guess, or a personality. I was used to being out of headquarters, dealing with lots of different kinds of people, patching up solutions on the spot. I think it was appropriate for me to have done it that way."

"Bob Francis is a very independent guy," Jim Hall says. "I had sent Peter Goelz up there as a sort of one-man family assistance team, because that's all we had. At one point I called and asked Bob if I could come up and help Peter, and he said no, he didn't want me there. And I respected that at the time, because we'd had an unwritten rule that members would not, you know, sort of be visible there during the camera time. So Francis and Kallstrom continued having their daily press conferences, and my investigators were chafing under the fact that Kallstrom was holding meetings with the vice chairman, sharing information, making decisions, and our structure was cut out."

Goelz recalls a touchy situation involving witnesses. "Francis made a decision early on to allow the FBI to exclude NTSB participation in witness interviews, and that was a serious mistake. I called Hall and he went nuts, because the FBI and the NTSB do interviews differently, and we have a different view of witnesses than the FBI does. We don't necessarily trust them as much. If you go back and look at initial press accounts of accidents, more than not you'll find a witness saying the plane was on fire when it hit the ground. Seldom is that the case. People, particularly in aviation accidents, really don't see things accurately. It's just such an extraordinary event.

"We take verbatim records of our witness interviews, and we do them as quickly as possible after the accident, before the press begins to intervene. There's a professor out in Washington State who does studies of witness accounts. We've taken courses from her, and she's extraordinary. It's just so easy to manipulate eyewitnesses.

"The FBI does not take verbatim interviews. They don't tape record interviews. They have what are known as the infamous '302s'—handwritten remembrances of the agents. And they ask leading questions, such as, 'What did you see going up in the air?' Their notes at TWA 800 gave rise to all sorts of conspiracy theories and cost the taxpayers millions of dollars. Hall, to his credit, overturned that decision a day or so later, but it was just another example of how Francis wanted to accommodate the FBI. We weren't interested in having an institutional butting of the heads, but the truth is, we do airplane accidents. They don't. And it's hard for the FBI *ever* to believe that anyone might know just a tad more than they do about *anything*. You know, Kallstrom is not a shy boy."

"I thought Bob and I worked things out splendidly," Kallstrom says today. "There are issues that have to be worked out, but it's not a function of people bullying or people taking over. It's a function of the law. It's a function of maintaining the evidence in such a way that it can't be contaminated and in a way that'll stand up in court later on. These things are well entrenched in common law and in the law of the United States. That's how you conduct a criminal investigation. NTSB doesn't have those requirements. So we had to make sure that our requirements were being met, and at the same time, to the extent possible, not interfering with NTSB's role. The notion that any one agency is in charge is ludicrous. Both agencies are in charge of what they are chartered and mandated to do. As for us not letting them go on the interviews, they had like five people. We had literally thousands of interviews to do. We couldn't wait for them to show up. They just weren't able to deal with something of this magnitude."

"We got our guys back in the witness process," Goelz recalls, "but we finally pulled out of it after a relatively short time. Simply because we realized that the overwhelming publicity had influenced the witness recollections and they were not useful. The FBI ended up interviewing three or four thousand people, of which maybe seven hundred actually saw something. But there was nobody who saw the whole event. The majority of people were eight to ten miles away, and it's pretty difficult to see anything from that distance at dusk, when a plane's at 13,000 feet."

THE CAMERA DOESN'T lie, they say, and I do think it's astonishing how clearly conflict comes across on a TV screen. FEMA doesn't handle airplane accidents, so I was in Washington watching the news just like any other citizen. On any given segment, I might see Bob Francis, or Jim Kallstrom, or Rudy Giuliani, or George Pataki, or any number of Suffolk County officials, or supposed eyewitnesses, or the occasional distraught family member—a wild cacophony of eyes, noses, and especially mouths—holding forth on the situation at hand. The message that came across, however, was total confusion.

This very impression had been noted much, much earlier across town in the West Wing of the White House. "From the moment the accident happened, I was at the FAA command center," says Kitty Higgins, then assistant to the president and secretary of the cabinet in the Clinton Administration. "Right away I met with Harold Ickes and George Stephanopoulos to determine what we needed. Because it was New York City, media capital of the world, and because of the speculation about terrorism, the level of interest in this event was extremely high."

Perception, Jim Hall said earlier, sometimes becomes reality. That was the case here. From the administration's point of view, the ValuJet crash had not been handled particularly well by those speaking for the government. And now the perception at the White House was that TWA was becoming a disaster atop a disaster. "Once there was daylight, we really saw the chaos," Higgins says. "Nobody had taken charge. It was a feeding frenzy. The question was, Who were we going to get to speak for the government at TWA?"

Which is how I found myself involved. Very early on, I got a call from Chief of Staff Leon Panetta asking me to come see him. I remember it was night, so maybe it was twenty-four hours after the crash. There were a bunch of people in a room, Higgins among them, and everybody was tired. Something had to be done, they told me. The president wasn't getting any situation reports. They were having too many press conferences. The families were complaining about how they were being treated. The bottom line, Leon said, was that they needed someone to go up there and get the situation under control. And that person would be me.

As you can tell from the accounts of the NTSB and FBI, there's no shortage of opportunities for conflict in a crisis situation. This wasn't something I was looking forward to. "Okay," I said to Panetta, "if I go up there, I'll go very quietly. I won't do any media. And I'm not going up there to take over."

"Fine," he said.

"And another thing. I request that you call Director Freeh at the FBI, Secretary Pena at Transportation, and Chairman Hall at NTSB, and tell them the president has requested me to go up there and help them pull some things together."

Panetta picked up the phone and started dialing.

Meanwhile, in New York, Goelz was giving his family briefing, which lasted from 7 P.M. till after 1 A.M. It was emotional, combative, exhausting, agonizing. There was no identification system, so some people asking questions weren't even family members; Goelz had no idea who they were. The Italians and French were terribly frustrated, because they couldn't understand the briefing. There was a bottleneck with the Suffolk County medical examiner, who was being asked by the FBI to do time-consuming forensic tests on the bodies but who refused Governor Pataki's offer of outside help. Mainly, the families wanted answers Goelz simply didn't have, and wouldn't have for weeks.

"What happened to the airplane?" they insisted.

"We don't know," Goelz replied.

"Was it a bomb?"

"We don't have that information."

"Where is the airplane? We saw it on the water—why can't you find it?"

"Because the ocean is a big place," Goelz said. In his office today, Peter Goelz shows me a chart that was made up after sonar equipment came in and located the wreckage, which fell in three main sections. Over to the left of the chart is a depiction of the airplane, drawn to scale. In the context of the vast area to be searched, the 747 jetliner is about the size of a housefly.

◆ ◆ ◆

A TERM YOU hear bandied about in Washington is *bigfooting*, as in, "I wasn't in a mood to be bigfooted by James Lee Witt."

That's actually a quote from Peter Goelz, after he heard I was coming to Long Island. I had sent Morrie Goodman, our director of public affairs, up a few days in advance to talk with his old pal Goelz and to scout out the lay of the land. I'll never forget Morrie's description of seeing Peter on Long Island for the first time. "I got to the Ramada where all the families were, and it was pandemonium. Peter, trying to find a little privacy, was sitting *under a table* talking on the phone."

In the midst of a crisis like this, even help can look like a nuisance. "When I heard the president was sending James Lee up to interfere," Goelz recalls, choosing his words, "I was already beat up. The last thing I wanted was to be bigfooted—by either the director of FEMA *or* the president of the United States!"

Goodman assured Goelz that bigfooting was not the intention. "Okay," Goelz said. "You want to know what we need? Come with me." And he took Goodman on a tour of the Ramada, the Sheraton (where the press conferences had been held), the Coast Guard station, the hangar where pieces of the plane were being brought in. One problem for NTSB is that they have no emergency fund, and by law they're not allowed to exceed their budget. So while they needed expensive items like simultaneous translation equipment (not to mention high-ticket dredging equipment, over which Kallstrom and Hall later butted heads all the way to the White House), their hands were essentially tied. "We were spending like bandits anyway," Goelz recalls. "And I was in the middle of this battle between Hall and Francis, because Hall was trying to figure out how much Francis was committing the agency to, and he was trying to get Kallstrom to calm down a little, but Kallstrom wouldn't take Hall's calls. Because he knew he had Francis rolled. Every time Francis would raise a question, Kallstrom would take him on a helicopter ride, and that was the end of that."

Anyway, Goelz listed about six items they needed. "If James Lee can do that," he told Goodman, "then he should come. If he can't, then he should stay away." Goodman passed along the message verbatim.

I got there maybe a week after the plane went down. With me were our

FEMA attorney, John Carey, and Mark Merritt, a top aide from Dardanelle, Arkansas. Mark and I go back a long, long way. His grandmother was my secretary when I was Yell County judge. Mark is a West Point graduate, was an aide to three generals in Desert Storm, and knows how to get things done. Sometimes I don't want to know *how* he gets them done, just *that* he gets them done. We landed at the airport early one morning and drove to the Coast Guard station at East Moriches, where everyone was waiting to brief us. My impending presence had obviously created a certain edginess among the people on-site. I don't mind admitting that I felt a little edginess myself.

First, we had a general get-together, with representatives from the FBI, NTSB (Jim Hall had flown up for the meeting), the governor's office, the mayor's office, the Coast Guard, and the county and local officials. I told them I wasn't there to take over, but that the president wanted some changes made. At the end of that larger meeting, I asked everyone to leave but Kallstrom and Hall. Maybe Francis was there, too. To me, the working relationship between Kallstrom and Francis seemed okay, but I impressed on all present the importance of presenting a unified front.

Today, most of those in that meeting say they don't recall anything that was actually said there, and that's fine with me. I wanted it to be low key. The important thing is that the situation—especially the situation for the families—improved. Instead of competing press conferences from city, state, and federal, there would be one daily press conference at 10 A.M., chaired by the NTSB's Francis, and the families needed to be briefed prior to that press conference. "Things changed dramatically," Peter Goelz says. "Somebody had to say, We're going to put aside the bureaucratic hurdles and just do what needs to be done, and we'll figure out how to pay for it later. With the president's backing, James Lee could do that. Within a day, we had simultaneous translation crews from the UN setting up shop, we added security so we could lock up the area so that it became a much less chaotic environment, and he had the president designate NTSB, and specifically me, to handle the families. Before, we had a bunch of competing agencies from the city and the state, and the way things had been going, I could foresee a Family Center in Perpetuity. The key is to get people home. It's not healthy to have them sitting around this hotel. Things also improved with the medical examiner. It's one thing to tell the governor that you can do the autopsies yourself; it's another to tell the president of the United States. James Lee's presence up there broke the logjam."

That night, Peter Goelz and I met with the families for a long time, and I told them things were going to get better. As I was leaving, a man asked me if I had a minute. He showed me a picture of his daughter, who had been on the plane. All he wanted, he said, was to get his daughter's body released so he could bury her. I asked Mark Merritt to look into it. The man took her home the next day.

The president and first lady flew up to meet with the families a week or so later. They stayed for hours, listening to stories, looking at family pictures, sharing tears and laughs and words of comfort. At the end of the session, the last person to talk with the president was Ann Carven. "Bill," she said, as only a mother can, "I lost my daughter and my grandson in this accident, and I have a story for you." It seemed that Jay Carven, in addition to all his other interests, was an actor who did commercials. His last acting job was to play "little Billy Clinton" in a TV spot. It turned out to be a political ad for the Republicans, and Jay had quit, saying "I'm a Democrat!" For Ann, meeting the president, and sharing her story about Jay with him, was a big step toward getting home.

SO ENDED MY part in the TWA 800 crisis. The families were there about three weeks in all, but the FBI and NTSB went at each other for months. Eventually, Jim Hall made internal changes that allowed him to be on the scene instead of Francis, which is when things fell apart, according to Kallstrom. "As long as Francis was involved, we were a well-oiled machine."

"In Washington," says Hall, "an independent agency's independence and authority must be jealously guarded."

By August of 1996, both the NTSB and the FBI agreed that TWA 800 had been brought down by an explosion in the center fuel tank. Once the voice and flight data recorders were recovered, and once the wreckage of the plane was found, several things became much clearer. "First of all," Goelz says, "it was highly unlikely that it was a missile. We found the engines fairly early, and if it was a surface-to-air missile, they probably would've honed in on the engines. The engines looked intact. So we always thought a missile was pretty low on the totem pole.

"Now a bomb, that was a real consideration. When we saw how the wreckage had fallen, that was a good tip. The things that come off first are where the event started. And we knew early on that the event had started in rows twelve to twenty-eight in the center of the plane. We knew there was a fuel tank there, and we knew the tank was empty—New York to Paris isn't a particularly long run, and they didn't need it. When we picked up pieces of the center wing tank, there were signs of a relatively low-order explosion, not something from a weapons-grade material. So we knew in August that the center wing tank had blown up. And we knew by September, when we had about seventy-five percent of the wreckage off the ground, that there were no signs of a bomb or a missile. The tank had blown up. We just didn't know why."

Despite the signs pointing away from criminal activity, Kallstrom insisted on bringing up the rest of the center part of the airplane and reassembling it in three dimensions. "We knew the center fuel tank had blown up, but the question was always what caused it to blow up. Was it something mechanical or electrical? Or was it a bomb that went off above the fuel tank and a piece of shrapnel went down into the fuel tank? Was it a bomb in the cargo hold, which is right behind the fuel tank? Or in the luggage hold, on the front side of the fuel tank? The tank was essentially empty, but you can never get that last forty gallons out. As the plane sat on the tarmac at Kennedy on that hot July day, taking a delay of two and a half hours, the air conditioners under the 747 model 100 were running the whole time, and all the heat from those air conditioners was going up into the fuel tank. So that thirty or forty gallons vaporized, and even though Boeing obviously designs these things not to blow up no matter how much vapor gets in there, what was it that introduced itself into that now-flammable mixture that caused it to explode? We couldn't really say it didn't blow up because of a piece of shrapnel until we actually put the plane back together and did a string analysis of every little puncture in the plane. So we had to get down to the nitty gritty. Could a missile have blown up *outside* the plane and a piece of shrapnel gone in? We had to close out all those possibilities or we weren't doing our job. NTSB was satisfied with a pile of airplane pieces lying in a linear array on the floor of the hangar—a million pieces. They wanted to say, hey, we know what it was. To my mind, that was totally preposterous.

"Because there was at least a fifty-fifty chance—or even a ten percent chance, the percentage is irrelevant—that this was an act of terrorism, we had to do what we had to do," says Kallstrom. "We had to complete our investigation. That's what we had told the victims' families we would do, that's what we had told the attorney general we would do, that's what we told the president we would do. I briefed the president, in the White House, two or three times on this investigation. This is what we had to do."

In November 1997, sixteen months after the crash, the FBI finally released a report saying it was satisfied that the explosion was not due to a criminal act. "The files for this investigation would be fifty feet high," Kallstrom says.

"Mr. Kallstrom's high profile at TWA 800 paid off bigtime in appropriations," says a still-skeptical Jim Hall. "The FBI got millions of dollars for terrorism."

The NTSB itself saw several positive changes in the wake of TWA 800. The Family Relief Act of 1996, which guarantees families of victims certain rights and on which the NTSB takes the lead, was a landmark piece of legislation. The NTSB has a new twenty-four-hour command center, which presumably will help speed up the agency's response time and allow investigators to do their work unburdened by administrative or travel-agent duties. Chairman Hall also made several changes in the way his board operated. "I tried, but was unsuccessful at, getting us a professional spokesperson, so the five board members wouldn't be essentially competing for camera time. However, one of the things that makes the NTSB members' jobs *attractive* is the public exposure, and the opportunity to be a national spokesperson for safety. So I made changes giving the chairman the prerogative of being on site in high-profile cases, such as the crashes of Egypt Air and John F. Kennedy Jr. In more ordinary events that appear likely to go on longer than three or four days, the spokesperson role reverts to the chairman. By then you're past the initial publicity and into a phase where you've got to make decisions about committing resources. I just think the present structure works a whole lot better."

As for the Carven family, they still travel together, and Paula is still a major force in their travel plans. Every July, for example, they all caravan up to beautiful Smith Point on Long Island to attend the annual July 17th memorial service for Paula and Jay and the other 227 victims who lost their lives in the dark waters just beyond. The Carvens all wear pictures of Paula and Jay on their lapels and dresses. And Ann drives to the site in a car that bears a simple bumper sticker: TWA 800—NEVER FORGET.

◆ ◆ ◆

I'M A SPORTS fan. I played football and baseball as a kid, and I coached my sons' Little League teams until I got into county government and it became unseemly—not to mention impolitic—for the Dardanelle team coached by the county judge to beat up on other teams in the county.

Even back in my coaching days, the bleachers included a few of those overactive parents you read so much about today. All they cared about was winning, and that's all they wanted their kids to care about. I've always been suspicious of that philosophy, feeling that it probably springs more from a deep-seated fear of being a loser than satisfaction at being a winner. In any case, while there's nothing wrong with winning per se, the notion that winning is everything isn't all that helpful to someone trying to build a well-rounded team.

In today's media culture, I think the aura of the almighty spotlight has fried more than a few brains. Those parents who come to their kids' ballgames and end up embarrassing themselves by getting into fights, they've probably just been blinded by the possibility that their kid could become the next Derek Jeter. In that mind-set, it's not too far a leap from Little League to limousines.

But self-aggrandizement and any resulting personal riches aren't, after all, the real point of teamwork. Teamwork is about the satisfaction of helping to build something larger than yourself, and about playing your part in that greater entity's accomplishing its higher purpose.

Winning is always one of any team's goals. But individual stardom times nine (or five, or eleven) doesn't always equal team success.

IN BUILDING A team, the first thing you have to do is tear down the stovepipes. By that I mean the vertical imaging that sparks someone to play for himself and not the team. A bunch of stovepipes in a room never touch one another. How can you pull off a double play like that?

I'm not here to criticize my friend Jim Hall and his former group at the NTSB, but it's clear from the story of TWA 800 that in addition to the unwieldiness and disorganization caused by the uncoordinated response of local, county, state, and federal agencies, the NTSB itself had some inherent problems that caused it to function less than effectively—either within itself or with others—as a team. As Hall himself says, "There aren't five FEMA directors, each with equal or near-equal power." Thank goodness for that. While NTSB has carved out an enviable record of emphasizing and ensuring travel safety in this country, the agency's idealistic set-up, with its five autonomous and near-equal board members, strikes me as a formula for squabbling and inconsistency.

At FEMA, I did choose to be the agency's sole spokesperson because I understood, as I think Hall does, that the media can play a huge role in an agency's ability to do its job. In order to do your job—and that should be the goal, not getting more camera time—you need to do what you can to affect your "media presence." A consistent message and tone are an important aspect of that. As Jerry Ellig wrote in his study of FEMA's results-based management, "FEMA's [1989] efforts in South Carolina after Hurricane Hugo . . . were viewed as a failure in part because several prominent politicians immediately took to the airwaves and painted a picture of federal incompetence. . . . FEMA itself lacked a strong media presence. Its image was at the mercy of state and local officials, and more importantly, the agency passed up opportunities to get critical information to disaster victims."

I also—as someone familiar with the immediate requirements of crisis management—still believe that NTSB needs an emergency fund so it can do its job without fretting over pennies and/or having to constantly seek quick approval from the inevitably disapproving and notoriously slow government bean counters. But that's ultimately an equipment issue—like having batting helmets or shoulder pads—and not really a teamwork issue.

Teamwork issues are, first of all, about attitude. At FEMA, when I was trying to reorganize the agency, one of the first things I did was to switch around my department managers. Some of them screamed bloody murder, but my goal was simply to rip out the vertical structure that tends to grow up in organizations where managers stay in the same place year after year.

TEAMS OPERATE HORIZONTALLY, not vertically. A manager's job, then, is to disassemble the stovepipe structure and reassemble it as a maze of connecting pipes. But how are you going to get something flowing from one pipe to another? That's the real trick, isn't it? Especially in these ego-hyping times (and the media loves to cover a blowhard!), reconfiguring an organization's thinking away from individual stardom to team cooperation is perhaps the hardest task in team building.

I've been fascinated by what I've read lately about the City Hall office plan of New York mayor Michael Bloomberg. As I understand it, he's almost literally torn down the stovepipes—in this case the rows of fancy private offices that once were the much-prized domains of ambitious city department heads. Bloomberg has replaced those with a maze of cubicles. The twist is that he occupies one of the cubicles himself.

That's a pretty forceful statement about teamwork—about egalitarianism, colleagueism, anti-showboatism. "Bloomberg's success . . . can be summed up in one sentence," wrote Michael Tomasky in *New York* magazine. "Bloomberg—the mayor, if not the businessman-citizen—has lots of will but no ego." That's a good way to begin creating a climate of teamwork.

Another vital step is achieving buy-in to a unified goal. You can't just stand before your troops and say, "Okay, team, this is your new mission in life." It's a sure bet that they'll look at you blankly, glaze over while you're outlining your brilliant plan, and then drift away into little knots of defiant resistance. That's why, at FEMA, I had the employees work together to create their new mission. I gave them general goals, parameters, directions. They fashioned the specifics. And because they did it themselves, they felt that they owned that mission.

Did you see *The Rookie,* starring Dennis Quaid? A once-promising pitcher whose arm injury derailed a likely pro baseball career, Quaid is lecturing his team of high school ballplayers about giving up, letting down, letting *themselves* down. They turn it back on him. Talk about selling yourself short, they say. And they make him a proposition: If we get it together and win the season, you make another try for the big leagues. This is based on a true story, by the way. I won't tell you how the movie turns out, but I will say this: It's inspiring to watch a group become a *team* by pulling in the same direction.

EVERY BASEBALL FAN knows that when you've got a great lineup that's working hard but losing games, you don't blame the players. You blame the manager. It's the manager who's responsible for directing his team's skills toward a clear goal. If something's broken, the manager has to step in first to fix it.

A good example from the business world was outlined in a piece I read last fall in *Harvard Business Review*. It concerned the Marriott Corporation, whose legendary work ethic put a premium on "face time"—the more hours an employee spent on the job, the better. It's understandable how such a corporate philosophy could've developed, given the extraordinary demands of hotel work. "We have to provide 24/7 service 365 days a year," wrote author Bill Munck, a vice president and market manager for Marriott International. "So when a problem arises late on a Friday afternoon, someone has to fix it that night or over the weekend. Managers who have an attitude of 'I'll get to it on Monday' don't last long in our industry."

Then sometime in the mid-1990s, Munck was in Boston chatting with a young guy whom Munck considered one of the company's best entry-level managers. Munck asked the man where he saw himself in five years. The answer set Munck—and the rest of Marriott management—back on their heels.

"He said he really wasn't sure that he would still be with Marriott," Munck writes. " 'I'm working a minimum of fifty hours a week, sometimes fifty-five or sixty hours. . . . And I commute an hour each way, so it's not just ten-hour days for me; it's twelve-hour days. I don't know if I want to continue doing that, because I want to have a life outside of work.' "

Rather than writing the young man off as a deadbeat, Munck and his fellow managers instead saw the writing on the wall: "Other Marriott employees were saying the same thing, albeit in different ways. From exit interviews and from word of mouth, I knew we were losing a lot of very good managers who wanted greater flexibility in the workplace."

The bottom line is, Marriott instituted a new program shortening the hours of managers. This was a basic institutional change of attitude, which required much heart-to-heart discussion within the corporation. But it was clearly an attitude aimed at fostering teamwork, rather than chipping away at it as the old attitude had done.

At the end of his article, Munck himself knocks off early to go to the gym—leading by example. "They needed to see that I had a life outside of work," he writes, "and that when business was slow, I wasn't going to hang around just because it wasn't six o'clock yet."

Tearing down the stovepipes can't be more important than when two companies are working together in partnership—especially when those companies come from entirely different cultures, speak different languages, and have different assumptions about how to do business or even how the partnership is supposed to work. Take, for example, the story of Northern Telecom (known more familiarly as Nortel) and Tong Guang Electronics. Business students have taken to studying how the Nortel and Tong Guang partnership to manufacture telecommunications equipment in China nearly fell apart when Nortel imported a management team without getting buy-in from their Chinese partners. Reading that business case study, I didn't feel that things were that much different from trying to get the FBI, the NTSB, and everyone else working together.

Nortel, a Canadian company, had had success with some previous joint ventures, especially one with a French company, Matra. One of the key elements of that partnership was the simple fact that they choose managers who had rotated through many different assignments beforehand, managers who had actually had experience working with companies in other countries. When the Nortel–Tong Guang managers were having trouble seeing things eye-to-eye, both sides decided they needed to learn more about each others' business practices and culture. A lead manager from Tong Guang was rotated to Canada for three months, and when he returned to the China-based joint partnership he was able to translate the ideas behind business decisions from both the Nortel and Tong Guang perspectives, a role that helped the joint venture thrive when managers disagreed or were faced with other problems. At the same time, Nortel managers were given a crash course in Chinese business and culture, and the manufacturing director even learned basic Mandarin to ease communication—and connect the stovepipes at the bases, so to speak.

In summary, then, here are some key principles for fielding a well-oiled team:

• **BUILD EMERGENCY TEAMS WITH CUSTOMIZED STAFFING AND REPORTING LINES.** First, tear down the stovepipes—as I said, successful teams operate horizontally, not vertically. Mixing managers around helps to reduce fiefdoms when you aren't in a crisis, and it also goes a long way to getting managers to work with lots of different people and to build relationships with them. Those skills and relationships are essential to leading people when a crisis hits. And even when you're *in* a crisis situation, you shouldn't be afraid to move people around. If you've rotated them as part of their regular work, they'll know the workers they're teaming up with or managing from their past assignments. This means you'll get the right combination of skills and networks working on every aspect of a crisis. Be sure to map out how your communications plan will work in any new team. And make sure everyone knows who's in charge of the team and who's in charge of coordinating all the teams, if there's more than one.

• **RECONFIGURE THE GROUP'S THINKING TOWARD A COMMON MISSION.** Without specific goals, a team's purpose can get lost in the haze. That's especially true if the group is working together for the first time in a crisis situation. Break down goals into benchmarks, and chart the team's progress toward getting the crisis under control. When you've got more than one team working on different parts of the same problem, let them know how their work fits together and when they've accomplished something that allows another team to meet its goals. When things get prickly between teams that seem to be competing—whether it's a case of needing the same staff, money, and equipment or they're sending mixed messages to a client—collapse the teams into a single unit, if only for a little while. There's no better way to get people on the same page as to give them only one book.

• **ASSESS THOSE EMPLOYEES WHO THRIVE IN CRISIS—AND THOSE WHO DON'T.** No matter how hard you try to get people prepared for a crisis, or how hard you to try to give them the support they need to fix a problem, there are some who seem to perform better than ever under the heat and those who seem to melt every time. You've hired these employees for their skills and talents, so unless you're in a constant state of crisis (and we all hope that's not in the cards), you've got to find a way to take full advantage of everyone. First, identify what makes those thrivers excel. Are they great connectors or smoothers or communicators? Are they creative about getting around resource shortages or bottlenecks? Are they more productive when they're getting assignments dropped in their lap for quick turn-around? Have they had lots of practice looking at your crisis plan and making it happen in the real world? Are they the kind who stays calm and precise no matter what gets thrown at them? You need to know what makes them so good at crisis management so you can plug them into teams where you need their skills.

Next, identify what sorts of issues are facing those who don't thrive in a crisis. Do they build fiefs and have problems working outside of them? Do they need stardom rather than teamplay, and therefore angle for responsibilities that aren't a good fit for them? Do they have a hard time making decisions without approval from a supervisor, even when there are guidelines in place to speed up decision-making? Do they freeze up and get overwhelmed? Before you make any changes to your crisis staffing, you have to figure out if the problem is with the person or with your communication system, your crisis plan, or your leadership.

After the crisis, you'll learn to collect information to see how well your plan worked. You should also take this time to see if your employees could learn to work better in crisis. For many people, especially those who freeze up or can't connect to others, working very closely with another team member or team leader will smooth those difficulties. For others, you can utilize them as communication coordinators or put their talents to work keeping the rest of your business on track.

• **WHEN WORK GETS STALLED, ROTATE NEW PEOPLE ONTO THE TEAM AND SET NEW BENCHMARKS.** It may seem like an obvious point, but teams as well as the people on them burn out after working at high alert for a long time. A long time can be several hours, several days, or several weeks, depending on what's going on. The only way you'll know is when you track the progress to your benchmarks and find that you're always slowing down. It could mean that you're ready to move on to your recovery plan, but if you've still got angry clients, a malfunctioning product, or no way to get supplies to your factory, you have to finish responding to the crisis before everybody can go home. It's not always easy to get people to rotate off, however. They tend to get knotted up in a crisis and start to make putting everything back to normal (or as close to normal as they can get) the driving force of their lives or careers. There are two possibilities: Either move them back to their regular work, or move them to a team that's less of a pressure-cooker—for instance one that's starting to roll out your recovery plan. As you assemble your new team, change the benchmarks for getting to your goal. You don't want to break down morale by making one team a star at another team's expense.

• **REMEMBER, IT'S THE MANAGER'S JOB TO HELP THE TEAM SUCCEED.** A leader's first responsibility—and most important skill—is to give his or her people the tools they need to beat the crisis. Sometimes that means brokering a game plan between two competing egos; sometimes that means taking a few minutes aside to coach someone before, or even after, a rough patch; sometimes that means giving a morale-boosting pep talk; sometimes that means revising the lines of communication, getting money and resources, or quietly sitting everyone down to make sure they're working the same crisis plan. Find out what the team needs, and get it for them.

Now, let's see what systems and ideas you need to have in place in order to make that essential transition from responding to a crisis to recovering from it.

IV

RECOVERING FROM
CRISIS

8

A LIGHTNING ROD WORKS BOTH WAYS

*Don't Underestimate the Energizing Power
of One Strong-willed Soul*

The year is 1944; the scene, Miami, Florida. It doesn't look much like wartime. Palm fronds rustle on the ocean breeze, while ladies and gents in tropical weaves sway to the strains of Johnny Mercer's "Dream" and Les Brown's "Sentimental Journey." Even as, a world away, General Dwight D. Eisenhower prepares his troops for the invasion of Normandy, Biscayne Bay shimmers under a topaz sky.

Unfortunately, Abe Wyatt is lost somewhere on the teeming blossom-lined boulevards of Miami. That wouldn't be so bad except that Abe is a bus driver for the city transit line, and he's sitting behind the wheel. "Oh, at first he used to ride those people around for a half hour or more, trying to find his way," laughs Ruby Wyatt, Abe's widow. "He was a fish out of water."

As a country boy myself, I can sure understand that. To say that the Wyatts of Falmouth, Kentucky (today's population 2,642), were far from home would be an understatement. Miami was everything Falmouth wasn't, and vice versa. The first settlers in the northernmost section of Kentucky, where the Licking River branches south from the mighty Ohio, came from Virginia and Pennsylvania all the way back in the year of the American Revolution. Falmouth itself—named, probably, for Falmouth, Virginia—was established in 1793 at the spot where the South Fork of the Licking meets the main stem, and the county of Pendleton, of which Falmouth is the seat, was formed in 1798. By the 1940s, Falmouth was a lazy, entrenched little town—which is to say, comfortable and cozy—built around one of its earliest residents' log cabins. It was a hamlet whose residents all knew one another and often waved from car to car on their way to do their *real* shopping an hour north, in Cincinnati.

But in that year that Abe Wyatt struggled to find his way through the web of sun-drenched streets, Miami was scarcely fifty years old. A gleaming and well developed Johnny-come-lately, it had been the brainchild of Henry Flagler, the legendary railroad tycoon who had developed St. Augustine and, later, Palm Beach. Flagler had a penchant for large, extravagant, and luxurious homes and hotels, so it's probably safe to say that Abe didn't pass too many log cabins on any version of his daily route.

The Wyatts had come to Miami because their seven-year-old daughter, Pat, had a terrible case of eczema, and doctors in northern Kentucky had told Ruby and Abe that their best bet was to take Pat to Miami, where she could soak daily in the healing sea water. This was a wrenching change for the young family, even in wartime. Married in 1934, the Wyatts had spent almost their whole lives in Falmouth. Ruby, daughter of a successful farmer, had grown up in a fine Victorian house on the banks of the Licking, while Abe—his given name was Earl, but someone had pinned this nickname on him during childhood and it had stuck—had had a slightly different upbringing. "He grew up working in his father's restaurant and poolroom," says Ruby, "and he played a lot of the time. Later he worked in a brewery. This was in the Depression, and you took what you could get."

When war broke out, Abe was rated 1-A and expected to be drafted at any time. Meanwhile, he found a job with Rice Aeronautical in Cincinnati, building airplane engines. The family lived in Covington, Kentucky, just across the Ohio River from Cincinnati. "I think we were there a couple of years," Ruby says. "Then Pat came down with this terrible eczema—just breaking out all over and being miserable. In fact, it was so bad that the doctors didn't know what to call it. We took her to I don't know how many doctors." Finally, one told them there was nothing more he could do—but that some patients had been helped by daily ocean baths.

"Well, we set out like gypsies," laughs Ruby. "We had this old car, I think a Chevy, that was worth about twenty-five dollars. We packed it up and headed for Miami." Near downtown, off on a little side street, they found a development of cottages; their place was only three rooms. "We made good friends with some people in the neighborhood, and they were really helpful when Abe got the notice that he was going to be drafted back in Falmouth." This would've been the spring of 1945, just as the war in Europe was winding down. "Coupons for gas were hard to come by in those days, and we had almost nothing to get home on," Ruby recalls. "This older man we knew gave us a lot of gas coupons. We didn't know where he got them, and at the time we didn't care. They turned out to be not quite enough. Before we reached home, we ran out of coupons and had to sell the car. We finally arrived back in Falmouth on the train."

THERE IS IN this story an undercurrent of steeliness that anyone who lived through the Great Depression and World War II will identify with. Times were tough, and you learned survival from the times.

But if you probe deeper into the lives of Ruby and Abe Wyatt, you find other, more personal, traits that were bound to make them successful. They loved life, and they learned early on to roll with the punches. People wanted to be around them. Abe was a clotheshorse with a hundred-watt personality. He never met a stranger. "One day after we'd started our business," says Ruby, "we were driving down the street and Abe was waving to this person and that person. Finally I said, 'Who *is* that?' 'I dunno,' Abe said. 'Might be a customer!'"

Ruby was a singer and entertainer whose natural habitat—she thought—was in front of an audience. Before she and Abe married, she and some friends spent a weekend at the nearby resort area of Indian Lake. "Well," recalls Ruby, "they had a talent contest at a club called the Wooden Shoe. And I won." She sang "Dinah/ Is there anyone finer/ In the state of Carolina . . ."

The next day, as Ruby and her friends were packing to leave, a man came over and said he wanted to hire her to sing in the club. "I was amazed. I was foolish. I was very young," she says. "I thought I had really hit the big time." She sent her friends home without her.

Within a week, the life of the entertainer had begun to pale. "It got so wild, and I was a little girl from a country town, I was frightened to death." A friend of hers from Falmouth ran a boat dock at Indian Lake, and one night Ruby went to him and asked when he was going home for a visit.

"Saturday," he said.

"Well, I'm going with you," she said.

And that, as she puts it, "was the end of my singing career," though it wasn't entirely. All her married life she would find herself in charge of putting on school and community shows, and she didn't always watch from the wings. Ruby and Abe, both avid dancers, loved to get dressed up and go to clubs where big bands would play and they could dance to their special song, "Stardust." "Inevitably, after a while Abe would leave the table and go talk to the orchestra leader," laughs Ruby. "I knew exactly what he was doing—asking if I could sing. And you didn't have to push me to get up there. I enjoyed every minute of it."

This, then, was the kind of couple who moved back to Falmouth, Kentucky, in the eventful spring of 1945. The plan was for Ruby and Pat—whose eczema had not been appreciably improved in Miami—to go live with her parents while Abe went off to war. But life soon threw them another curve: The Germans surrendered, and soon so did the Japanese. Abe was staying in Falmouth. But he had no job, no money coming in.

"He had saved some war bonds," Ruby says, "and his brother-in-law had an old rolling store—what was called a 'huckster truck.' Abe cashed in some bonds and bought that truck, a 1929 Studebaker with a front door and a back door and shelves against both inside walls. Outside under the truck on both sides were cages for chickens, which farmers sometimes bartered for other goods. Suddenly we were in the grocery business."

In the mid-1940s, the supermarket boom was just getting under way in the United States. The grocery business has always been cyclical: in the early days, general stores sold a little of whatever goods were available. Then specialized shops came in, such as the bakery, the butcher, the produce store. During the Depression, hard times decreed lower prices, which required higher volume. Someone came up with the idea of "warehouse stores," larger barnlike general stores with night hours, self-service, and heavy advertising. By 1940, there were six thousand supermarkets in the United States. Ten years later there would be fourteen thousand. They were the wave of the future.

But in small towns like Falmouth, Kentucky, which were surrounded by miles and miles of farmland, you could still find a lucrative niche for yourself by taking the market to the shoppers. "Up in Covington, there was a wholesaler called Dixie Wholesale. Abe drove the truck up there, and they filled it up to the extent that our money allowed. We never used credit—not *ever.* I was never in debt in my life, until the events of 1997."

In addition to the groceries and the chicken cages, they also carried a tank of coal oil so the farm families, none of whom had electricity yet, could replenish fuel for their lamps and stoves. Finally, the men who delivered bread and produce to Falmouth were friends of theirs, so the Wyatts stocked up daily with those perishables. Ruby didn't drive, but she rode along with Abe in the earliest days of the business. "It was great fun," she says. "Each day we would take a different route out of town, and we would go to the end of the line, or until Abe got tired, or until we were about to run out of gas, which did happen occasionally. We would stop at each farmhouse, blow the horn, and here would come the farm ladies, some of them carrying a baby, with two or three toddlers running along behind them, and nearly always a dog. The dog would be the first on the truck. We'd give the children cookies and candy, and the ladies would usually have a basket of eggs, or maybe a chicken or two. We would buy the eggs and chickens and give the ladies credit on groceries. Then when we got home, we would drive to the wholesaler in Covington and trade the eggs and chickens for more groceries. With those chickens squawking under the truck, we were a pretty noisy bunch."

BY 1946, THE business was healthy enough for Abe and Ruby to branch out with a permanent store. Abe published the following ad in the local newspaper:

AT LAKE VIEW
I have opened a grocery in West Falmouth, and will handle
all kinds of groceries, vegetable and meats. I will also

continue to operate a rolling store and buy country produce. My prices will be in keeping with the times, and the
public is cordially invited to call.

EARL WYATT

"There was a tiny little one-room building near where we lived at the
time, and we decided we would fill that with groceries," says Ruby. "I would
run the store, and he would run the huckster truck."

With their built-in customer base and the new postwar prosperity, their
small store was an instant success. The next year, Ruby gave birth to their
second daughter, Dixie (Ruby denies that they named her after their grocery wholesaler!), and with that development Abe gave up the truck route to
work solely in the store. Then, in 1949, they built a larger store on a piece of
property very close to where Ruby had grown up, facing Shelby Street and
backing up to the South Fork Licking River. On the second story, just above
the grocery, they built a four-room, one-bath apartment for themselves and
their young family. On the east side of the store they built steps up to a large
second-floor porch and the apartment entrance.

Ruby's description of the way that first Wyatt's Grocery operated
reminds me so much of going shopping with my mother when I was a child
in Dardanelle, Arkansas. "We didn't have a cash register," she says, "though
we had a cash drawer built in underneath the counter. When a customer
would come in, he or she would come to the counter and I would wait on
them. 'I'd like a box of salt,' they might say, and I would go get the salt and
bring it back. Then I would jot down the item and price on a brown paper
bag at the counter. 'Now I'd like some black pepper,' they would say, and, of
course, the pepper was right next to the salt, so I would go over there again
and get the pepper, bring it back, and write it in on the paper bag. When the
customer was through shopping, I would add everything up and write the
tally on the front of the bag." Although Ruby and Abe always paid cash for
the things they bought, they did eventually extend credit to their customers.
"So many of them were farmers," Ruby says. "They had to wait until they
could sell their crops before they could pay us."

To people like that, a grocery store is so much more than just a place to
get groceries; it's almost an adjunct of the bank. I know my family sure relied
on our local store. I'll never forget my dad borrowing $18 from the bank to

plant his cotton crop, and our charging our groceries until the crops came in. That year was incredibly hard—it was the year he brought in only two bales—but somehow he made enough to pay back the $18, pay off the groceries, and get ready for the next year.

Wyatt's Grocery outgrew the new store almost immediately, and in the spring of 1950 Abe expanded. This began an almost yearly ritual of add-ons. "And every time he enlarged the store, he added a room to our apartment." With every expansion, they also "expanded" the name of their store. "We would become 'Wyatt's Food Market,' or 'Wyatt's Supermarket'; at one time we were called 'Wyatt's Best Way.'"

Whatever they called it, Wyatt's became a place for the community to gather. They had an old potbellied stove in the back with a bench nearby, and that drew coffee drinkers and kibitzers throughout the day and husbands and wives on Saturday night. Vendors would drop in, trying to get them to carry some product or another, and whether or not they made a sale, the vendors eventually became the Wyatts' friends. After school, Dixie and her pals dropped by for after-school snacks. Ruby laughs at the memory: "I tell you, they just took over the store—the cookies, the candy, the soft drinks. I'll never forget one of her friends saying, 'I wish my daddy owned a grocery store so I didn't have to pay for anything!'"

Most of the town's teenagers got their first working experience at Wyatt's, and those who had gone on to college or to other jobs would occasionally stop by to say hello. To them, the store had been a kind of second home. In recent years, on the occasion of a birthday celebration for Ruby, a man named David Shipp wrote a letter to the local paper, The Falmouth *Outlook*. "I consider myself very fortunate to have worked for them," he wrote. "Not only was I able to make some spending money, but the life lessons I learned at Wyatt's have followed me every day of the past forty years. . . . Honesty was at the top of the list, as evidenced by this example. Grocery orders were checked against the bill of lading. Once I remember telling Abe that we received one case for which he was not charged. He promptly called the wholesaler and said he would pay for the extra case the next week. . . . Another time I saw Ruby going through the check-out with her personal groceries. Since she already owned the groceries, I asked her why she was going through the check-out. She reminded me that a 3 percent sales tax had just been put into effect and that the law required her to pay. . . ."

There were no set hours for the store to close. "Everybody would usually be gone by nine or nine-thirty," Ruby says, "but many's the night we'd be sitting upstairs in our apartment after ten o'clock and there'd be a knock on the door. Abe would open it and somebody or other would be standing there apologetically, but his baby was out of milk. Well, Abe would go downstairs, open the store, and get him whatever he needed."

Despite the Wyatts' progress and prosperity, there was one particularly large cloud hanging over their lives, and it had the potential to shadow everything they were trying to accomplish. "Abe had been drinking since he was young—beer, liquor, anything that came down the road," Ruby says. "I knew he drank when we met, though I never saw any awful side of it. There never *was* any awful side of it—he would just get drunk and go lie down. His companions at the time, from a bar down the road, were just the wrong people for him. Dixie says she doesn't remember ever seeing her daddy drink or drunk, but Pat does. And it really broke her heart. She hates alcohol to this day, as I do.

"Anyway, I guess it was the early '50s when a doctor told him: 'Well, Abe, I can get you over *this* drunk, but you're going to have to change your companions.' It was like turning on a lightbulb. He stopped it immediately. I had always gone to church, had been raised in the Baptist church, and I took my girls from the time they were little. Finally, I got Abe to go. And you know, he just turned his life around. Suddenly he hated alcohol as much as he'd drunk it.

"People would try to get him to sell beer at the store, and he would tell them, 'I don't intend to do it. If I sell to some young kid who goes out and kills somebody—or gets killed—it'll be on my conscience. They might get it, but they're not gonna get it from me.' When we had a local option vote here in Falmouth, he strung a big piece of butcher paper across the store with the message VOTE NO."

RUBY RECALLS THE '60s and '70s as being "glory years" for their business, as well as for their family. Pat had long since outgrown her eczema, and Dixie had become an outgoing teenager. The store and the apartment had expanded several times, always straight back. "Sure, we probably could've built a large dream home in a nice neighborhood," says Ruby, "but we couldn't leave our cozy apartment above the store. We would go out looking at houses or lots, and when we would come back and open the door to our apartment, Abe would pucker up his lips and go, 'Mmmm, mmmm, mmmm,' kissing the air. This was our home, and it had everything we needed." When Dixie turned sixteen, Abe roped off the parking lot in front of the store and threw a big party for her. "There was this band made up of a group of young local boys, and they played. I tell you, this place was packed. The police came and watched, but there was no trouble whatsoever. Just all those teenagers dancing their heads off on the blacktop."

Money was rolling in, and Abe and Ruby often took their family to Cincinnati on shopping sprees; at night when they drove home the girls would be asleep in the back of the car surrounded by presents. Of course, some of the gifts were for Ruby and Abe. "We both loved clothes," she says, "but, oh, my husband, he was a *dresser.* He had expensive shoes, and he loved sport coats. I don't know how many he owned. It was nothing for him to spend $250 dollars on a sport coat. He wore sweaters to work—he had gorgeous sweaters. But when we went to church, or if he had to go to a meeting or something like that, he put on a suit. He was always going to be very correct and proper."

In addition to her work at the grocery, Ruby was active in civic affairs. From 1966 to 1968, she was president of the Women's Club of Falmouth and later served as an adviser to the club officers. Nineteen-sixty-nine was the Golden Anniversary of the Women's Club, and records show that she participated in at least two programs that fall: In October, she was one of the hostesses for a program called "Changing Picture in Europe." Two months later she was in charge of the Christmas party.

By the 1970s, Wyatt's had affiliated with a grocery company called Malone & Hyde. "Every year the company would take a trip, and we couldn't wait to buy all our fancy clothes and go," says Ruby. "We had the privilege of visiting seven different countries in Europe. We loved London, but we loved Hawaii, too. Times were good, and these companies had everything planned for you."

Their fortunes changed with the tick of a new decade. In 1980, Abe suffered a heart attack and had to undergo quadruple bypass surgery. He recovered fine, and in the early '80s Wyatt's changed affiliation from Malone & Hyde to Supervalu. Then, in 1983, Abe was diagnosed with bladder cancer.

"That started the years of agony and strife," says Ruby. Abe died in February 1985 at age sixty-eight. The Falmouth *Outlook* published a glowing obituary, saying that during his forty years in the grocery business Abe was "a leader in making Falmouth a great trading center for all Pendleton [County] merchants, and could always be counted on to do his part and take the lead."

A CRISIS IS a test of mettle. No one who knew Ruby Wyatt doubted that she would rise to the occasion.

"I was *determined* to continue with the store," she says. Her way of doing it was to gather her family tight around her. "After Abe died, I incorporated the business with my two married daughters, Dixie Owen and Pat Simmons." Pat lived out of town, so she didn't take part in the day-to-day running of the business, but Dixie—who had been doing the payroll for the store for nearly two decades—increased her participation dramatically (Dixie is now president). Besides giving her support at work, Dixie and Pat often traveled with their mother, going to England, Hawaii, and on several Caribbean cruises.

The Supervalu brass up in Xenia, Ohio, were also especially attentive. "The president of the company would call me, and sometimes he would come down to visit," says Ruby. But by 1987, Supervalu executives were telling her that her store was out of step with the times. This was the period in which supermarkets and discount stores, led by the rapid rise of Wal-Mart, had grown increasingly large and varied in their product lines. Other kinds of stores were carrying grocery items. In contrast, Wyatt's home-grown, add-a-room shotgun store wasn't just less shopper friendly, it also lacked the space required in order to be competitive. "You need to make a change," the executives told Ruby. "If you don't, we're afraid that in five years you'll be closed."

Ruby was seventy-five years old when she heard this news. She could easily have sold the store—she had several offers—but what would she do with herself? She was still active, still engaged in life. She went to movies, listened to music, stayed up late watching Jay Leno, kept CNN on constantly in her apartment above the store. The truth is, challenges got her back up. When those men told her she might go out of business after forty-five years, something inside her said, *No way.* To the Supervalu executives, she replied, "That's not going to happen to *me.*"

By this time, she owned a parcel of land on the river just west of the store. "It wasn't quite big enough, but it was the best I could do," says Ruby. With plans for the big new supermarket under way, Ruby and Dixie realized they needed additional managerial talent. They turned to Roger Craig, Ruby's nephew and Dixie's first cousin. Roger, Ruby's sister's son, had grown up at Wyatt's, like so many other kids in Falmouth. "I was nearly born in the backseat of Ruby and Abe's car," Roger says. He had gone off to college, gotten a business degree, and by the late '80s was in Richmond, Kentucky, outside Lexington, working for Kroger. "Ruby called me one day in 1987. It was an opportunity for me to come home, and my wife's from here, too. We talked about it and decided to make the move." Roger, now general manager of Wyatt's Supervalu, came back to Falmouth to oversee planning and construction of the new seventeen-thousand-foot, state-of-the-art supermarket.

The grand opening was in September 1990. Most people involved didn't know it then, but Ruby had just built herself a theater. "The Supervalu people would send down these memos about what they called 'spectaculars,'" she says. "For example, 'We're going to be promoting Halloween,' or 'We're going to feature a western theme.' Then it was up to the individual stores to decorate, to come up with costumes for the employees, that kind of thing." For the first Oktoberfest in the new store, Ruby went all out, creating a template for spectaculars to come. "I had everybody a-workin' and a-goin'," she says, still amused by the memory. "All the employees had on these Oktoberfest vests, and somewhere I found this great big farm wagon. You know, the Germans would put these huge barrels of beer on a wagon and the Clydesdale horses would pull it around. I put that out in the front. We had things going on all over the place. People brought me barrels, which I decorated. Of course, I *always* had music. By that time, we had a lot of high school boys and girls working for us, and I wanted them to be able to dance the polka. There was a young teacher at the school who was quite a dancer, and she came out and taught them. The kids were into it tooth and toenail. The radio station was there. I'm telling you, the joint was jumping!"

In the mid-1990s, the glory years seemed to return for an encore. Business was good, Wyatt's employed a record fifty-two employees, and Ruby—whose apartment now looked out over the gleaming new store and its jam-packed parking lot—seemed to be having the time of her life. In 1995, she was named the Kentucky Grocer Association's Retailer of the Year, the first woman to win the award. That honor came, as if on cue, in time for one of the biggest spectaculars Wyatt's Supervalu had ever staged: a no-holds-barred celebration of its own fiftieth anniversary in business. In February 1997, Ruby was named 1996 Woman of the Year by the Women Grocers of America.

And then the Licking River began to rise.

"I remember the river being discussed when we built this building," says Roger Craig. "Ruby said, 'Aw, that river will never get up there in a thousand years. Don't worry about the river.' That's the way Ruby is. We'll be worried about something here, and she'll say, 'Oh, that's a tempest in a teapot. Don't worry about that.'"

Of course, Ruby had reason to believe the Licking would stay within its banks. She and her siblings had grown up a few yards from where her big store now stood. They had swum in it, fished in it, played in and along it all their lives. True, the river had flooded in 1964, but that was a long time back.

On Saturday night, March 1, 1997, Roger was preparing to close the store as he had a thousand times before. The river had been rising, but it still didn't seem to be anywhere near crisis level. "I remember going and checking on it," Roger says. "It was coming up like five inches an hour, and we had five feet before it would be over the bank. Doing the math, we thought we'd have at least until the middle of Sunday. Then about seven-thirty that night, that river jumped two feet."

Dixie and her husband, who lived a couple of blocks from the river, were in the process of getting things out of their basement. When the Licking made its dramatic rise, Dixie took Ruby and went to Roger's house, which is ten miles from town on one of the highest points in the county. "If the river ever gets my house," says Roger, "it's time to call Noah." Meanwhile, Roger and a few others stood out behind the store watching the water's steady climb. "I guess we were out there till almost midnight. Then somebody told us we had to get out of there *now* if we were going to get across the bridge."

The next morning, Roger drove back to town. The bridge was under water. "Looking across the river, I could tell we had about six feet inside the store." He turned around and went back home. Ruby, Dixie, and the others heard him coming. "It's not good," he told them.

It was the following Tuesday before Roger could actually set foot inside the store. "It was nasty," he says. "I mean, it was a mess. The dog food, which was probably the grossest of all, was rotting near the front door. Diapers had swollen up like turkey breasts and were floating around the store. However bad you think it would be, it was worse."

AT THE TIME of the flood, there were three grocery stores in Falmouth. Two of them didn't reopen.

This is the insidious part of disaster, the destruction that doesn't show on the surface. Whenever you see a town besieged by floodwaters—or ravaged by tornadoes, battered by hurricanes, swallowed by earthquakes, or scorched by fires—you see only the iceberg tip of the hurt. I don't care how much government assistance they get, disaster victims sustain astounding body blows—financial, emotional, spiritual. It takes great will and depth of character to bounce back.

Two days after Roger Craig got his first look at the supermarket, Ruby Wyatt—age eighty-three—came to survey the damage firsthand. "Ruby took two steps inside the building," Roger says, "her boots sticking to the floor. 'Well, clean it up!' she said, and that was that."

Never mind that they had to throw out a quarter million dollars worth of inventory, or that refurbishing the paid-off building was going to force her into debt for the first time in her life. "I never shed a tear," Ruby told a radio interviewer, "nor will I. I will rebuild my store and move on with my life."

Dixie's house was totally destroyed, and Ruby's hot-water heater and other ground-floor systems had to be replaced before she could move home. They stayed at Roger's for about three weeks. "Ruby didn't miss a bit of sleep, and she ate as well as she always had," he says.

Meanwhile, recovery and clean-up started immediately, thanks to Supervalu, which made Ruby a $750,000 bridge loan to tide her over until she could get government and private disaster relief assistance. The total damage came to more than $1 million. "We had to gut the building and start over," Roger says. "We took the tile up off the floor and stripped out all the drywall. When we got through cleaning, all we had were a concrete floor and concrete walls." But just as this store had long been more than brick and mortar to this community, now the community was able to pay back a little of its debt. "We had customers come in and help us, family members, truck drivers, employees from fifteen years ago. One man now lives in Charleston, South Carolina. He drove up here with a pressure washer and stayed a week."

Ruby ordered a huge banner hung over the front of the store: "WYATT'S SUPERVALU WILL BE BACK . . . BETTER THAN EVER!" it said, and it was signed "Ruby Wyatt." That signature on that promise energized the whole town. "Folks here are so thankful to Ruby and Dixie for sticking around and bringing back the groceries," said longtime Falmouth resident Kay Williams right after Ruby vowed to rebuild.

Never for a second did Ruby consider otherwise. "I was rocked back on my heels," she says. "I had been set down. But I was going to get up. I was not going to stay down." She had her employees to think of. She had her family to think of. She had her community to think of. She had *Abe* to think of. "This store was his *dream*," Ruby says.

On May 7, sixty-six days after the flood, Wyatt's Supervalu had its second grand opening. Not only were the original fifty-two workers back, but Wyatt's hired thirteen new ones. For their leadership as business owners, the Small Business Administration recognized Ruby and Dixie with a Phoenix Award.

NEARLY FIVE YEARS later, a visitor to Falmouth would be hard pressed to see that anything momentous had happened here. On any given day, cars and trucks fill the parking lot of Wyatt's Supervalu, in whose window hangs an American flag and a banner reading GOD BLESS AMERICA. Out back, the South Fork of the Licking seems to be behaving itself. Ruby still lives in the apartment that she and Abe moved into in 1952. All the store mail goes first to Ruby, the way it always has. Meetings with Supervalu executives are still conducted around Ruby's kitchen table, where Dixie still figures the payroll by hand. "And," says Roger Craig, "Ruby still phones me every day to tell me to have someone get the grocery carts out of the parking lot."

For Ruby Wyatt, there's a way to do things and a way not to do things. "Life goes on," she says. "We're planted here. We're not going anywhere."

CRISES ARE MADE for heroes. Sometimes I even wonder if crises aren't made to *make* heroes. How can we know our truest selves if we're never tested?

I think of the brave band of travelers who boarded United flight 93 on the morning of September 11, 2001. Standing in line at the airport, they looked like ordinary people—husbands, fathers, sons, brothers—all preoccupied with the mundane hopes and hoops of daily life. Then they buckled their seat belts, and that big jet lifted off, carrying a handful of extraordinary passengers into the history books.

As I said in the introduction, I've been privileged to mingle with many, many heroes over the course of my career. Most of them, I don't even remember their names. They're just people who stepped up when the chips were down. Sometimes the heroic acts were private gestures that rippled among a select few. Other times, someone's single act of courage—or defiance— caught fire in the hearts of a community and changed the outcome of a crisis itself. I believe that's what happened in the case of Ruby Wyatt in Falmouth, Kentucky. Had she decided not to rebuild her store, the town might never have recovered. Fortunately, the opposite was true: Ruby's bold stance brought out strength in others.

As crisis managers, we should seek out the Ruby Wyatts of the world. How do you know who and where they are? Look for the lightning rod. It's been my experience that personalities capable of sparking others tend to attract their share of sparks. They're passionate people, and passion doesn't sit quietly by while everything falls to pieces around it. As a manager, you want people who identify with your leadership role. You want someone who instinctively grasps the need to pick up the flag and inspire others to follow.

When I took over as FEMA director, I chose as my chief of staff a career employee named Jane Bullock. On the surface, Jane and I were about as different as night and day. A native New Yorker who tends toward brashness, she loves to tell the story of her mother coming to visit shortly after Jane started working with me. " 'Jane,' Mother said, 'I can tell this man is having a good influence on you. We've been talking two hours and you haven't said one curse word.'"

Even so, Jane's take on things was always colorful. "Running FEMA is like running a day-care center," she said, explaining the job I had ahead of me. "People are fighting over the toys. People are fighting to decide who's going to get to sit on the teacher's lap during storybook. It's terrible to say, but it's true. And I don't think this is atypical." Though Jane and I were different on the surface, we both abhorred bureaucracy, with its stress on rules over results. Clearly, Jane Bullock was the kind of strong person around whom I could start building FEMA's recovery.

Another lightning rod was our outspoken director of communications,

Morrie Goodman. The following is from the FEMA History Project, a series of oral histories we took from people who had helped effect the changes in the agency. Here's Morrie talking about his first impression of FEMA: "Well, I started there a couple months before James Lee did. . . . I was maybe the third or fourth political appointee sent there in the Clinton administration. . . . I thought the agency sort of sucked, and I didn't know anything about what it did, and I really didn't care. All I knew was they screwed up in disasters, and I was in the news media, so I was one of the persons who wrote stories like that. I kept calling the White House saying, 'Get me out of here.' And they said, 'Just sit tight.'"

Now here's Morrie talking about his first impression of me: "I asked for five minutes to see [Witt] when he was first sent there as an intent to nominate, and he was in a little teeny office just big enough for a desk and a chair. He pulled out one of the drawers and put his foot up on it; he had his ostrich cowboy boots on and he had jeans on that day, and he was chewing tobacco. He kind of spit in the wastebasket and said, 'Let me tell you something— we're going to have to market the hell out of this place.' I tried to get a couple words in edge-wise, but people kept knocking on the door and finally my time was gone. But my impression from that five-minute meeting was if he said we had to 'market the hell' out of this place, that's a pretty insightful thing. In government they do too little of that. You have to have something to market, and I hadn't talked to him about what we had to market. But I thought, wow, that's a remarkable thought coming from this guy. I still thought he was a little bit of a hayseed from Arkansas. But I liked that idea of marketing. That set off a lightbulb in my head with him."

As you saw in chapter 2, marketing the new FEMA was part of its reinvention in the minds of its customers—skeptical disaster victims, jaded state and local agencies, naysayers on Capitol Hill. What manager worth his salt wouldn't send irreverent Morrie Goodman out there to hack through the doubt and hammer home our message?

CRISIS PLANS REVOLVE around strong individuals all the time. Back in the 1970s when New York City was on the verge of bankruptcy, financier Felix Rohatyn stepped into the breach and masterminded a bailout strategy.

When Chrysler was on the ropes, Lee Iacocca came in and re-created the car company. When Jerry Jones became owner of a losing Dallas Cowboys football team, he and coach Jimmy Johnson restructured the future multiple-Super Bowl–winning club around a new draftee—quarterback Troy Aikman.

Lately I've been fascinated by the news surrounding Kmart's January 2002 chapter 11 filing. To lead it through the rigors of reorganization, the company turned to one of its longtime board members, James B. Adamson. Chairman and CEO of a successful restaurant chain, with bench experience as executive vice president of merchandising at Target Stores and as executive VP of marketing at the Revco drugstore chain during its chapter 11 restructuring, Adamson had the perfect business credentials to lead Kmart at this time. But in the end, a résumé is just a piece of paper. By all accounts, it was Adamson's energizing personality and galvanizing presence as an executive that made him the right man at the right time.

Ironically, though, the big question in the press hasn't been so much about who's leading Kmart, but whether or not the company would be able to hold onto Martha Stewart and her premier brand of housewares. I know nothing of the inside negotiations, or even whether Stewart seriously considered cutting her ties with the company. But the message inherent in the pundits' commentary was unmistakable: A huge retailer was in trouble, and one of its high-profile vendors was a—maybe *the*—factor in determining the company's future. Martha Stewart was a lightning rod around which to build a recovery. Fortunately for Kmart, Stewart stuck by them.

The larger message I'd like to get across here is about understanding and embracing the role of lightning rod yourself. I don't mean you should be what we in Dardanelle used to call a "showboat"—the kind of person, or employee, who brags about being the stick that stirs the drink. But by knowing what you believe and being willing to take a stand, you can be a strong and energizing influence for good—in other words, the kind of person everybody needs in a crisis.

Last fall I read a story in *Stanford Business Magazine* about a Richmond, California, company called MBA Polymers, which has figured out a way to solve a huge societal problem. Because we as a culture generate so much refuse and have no idea what to do with it, our landfills and garbage dumps are overflowing with junk. But MBA Polymers, which was developed by a former Dow Ph.D. named Mike Biddle, has researched and refined a technique for recycling old plastic from computers and printers into little colored pellets that can then be used to make new plastic parts.

In 1999, the company received its first outside funding—$6 million. They staffed up (to a hundred employees) and went to three shifts. Then disaster hit in the form of a plant explosion—probably caused, says *Stanford Business* writer Janet Zich, "by an electrostatic charge in a grinder that ignited an accumulation of toner-cartridge dust." One employee was killed, and the resulting fire's thick acrid smoke closed a dozen schools and sent some two hundred people to see their doctors.

The devastation to the company was difficult enough to overcome— CEO Biddle and his management team, led by COO Richard McCombs, persuaded their investors to keep half the employees on the payroll, and McCombs negotiated with their insurance carrier to keep the other half on for a few months doing cleanup. But where MBA Polymers became its own lightning rod was in its dealings with the city of Richmond. A frightened community that had suffered four major industrial accidents in 1999 alone, Richmond could've become a major obstacle to MBA Polymers' rebuilding and future success. "Another company might have hidden behind a wall of lawyers or revved up its public relations spin machine," writes Zich. "Instead, MBA Polymers quickly and publicly offered to pay medical bills for anyone worried about the effects of smoke inhalation." The company takes an active role in the Chamber of Commerce, invites the community into the plant for open houses, and regularly sends representatives out to monthly neighborhood council meetings. Instead of slinking back to a comfortably (but disastrously) low profile, MBA Polymers boldly took the offensive. Its leaders stood up and became leaders in the community, thereby drawing Richmond into the company orbit and heading off what could've been a much worse crisis. Obviously, Biddle and McCombs have also learned a thing or two about recycling reputations.

It might dawn on you that motivating people in a crisis has to happen from the get-go, not just when you're at the recovery stage. But by the time everyone has put in the hours and energy to respond to a crisis, they're exhausted. That's when lightning rods can do their most important work. Because, as you'll see in the next chapter, you've got to do more than just clean up the loose ends; you've got to inspire people to carry on, gather up information about what just happened so you're better prepared the next time, stay alert for any fall-out, and muster the enthusiasm for rebuilding regular life—which can be a long, slow, hard process. Knowing who and what can be a lightning rod for you, ready to step up to the plate right away, will save you a lot of headaches, and possibly a few crises, as well.

In summary, then, here are a few points for finding and managing those corporate lightning rods:

• **CAST YOUR NET WIDE, DEEP, AND FAR.** The knee-jerk reaction for most everyone who manages people is to think that you are the best person to motivate your employees. That's just not true. Some days you may be the lightning rod, but oftentimes the best sparks come from the unexpected places—and that has the extra bonus of leaving you free to lead in other ways. Who would have thought that Ruby Wyatt, at eighty-three and with a lifetime of success to look back on with pride, would rejuvenate her town? Well, maybe not you or me, looking from the outside, but anyone who knew Ruby wasn't surprised that she could rally all of Falmouth with her energy. The ones you want are those who run toward a crisis, not away from it. Remember that a résumé isn't a reliable predictor of genuine fire. Who in your organization keeps everyone's spirits going strong and can even make someone having a tough time with a client, a boss, the workload, or personal matters see how things can turn out for the better? It could be a forty-year veteran who has seen it all and provides organizational wisdom to younger employees. It could be your assistant, who everyone knows has your ear when you're busy and who knows better than you do what your priorities are at any given moment. Or it could be a member of the board who brings their passion from outside the company, or a retired executive who's still very much a part of the team. But don't limit yourself there. Could the encouragement or testimonial of one of your partners help employees realize that there's a future for them after the crisis? Know who these people are and nurture their team-oriented leadership before a crisis so it won't seem as though you're bringing in—or expecting—a showboat.

• **THEY MAY MAKE SPARKS, BUT EVERY MANAGER (AND EVERY CRISIS) NEEDS A FEW GO-TO PEOPLE.** A different sort of lightning rod is the person or people who keep you motivated throughout a crisis and afterward. Who can give you counsel, help you keep your eye on your plan for handling a crisis, or serve as your proxy when you'd like to be in two places at once? They should complement your talents, even outshine you, so don't be afraid to hire people you think might be better than you are.

• **REMEMBER THAT THE MESSAGE YOU CHOOSE CAN, AND SHOULD, BE AS ELECTRIFYING AS THE PEOPLE WHO DELIVER IT.** When a lightning rod doesn't have the right message, you can send morale into a tailspin. First off, sit down and figure out who you're trying to motivate and what you're trying to motivate them to do. Are some individuals or teams—or partners or customers or the community—in the doldrums, really down on the chances of pulling through the crisis to a renewed and even better position than you were in before? Who do you need to electrify to action first? Turn back to your priorities, which you identified long before you got to this stretch of the road, and use those priorities to triage motivation as you would anything else.

• **ELECTRICITY IS ABOUT POWERING ACTION.** As you figure out *who* you need to shape your message to, think about *what* their role in the recovery will be. Everyone should be thinking about how to learn from the mistakes and successes you've just lived through, so any lightning rod should be putting some sparks in that direction. Everyone should be on the lookout for what I call a recovery crisis, the crisis that rears its head because you weren't paying attention to a project or client while you were directing all your resources at the disaster in your midst, so your lightning rod should be shooting some other sparks toward that. The specifics of your recovery process will determine where the rest of the sparks go. List the actions you need from the who's of your recovery plan, and roll out your motivational messages to match them.

Can you really recover from a crisis? And be stronger than you were before? In the next chapter, I'll give you some final lessons on how to manage crisis so you succeed in the end.

9

STRONGER IN THE BROKEN PLACES

Life Does Go On—Sometimes Even Better Than Before

COLLEGE STATION, ARKANSAS
MARCH 1997—MARCH 1998

It was one of those days when the weather was too warm for its own good. March in Arkansas isn't frigid, even though for most of the month it's still technically winter. Those of us brought up in the state generally think of it as a time of great promise, a pledge backed up by budding daffodils. But there was something very wrong with this particular Saturday. The air was still, the sky sallow. It was full of portent, not promise.

And yet the Reverend Hezekiah D. Stewart Jr., a man who appreciates the nuances of God's creation, was at first enjoying this day immensely. Reverend Stewart was, and is, pastor of the Mount Nebo African Methodist Episcopal Church in College Station, Arkansas, an unincorporated community near the Little Rock airport. He's also executive director of Watershed, a not-for-profit community development agency that he calls "the world's first social hospital." On this first morning of March 1997, the reverend and his wife, Diane, had driven from Little Rock to the University of Arkansas at Monticello, in the southeastern part of the state, so that the reverend could deliver a speech. The talk had gone well, and the Stewarts had been uplifted by the program put on by a group of black students. After a nice lunch, the reverend and his wife took a leisurely drive home. "It was just one of those very pleasant days," he recalls, "spending time with someone you love."

Working her custodial job at the Little Rock airport, however, Tressie Robierson wasn't feeling so carefree. She stopped her sweeping and stared out the window. "It was real dreary-looking," she recalls. "It looked like it wanted to rain, or maybe to snow. But it was hot and hazy. It would be very sunny, and then it would cloud up." As she picked up her broom again, she heard a disturbing voice in her head. "Go home," it said. "You should go home." She heard the voice the rest of the morning. When lunchtime came, she had no appetite. "What you gonna eat?" a coworker said.

"I'm not hungry," Tressie said. "All I want to do is go home."

She thought about punching out early, but she didn't feel that she had a good enough reason. About two o'clock she looked out the window again. "It had been raining, but then the sun had come out." That lasted a half hour or so, and then the sky got very dark. Tressie finally clocked out at three-thirty, her usual time. But instead of sitting around and gossiping with her coworkers, she headed for her car.

"I pulled out of the parking lot, thinking I would go to Kroger. Then the voice said, 'Tressie, go home.' I turned that car around in the middle of the street. I knew better but did it anyway. The rest of the way home I kept my eyes on the rearview mirror to see if I saw blue lights behind me."

She crossed over the interstate and took a right on Bankhead Drive. At Frazier Pike, she thought about stopping at the little grocery store there. "I turned my blinker on; there wasn't anything coming. There wasn't a reason in the world why I shouldn't pull in." But the voice changed her mind: "Go home, Tressie," it said. She switched off her blinker and kept going. At her house by the railroad tracks, everything looked normal—except that her husband, Red, wasn't out in his little bait shop next to the road. Instead, he was standing in the door. "I thought, as women will, *I don't know what he's standin' in that door for. I'm not goin' back to get him any cigarettes.*" She pulled into the driveway—and then the voice told her to back the car in. "I never had done that in my life, but this time I did."

"Well, girlie, you made it," Red said when she got out of the car.

"I sure did," she said. "What is it?"

"Tornado warning."

"Oh," Tressie said, "it's just cloudy, wind blowing. It's gonna pass over."

"Touched down in Arkadelphia," Red said. "It's headin' this way."

"It'll pass," she said, and headed into the house. Red pulled up a chair on the porch. Tressie couldn't believe it. "What you doing, sittin' out here with a tornado comin'. You gonna fool around and get blown away."

Red didn't say anything, but he did follow her into the house. As she tossed her purse into the bedroom, he spoke up. "I'm tired of you raisin' hell," he said. "I bought some material today. I'm gonna remodel the bathroom."

Tressie was glad to hear it. This house, once owned by her grandmother, had been home to the Robiersons for more than forty years. It had seen eight children raised. Now it was tired and showing its age. The rest of it didn't matter to Tressie—just the bathroom. "All I want's my bathroom remodeled," she told Red.

"Well, girlie," he said, "I'm gonna remodel it for you— one more time." He started showing her the receipts for the materials he had bought. "We were both in the living room," Tressie says, "when we heard the train coming."

HEZEKIAH AND DIANE Stewart noticed traffic backing up on the interstate five or so miles outside of Little Rock. For a long time they poked along bumper to bumper. The sky was much darker in the city than it had been on the drive up, and a steady rain was falling. Eventually they saw flashing blue lights ahead, but by then Stewart already knew what had happened. In the dusky winter woods the tops of the trees had been twisted off, leaving splintered scars of ghostly white. "Honey," he said, "a tornado has gone through here."

They turned on the radio and heard the announcer talking about several storm systems that had swept through the state. "Let's go to the church," Diane said. "The kids are there practicing." Passing Watershed headquarters on the way, the reverend slowed on Confederate Drive to see if he could detect any damage. The outreach group's main offices are in an abandoned elementary school, which the city allows them to use for a dollar a month. Reverend Stewart strained to see in the rain, but he thought the building looked okay. A few trees were down, but they could live with that.

They continued on across the tracks and up the hill. The damage so far appeared minimal. Branching off at 3M Road, they wound down by the shingle plant and quarry to the entrance to College Station. There the road climbs again, and at the crest of the hill they saw a huge tree lying across the road. It had fallen from the yard of Dimples and Cornelius Henson. The limbs obstructed not just passage but sight. Stewart pulled over and got out. The Hensons' driveway sloped upward to slightly higher ground, and Reverend Stewart walked up as far as he could. He peered over the splintered tree trunk. What he saw made his heart sink. "Diane," he said to his wife, "I can't tell you about this. This is something you must see for yourself."

College Station, in Stewart's words, "was flattened." From his vantage point by the fallen tree, he could see heavy damage at Annette McClain's place. And beyond that, just across the tracks where the houses of Alice and Ira Akins, Vera Mae King, Kid Henry Williams, and Tressie and Red Robierson should have been, there was nothing but debris.

Reverend Stewart told his wife to take the car and double back to the church. He was going to walk. The path of a tornado is an exercise in humility. All along where the storm hit, Stewart saw the cherished items of private lives hanging from trees, strewn along curbs, flung into fields. The modesty of walls and doors was ripped away, baring closets. At the next corner he found Annette McClain and her family standing in their yard in shock. Their house was severely damaged. "Their roof had been lifted off and dropped onto Mr. Wooley Thompson's rent house that sat fifty yards behind the McClains' house." On past that, he saw that several other houses were pretty torn up, though still standing. There, on a slight rise, was where the tornado had apparently begun to descend.

"But where it really struck was right there where Red and Tressie Robierson lived," says Reverend Stewart.

"Since we do live next to the train track, I thought it was a train we heard," says Tressie Robierson today. "But suddenly the house started to shake. I went to fasten the front door, but I couldn't lock it. I turned to go to the kitchen to cut off the light, but I couldn't get to the kitchen. Something was holding me. I looked at the curtains, and they were blowing in a way I had never seen before. Instead of going out to the side, they were just churning over and over. I hit the floor right by the front door, and that's all I remember till it was over."

Her husband had been standing not far away when she fell. Tressie remembers being unable to move but not knowing why. "Red!" I called. "Red!" He didn't answer. "I thought, *Oh, he's back in the garden.* He had told me that morning that he was gonna plant me some greens. 'You love greens,' he'd said, and he had gone out and made a furrow."

Tressie isn't sure how long she lay there, how many times she called out for Red. She does remember hearing the same voice she'd been hearing all day long. "He doesn't hear you," it said. Then the voice told her to pray.

"I said, 'Lord, here I am down here, I'm one of your children. Whatever it is, take care of me.'"

Finally she heard other, more positive voices, those of her rescuers. The earliest on the scene were a handful of young men whom most in the community would've guessed to be the last to pitch in. "I always say that the first line of defense for recovery was the guys who spend Saturday afternoons hanging out on the corner across from Pete's market," says Hezekiah Stewart. "The ones having their 'snoot,' or whatever. But they rushed out to these demolished houses and started rescuing people from the debris. Those guys were the original heroes."

Tressie could hear the boards slapping as they threw them off. When they freed her from the pile, she could hear but she couldn't see. She knew the paramedics were there, and so was the Reverend Mr. Stewart. They got her out into the street and had her sit down in a broken chair. Finally her eyesight came back. She looked herself over. She was wet and gritty, but she didn't seem to have any serious injuries. Only a skinned place on her hand.

"You need to go to the hospital," one of the paramedics said.

"No I don't," Tressie said. "I don't see any blood, so I'm not hurt."

"You are hurt," the medic said.

"I'm not going to the hospital," said Tressie. "Not till you find my husband." Nobody said a word.

"What's wrong?" Tressie said, but still nobody could bear to tell her. Every time she brought up Red, the others just seemed to drift away. Then she spied something lying in the side yard. "That looks like my husband's clothes," she said, and started walking toward it.

Somebody stopped her. "Tressie, no," he said. "Your husband's gone." She got to within ten feet of him and saw the blood. She agreed to go to the hospital only if they took Red there, too.

◆ ◆ ◆

ACROSS FROM THE Robiersons, the Akins house was totaled. Their grand-daughter LaToya was trapped for hours in the rubble. Next door to the Akinses, at the seventy-year-old house where Vera Mae King had reared twelve children, the aged wood gave up the ghost and Vera Mae's forty-year-old daughter, Betty, who lived out back in a trailer, was killed. Betty's eight-year-old daughter, Shandra, was critically injured. On the corner opposite the Kings, Kid Henry Williams's house was blown away. Up the street from him, Minnie Lee Davis was caught by the wind and killed as she tried to get into her truck. On the west side of 3M Road, Tuck Porter was buried beneath the rubble of his house; it would be days before anyone would find his body.

As Reverend Stewart walked through the streets, he was stunned at how suddenly and completely the tight little community he had left just that morning had been rent by death and devastation. Everywhere he looked, people were standing stunned, getting drenched by the rain. "They were just huddled around their brokenness," Stewart recalls. "What you do within an hour of a disaster like that somehow gives vent to what happens after that hour. You have to position people for recovery."

Stewart instructed William Thompson, one of his church members, to get to Mount Nebo AME, put candles in the windows, and set up the church as a relief station. Then, looking into the eyes of these people he knew and loved, the reverend began to hear a voice as powerful as that which had spoken to Tressie, but this voice turned out to be Stewart's own. As he moved along street by street, block by block, he called out to all he saw: "The Devil meant this for evil!" he shouted. "But God meant it for good!"

COLLEGE STATION SUPPOSEDLY got its name from a huckster who had blown into town to take advantage. "It was before my time," says Vera Mae King, who is seventy-two and has lived here all her life, "but I've heard the story." As she tells it, a stranger showed up one day in the mostly black community, which was then known as Big Rock, and told the residents he wanted to build a college there. He accepted donations from the hopeful cit-izenry, posted the sign COLLEGE STATION on the train depot, and promptly absconded with all the money. But the people liked the name, which matched their aspirations, and so they left the sign.

There is a long history of community activism in College Station. Annie Mae Bankhead, Vera Mae King's much older first cousin, was one of the early leaders. "A community's not a community without a health clinic and a school," Annie Mae used to say, and she was instrumental in forming a group called the Progressive League, which rallied residents around civic projects. But one goal Mrs. Bankhead and her fellow volunteers failed to meet: They never got College Station incorporated into Little Rock, with its money for better roads, sewers, and other improved standards of living. Reading between the Reverend Mr. Stewart's eloquent lines, you get a sense that the people in College Station felt some lingering resentment toward Little Rock—or, more specifically, toward white Little Rock. A kind of wall went up between the two communities. And though every Little Rock resident who goes to the airport turns off the freeway at an exit marked Bankhead Drive, few have any idea who the road was named for. Nor would they con-sider turning right toward Bankhead instead of left to the airport. "Be care-ful," a white colleague of mine was told when he announced that he was headed to College Station to conduct an interview. "It's dangerous over there."

Imagine, then, the scene in College Station two days after the tornado, when the Mennonites came calling.

The Mennonite Disaster Service (MDS) has been helping disaster vic-tims for more than half a century, ever since a Mennonite Sunday school class in Hesston, Kansas, pitched in to help some needy neighbors rebuild their home back in 1950. The next time somebody had a crisis, they called on the Mennonites. "And so," says Lowell Detweiler, former head of MDS and author of *The Hammer Rings Hope: Photos and Stories from Fifty Years of Mennonite Disaster Service*, "that became an organized effort to respond to people. It grew so that it was not only neighbors, or at least next-door neighbors, but people across the country. Soon it became binational, includ-ing Canada. Today, MDS has over fifty state or provincial units supplying volunteers for disaster response, particularly in the areas of cleanup and repair and rebuilding."

On the late afternoon of March 1, 1997, Mennonite Willie Miller of Harrison, Arkansas, in the far northern part of the state, heard the tornado warnings, walked outside, and started praying. The next morning he was assigned to Little Rock. At about the same time, the announcement was being made from pulpits throughout College Station that someone would soon be there to help.

Tressie wasn't in her pew at Antioch Full Gospel Baptist Church that morning. After being released from the hospital, and having given instructions on where to take Red's body, she had returned to College Station to stay with her daughter. She had passed the night crying, and when Sunday dawned, wet and cold, she walked over to where her house had stood. Cleanup crews were already there, working that devastated block. But they weren't all. "There were people crawling around in the ruins of my house like flies on something sweet," Tressie says. They weren't neighbors, or even people who lived in College Station.

I can tell you, from personal experience, that you feel a great many conflicting emotions at a time like that. You're grateful to be alive, grief-stricken and angry at your loss, humiliated to be so vulnerable and needy. Tressie had no clothes, only the uniform she'd been wearing when the tornado hit—a uniform taken and washed by her sister as Tressie waited to be examined by the doctor the night before. A cousin had brought her some shoes. Now she stood in the rain looking at the flattened ruins of her home. She must've thought of her grandmother, who had come from Louisiana in the 1940s to chop cotton on a plantation down by the river. She must've thought of her grandfather, who had given her this house on his deathbed. "This is your land," he had said. "Stay on it and take care of it." She must've thought of this neighborhood—a homey place where people watched out for one another, thanks in great part to Vera Mae King, whose house across the street had been a kind of hub of humanity where working mothers with sick children could count on last-minute baby-sitting and inebriated down-and-outers could count on a solid meal, even if it did come with a maternal lecture.

And, too, Tressie must've thought of Red, a good-timing man who used to wrap a couple of $20s around a wad of $1s and strut around like he had money. "Woofin'," Tressie called it.

Now the looters disgusted her. "I could've probably dug through the rubble and found some things I wanted—pieces of my mother's silver, antiques from my grandmother," she says. Instead, she instructed the cleanup people to scoop everything up with a bulldozer and haul it away.

"Are you serious?" they said.

"Yes I am," said Tressie.

That afternoon, while Tressie was crying at her daughter's house, Willie Miller drove into College Station to survey the situation. "Pastor Stewart helped us find a trailer to set up an office," Miller says. "That night I stayed in it, and I was scared. I had noticed several bullet holes in the windows. Before I went to bed, I made sure all the doors were locked, and I prayed for God's protection. The next morning I was looking for the keys and found them outside, sticking in the lock. 'Thank you, Lord,' I said."

On Monday morning Tressie Robierson walked down to the original Watershed office across from Mount Nebo church. A note in the window told her to go to the trailer by the post office, where she would find people to help. She climbed the steps and, through a tiny window, saw a lone bearded white man inside. Working up her courage, she knocked on the door, then backed off to the far edge of the steps. The man cracked the door a ways and stuck his head out. Tressie told him what she was there for. He took her name and told her to come back Wednesday, when Willie Miller would be back. Tressie said she would, and she eased down the steps. The bearded man cautiously closed the door. "I was scared of him," Tressie says. "And I think he was scared of me."

SUCH WERE THE first tentative interactions between two vastly different cultures at College Station in the cold depressing post-tornadic March of 1997. But as Hezekiah Stewart will tell you, big things can grow from small beginnings. Stewart sees the world through the eyes of a healer. Consider his parable about the founding of Watershed: "There was a time when I felt that my work was all in vain," he begins, "so I took my feelings to God, and He told me to go fishing. I didn't know anything about fishing, but I got me a line and a hook and I tossed it into this little backwater of the Arkansas River. All day long I fished, and I didn't catch a thing. But at some point I noticed that there were all these fish around me, thousands of fish, and they were sticking their mouths up out of the water. I threw my hook right in among them, but they wouldn't take the bait. That's when I realized they were dying. This backwater where I was fishing had become isolated from the river, and all the oxygen was gone. Right away I went and got a plastic bag I'd brought, and I dipped up several of those fish into it and ran with them over to the main part of the river. When I put them in the fresh flowing water, they swam off immediately.

"So I ran back to where the other fish were, and now there were two men with sticks whacking at the water, trying to kill as many of the fish as possible. 'What are you doing?' I said, and the men explained that these were just shad, junk fish that take nutrients from the desirable fish. As they went back to their beating, I waded in right beside them with my plastic bag. And that's how I found my vocation, which is to try to save the people who're considered by society as useless, like the shad. God gave me the vision of the Watershed as the world's first social hospital, because we take a holistic approach to dealing with crisis. We feed people, clothe them, provide day care, and help them find jobs. We do alcohol and drug counseling. The word *watershed* means an event or series of events that releases new energy in and gives new direction to people. What we do is go and pick up broken humanity and try to put them back in the main stream."

I didn't know Hezekiah Stewart before the tornado, but I had heard a lot about him. He was already a friend of President Clinton's, from the days when Clinton was governor. In College Station, he and his Watershed had picked up where Annie Mae Bankhead had left off. We recognized him as our conduit to the community's recovery. "The people trusted us," says Stewart. "They knew we weren't playing games with them. When FEMA and the other agencies came in, there were a lot of people who didn't trust the process, and here you get racism involved again. But when we said, 'Go and register,' they went and registered for the help FEMA could give them."

In those first days after the storm, Stewart was everywhere—out in the streets hugging the people, helping them deal with insurance companies (if they had insurance), working with the National Guard to set up a food-and-clothing center at Watershed, meeting with Willie Miller and the Mennonite workers to establish some priority in house rebuilding, and talking dollars by phone with Rodney Slater, secretary of Transportation, and me.

"Miss Lena Broadway was the first person whose house they started on," says Stewart, "and it was the first one I got jumped on over. 'Why you buildin' her house first?' Because she was ready. She had insurance, and the Mennonites were here. We went and bought them an air hammer for $450, and they got *started*. You got to get to work in spite of the chaos and confusion, because every time something is completed, it brings the people closer together. It brings the healing. Of course, you have to communicate with broken people, and it's difficult. There will be fussing, cussing, and scratching all along the way."

Before long, other houses were going up, and not just by the Mennonites. "Second Baptist Church in Conway came and asked me to give them some families to build houses for," says Stewart. "I gave them Kid Henry Williams, Annette McClain, and Elijah Jones. Kid Henry had an insurance policy for $10,000. They took that insurance money and some monies from the Watershed and built him a brand-new house. Not only that, they planted flowers in the yard."

On the Monday after the tornado, I flew to Arkansas to survey the damage. When I phoned the president to tell him how bad it was, he wanted to come show his support. He and his entourage from Washington arrived the very next day, Tuesday, and I met them at the airport. I rode in a van with Senator Dale Bumpers and Congressman Jay Dickey. From there, we crossed the interstate and turned onto Bankhead Drive, tracing the route Tressie Robierson had driven just three days earlier. I guess to the people along those torn-up streets digging through rubble for their memories, that long line of black vehicles looked like a funeral motorcade. But then, at the intersection of College and Southern Streets, right on the corner where Vera Mae King's house had once stood, the president stopped the caravan and got out of the car. Hezekiah Stewart was there to greet him.

In no time there was a mob around him, and I never saw so many hugs in all my life. He seemed to know everybody, calling each one by name. The president, FEMA regional director Buddy Young, and I started walking, and the Secret Service began getting nervous. The president would climb up on a pile of rubble to high five or shake hands with somebody he knew. Even the houses still standing were treacherous, with nails sticking out and wires dangling everywhere. At one point President Clinton went over to talk with a man and woman standing in front of their battered home. The rest of us dropped back to let them visit. When he started to go inside, a Secret Service agent said, "James Lee, get him *out of there!*"

Later, standing in front of Mount Nebo Church, the president gave a moving speech, as did Senator Bumpers and several others. Senator Bumpers promised to include College Station in the disaster package going to Congress for sewage. Secretary Slater promised new and better roads. Then the Reverend Mr. Stewart spoke up: "We thank God for the Red Cross and for Blue Cross, but in the March 1 tornado at College Station, people got help at *the* Cross."

TRESSIE BURIED RED at the Veterans Cemetery on Thursday. All her scattered family came home to be with her—her children from Wisconsin and Maryland, her stepdaughter from California, and, of course, her kinfolk from Louisiana and Arkansas. Like every family, they told stories about the dear departed, they laughed and cried, and they filled their empty place with chicken and greens and corn bread and pies.

Willie Miller and Tressie had met by then, and he had told her not to worry, that things would work out. "He said he was with the Mennonites," Tressie recalls. "I had never heard of them. But he was real nice. He gave me his home number in Harrison. Gave me his pager number. Told me to call him anytime. I phoned him once up in Harrison, because I was skeptical about him coming back. He said he would, and he did."

By the end of that first week, Tressie's insurance agent had handed her a check for $30,000, which included her household contents and car. She was worried to death. "I told Willie Miller, 'I can't have a house note and a car note, too. I don't make enough money.' He said, 'Don't worry, we'll work something out.'"

The next time he came back from Harrison, he brought three house plans to show her. Just looking at them almost broke her heart. "He was talking about two bedrooms each ten feet by ten feet. Well, the house Red and I lived in had eight rooms, with four bedrooms each fourteen by fourteen. Our family room was fourteen by twenty-eight and a half, the kitchen fourteen by fourteen, and the den fourteen by twelve. I wasn't in a position to argue about *anything*. I mean, when you haven't got money, you can't be too choicey. I was asking for help, and I couldn't have the finest. But I couldn't help tearing up, and my voice broke. 'What's the matter?' he said.

"'Well, I got to have three bedrooms.'

"And he said, 'Okay, we can redraw this.'

"Then I just blurted it out: 'And I just can't stand these *stinky-dinky bed-rooms!*' By then I was crying. He kind of laughed, but he was nice about it. 'Don't cry, Tressie,' he said. 'We're gonna figure something out.'"

The cleaning up, planning, and financing process was what took time. Once the Mennonites started pouring foundations and framing in walls, houses went up in a matter of a week or so. All that spring and summer the hopeful ring of hammers on nails sounded throughout the College Station community. Besides working for Tressie and Vera Mae King, MDS was to build houses for Austin Porter Sr., whose brother had been killed, and for Emmanuel Benton. "Mr. Benton, who was ninety-three years old, had come to my office with a great burden," says Stewart, relishing the memory. "You see, he lived in an old house, a shack really, a place that should've been torn down thirty years ago. And his yard was filled with—well, with *relics* that were important to him. An old car, pieces of metal, things like that. These were cherished parts of his past, and he didn't want to leave them. He was afraid something would happen to them. 'Reverend,' he said, 'can they build on the lot while I stay in the house?'

"I knew that wouldn't work, but I phoned FEMA and explained the situation. Then I told Mr. Benton, 'You can't stay in the house . . . but they're going to provide you a trailer to live in while they build you a new house.' Well, he started crying. He was so happy."

By the end of the summer, the first few houses were finished. I flew out from Washington to attend the key-presentation ceremony, which was held at Mount Nebo church. Willie Miller said a few words and then handed keys and a Bible to several people, including Tressie Robierson and Emmanuel Benton. "Mr. Benton had a smile on his face that would probably last him forty years," recalls Stewart. "He had a new house, new beds, had some bathrooms, a stove. Everything was absolutely new. When he walked into his new house, he looked around and said, 'Now all I need is a *wife!*'

"See what love does? Here's when the human heart begins to mend. Mr. Benton was a totally new man. At age ninety-three, he now wanted a wife. Of course, I advised against it, because I wanted him to enjoy his house."

In her own quiet way, Tressie was as thrilled with her house as

Emmanuel Benton was with his. She got her three bedrooms, all of comfortable size. She got the kind of kitchen counter she wanted. She got ample storage space, so nothing would have to be outside in the carport except her new car. And she got two bathrooms, which she didn't even ask for. She moved in in September, six months after the tornado. She didn't have much in the way of furniture yet, but the house itself more than satisfied what she'd told Willie Miller she wanted: "I don't want to be head over heels in debt. I just want a comfortable house, with a roof on it, where I can eat and sleep, and it's not gonna be raining in my face."

THIS, THOUGH, IS where the real healing of College Station comes in. The work continued all through the fall of 1997. MDS crews came and went, interacting with the locals, then moving on to the next community that needed them. But still other MDS teams came to College Station. "They'd never stayed in a place this long," says Stewart.

But there came a time, in late 1997 and early 1998, when the community was running out of places for the Mennonites to live. Tressie Robierson heard some of them discussing that and said, "Y'all can stay at my house."

Nothing came of that for a long time. "They must've thought I was joking," she says. But then the lodging crunch apparently got critical. Two new couples were in town—Russ and Linda Smucker from Ohio, and Henry and Pearl Dueck from Manitoba, Canada. The Smuckers were living in a small RV "that is semifunctioning," as Russ Smucker wrote to his family back home. "The AC outlets work. No furnace, no lights, leaks in the waterline, leaks in the roof. Fortunately, Linda and I are stubborn campers."

The Duecks, on the other hand, had no place to stay. One day an MDS leader came to see Tressie. "Did you mean it?" he asked.

"Yes I did," she said. "Y'all left your comfortable homes to come here and help me. I had nothing, and the Lord blessed me. And I'm opening my doors so you all will have a place to live."

The next day, January 18, 1998, Henry and Pearl came to see Tressie. By then she had some bedroom furniture for her room and a guest room. "I have very little," Tressie told them, "but what I have you're welcome to." And the Duecks moved in for the next two months.

No one who took note of this development was happier about it than the Reverend Mr. Hezekiah Stewart, who had been seeing all sorts of positive changes in his community, and I don't mean just the new and refurbished houses, the new roads, and the trenches for the new sewer lines. "I had told them that the tornado would bring more into College Station than it took out," he says. "And that's exactly what happened."

Over the next couple of months, the Duecks and the Smuckers blended into College Station in a way that no white people ever had before. "Sometimes in the evenings when we weren't working, Tressie's sister Pinky would come over," Henry Dueck recalls, "and they would lie on the floor laughing, and we would all talk about our lives. And Tressie fixed great meals—hot-water corn bread, okra, purple hull peas, turnip greens."

The Smuckers sometimes went over to Tressie's, but they also spent a lot of time at Vera Mae King's big new house, one of the largest ever built by MDS. "Vera Mae's brown beans, chow chow, and hot-water mush were great," Russ Smucker wrote to his Ohio relatives. "She tried to get me to agree that her chow chow was better than my mother's, but I wasn't going to touch that subject with a ten-foot pole. She's declared she's going to take on my mom next with her barbecued ribs."

Not every moment was carefree, of course. Henry, a farmer in the summers, remembers going to a farm show in Little Rock one night. "I listed my address as College Station, and people gave me the strangest looks." On the other side of the coin, Pearl recalls the night Tressie finally talked candidly with them about racism. "This was after we got to know her better. She told us that there was a lot of opposition to this arrangement from her black community. 'Why you letting those white people stay in your home?' they asked her."

The younger black people, especially, seemed to the Mennonites difficult to connect with. In one of his letters home, Russ Smucker described a group of them. "We celebrated Ash Wednesday together with ashes from the barrel just across the road behind our trailer. Most evenings there is a fire in the barrel, with five to twenty young fellows sitting around it on rickety old chairs, talking and laughing. Sometimes on weekends we can smell ribs roasting. Someone told us they don't need to work because they're living on drug money. Anyhow, we wave and greet them when we are walking home from work, but we don't sit down with them to visit. I would love to talk with them, but prudence suggests we keep our distance."

Henry Dueck did notice, however, that the young black people would respond more warmly if they were approached through an older person, especially their mothers. Russ Smucker recalls that one night some Mennonite tools were stolen—then shortly thereafter reappeared. "I felt that Vera Mae and Tressie were watching out for us," Russ says. "We always wore our MDS badges when we walked around town, but one day Linda and I were going somewhere and a man began verbally abusing us. He was drunk, or stoned, or something. Anyway, Vera Mae was out in her yard, and she made him apologize to us. When she explained to him that we were the Mennonites, he became abject in his drunken apologies. As we went on our way, I looked and saw that she had her arm around him and was taking him into her house. To try to get him sobered up, I guess."

Despite these undercurrents, for Pearl Dueck the highlight of those two months was when she and Henry went with Tressie to her grandson's basketball game at Little Rock's Shorter College. "We were the only two white people in the arena," she says, "and every time Tressie introduced us, she made a point of saying, 'These are my friends.'"

She told that to the community, too. On March 1, 1998, the first anniversary of the tornado, a special service was held at the Mount Nebo AME Church. Russ Smucker had described previous services to his relatives back home ("The choir at the Mount Nebo church is worth hearing—seven women dressed in red and yellow robes, they sang with spirit, and in tune . . . ," and, "The altar rail along the front of the sanctuary was clothed in white. The pulpit was clothed in white. The choir had on white robes (with pretty orange and green and black sashes). Rev. Stewart had on a white blazer. The five lady stewards in the left amen corner all had on white gowns and white hats . . ."), but on this day all stops were pulled. "We were in church nearly five hours . . . ," Russ wrote to his relatives. Tressie Robierson played a key role in that extended service. Standing before her neighbors and her new friends the Mennonites, she said, "When I opened my home to you folks, others asked, 'Why are you letting those white folks live with you?'

And I told them, 'After what they've done for me, how can I not invite them in? They are my sisters and brothers.'"

Now, some four years later, Tressie and the Duecks still stay in touch. "Whenever they come through town, they go first to Tressie's, then Vera Mae's, and then to Watershed," says Stewart—who not only has a stronger community over which to say grace, but a new receptivity to an old message. "I think the storm has been a blessing," Austin Porter Sr. told Lowell Detweiler for *The Hammer Rings Hope*. "A lot of businesses and homes are better than they were before the storm. I'd like to say that my brother and the people who died have made a way for us to live life more abundantly."

And during those long rich Sunday services at Mount Nebo AME Church—a church started years before when two black people were turned away from worshipping with whites—the reverend tends to focus on the changes of heart. "Be careful what you say about white folks," he tells his congregation. "You may be living in a house built by one!" To whites and blacks alike, he preaches about the hidden good things that sometimes can come from bad. "That tornado caused racism to take a back step," he says. "That's some of the miracle that happened here."

Stewart isn't the only one saying it. "The Mennonites coming in left a lasting impression on the people of this community," Austin Porter Jr. says in *The Hammer Rings Hope*. "Before the storm, a lot of people would have said there are no good white people around. Now we can see there are white people who have heart. They came in without fanfare, to work, not to be on TV."

"If you ever want to eliminate racism, get to know the person you hate," Stewart says. It's one of his favorite themes. "A lot of this stuff about racism is that we don't know each other. If you watch kids, we just need to do what kids do. You put kids in a room, they'll play. They don't care anything about whether they're white or black or Hispanic or alien. You put a ball in there, they want to play with it.

"We have to take that on, and that's one of the things we've been working on in Little Rock—to show people what fellowshipping and love can do. Sitting down and getting to know each other, and then learning how to respect each other. You can't do it without respect, and you can't do it if you're not operating out of a level of integrity.

"Once that happens—well, let me just say this: I've got some white friends now who've got a black friend forever. We've moved from being white friends and black friends to being friends. Isn't that wonderful?"

◆ ◆ ◆

THE CHINESE, BEFITTING a culture marked by age and wisdom, apparently choose to take the long view of the calamities that beset mankind: "Their character for crisis, *wei ji*, . . . is made up of characters for two other words," I read in the *Stanford Business Magazine*. "One is danger, the other is opportunity."

That's a wonderful fact, one we Westerners ought to remember. We have plenty of hopeful platitudes about clouds-with-silver-linings and it's-darkest-before-the-dawn, but most of us still tend to believe the light at the end of the tunnel is most likely a freight train. It never occurs to us that that train may be hauling a pot of gold.

Change, even unasked-for change, often turns out to be good. Nobody would ever say they're glad terrorists attacked the World Trade Center and the Pentagon, but it did happen. Now we have to try to find the positive, the hopeful in that. It's clear to me that, since 9/11, people in this country have felt a sense of kinship and unity that they didn't feel before. That won't bring back the people who were lost, but it may end up making us a better, stronger nation.

A crisis stops time for a while. When life is going along normally, it's like we're on one of those interminable moving sidewalks in airport corridors. I like the feeling I get at the end of those things—that sudden absence of velocity. In a crisis, another kind of time takes over, but you know it's temporary. Meanwhile, ordinary concerns become irrelevant. Who you are and who you want to be become more visceral, less intellectual questions. If we manage it right, a crisis becomes an opportunity for reinvention.

In the last chapter, I wrote in the notes about MBA Polymers, the plastic-recycling company that bounced back from an explosion and fire in one of its plants. Here's a quote from CEO Mike Biddle about the opportunity to be found in crisis: "You could never say the fire was a blessing, but there were some small silver linings. We were forced to step back and take that time to evaluate. We had brought Bechtel in before the fire to do test work and observe the process lines. After the fire they were able to spend more time on the line than if we had been in production. And the time-out helped accelerate our business overseas."

Blessed as I've been to have the career I've had, I often wonder how my life would've turned out if my great youthful plan to get out of Arkansas and make something of myself had actually worked. The year was 1962. I had just graduated from high school. I was driving a dump truck for a living. I had a terrible wreck in that truck. My thermos rolled off the seat and I reached down to retrieve it. In that split second I missed a curve, sailed off a cliff, and soared through the air into a concrete abutment. When I told my brother about it, I think he saw my life flash before his eyes. He was working in Groton, Connecticut, building submarines for General Dynamics, and he urged me to come work there with him.

Lea Ellen and I agreed our future was probably brighter in Connecticut, so we borrowed $250 from the bank, traded my '51 pickup for a 1953 Chevy convertible, and set out. We were on the Pennsylvania Turnpike when the car broke down. After a long time of waiting, we were towed into a little burg where the lone mechanic promised he could fix the car by the next day. Worried about money but having no choice, we checked into a seedy motel for the night. Later, on the way to supper, we noticed a bunch of motorcycles and tough guys in black leather. We came out later to find them all lying around bleeding on the street and sidewalks, bloody chains everywhere. We hurried back to the motel and bolted the door. The next morning, the car repair cost $90 of our very limited cash. As I was paying the mechanic, I asked how long he had lived here. He said he had just moved back. Until recently he'd been in prison—for killing a man in the same café where we had eaten supper.

We were glad to leave there and get to Connecticut, where I soon started a thirteen-week course in mechanical drafting and Lea Ellen worked for a publishing company. Then, just as I finished school, General Dynamics went on strike. We felt like the bottom had just dropped out of our lives. "Why don't we go home?" Lea Ellen suggested. I couldn't think of a single reason not to. Soon we were back in Arkansas, me working as a carpenter's assistant for her dad. Three years later, we started our own construction business and I got involved in the community that later elected me county judge. The rest, as they say, is a quarter-century string of ice storms and hurricanes and earthquakes and floods. A crisis usually isn't the end. More often than not it's the beginning.

◆ ◆ ◆

NOT LONG AGO, while flying to California, I read a fascinating feature in *USA Today*. It was an interview with James Morgan (not my collaborator!), CEO of Applied Materials, a company that makes the equipment that makes computer chips. The subject of the interview was "using recession to plan for the next level," and Morgan said some of the very things I'm trying to say here, only with more style. In tough times, Morgan said, "Problems show up like the rocks in a bay when the tide is out. You can develop a navigation plan. When the water is up, you don't know where the rocks are. Use downturns to find areas that need to be improved." That's a very healthy way to think about crisis. Sure, you have to get through it. But the time-out factor a crisis gives you is a perfect opportunity to see what you've been doing wrong, what you could be doing better, and to make plans accordingly.

Two other provocative Morgan quotes: "Recessions are a great time to start a new job. In good times, expectations are high." And, "Good news is no news, no news is bad news, and *bad news is good news if you do something about it*" (my italics).

Morgan doesn't just talk about making the best of a crisis—learning from it and mining for opportunities—he makes it a part of his company's business plan. Remember all those projects that you never have time for when you're trying to catch up to consumer demand? When CEOs around the country were freezing up their budgets for computers, Applied Materials, which was faced with much less demand for its inventory, fine-tuned its distribution so they could get parts around the world more efficiently and cheaply. Morgan has also kept his research and development budget intact and opened a new technology center on schedule. Not only will this keep them ready when consumer demand turns around, it will give them an advantage on the competition.

The 2001 recession wasn't Morgan's first, of course, and he learned from past experiences that while your competitors are stumbling, your employees can even expand into new areas to help cushion a crisis and get your recovery jump-started. "Get close to your customers," as Morgan says. "Make sure you know what they want, what they need." That strategy explains in part why Applied Materials was able to land a big contract in China to outfit a factory while the rest of the industry was hunkered down. And because the company has stayed focused on turning this recent crisis into a triumph, they've even gotten a lot more press ink than usual. For what *Newsweek* has called perhaps "the most important manufacturer you've never heard of," Applied Materials sure is getting the sort of attention that translates into business.

But you don't have to be a Fortune 500 company to turn a crisis to your advantage. A couple of years ago I read a story about a small family-owned coffeeshop in Long Beach, California. Polly's Gourmet Coffee, owned by a man named Michael Sheldrake, had long been "Coffee King of Second Street," as *New York Times* writer Joel Kotkin put it. And then came that nightmare of every mom-and-pop operation—one of the mega-chains moved in on their turf. In Polly's case, the nightmare wore the face of Starbucks. In 1994, the coffee giant opened a store four blocks away.

Polly's sales dropped around 15 percent as a result. Then, four years later, another Starbucks opened—this one seventy-eight yards from Polly's.

The good news is that Polly's took that bad news and did something about it. As Kotkin noted, Sheldrake got some expertise in the form of consultant Bob Phibbs and came up with a two-pronged strategy: Beef up their own business efficiency and figure out how to take advantage of the chain's weaknesses. "The problem with a chain is that it's like a mall. It's all mechanical, and there's no relationship with the customers," Bob Phibbs told Kotkin.

Phibbs encouraged Polly's to stress the fact that it roasts its coffee on-site, "which is impractical for a sprawling chain like Starbucks." Phibbs also "urged the store's management to adopt the chains' best organizational and management ideas, like putting an end to a plethora of special arrangements between employees and longtime customers for free or cut-rate services and tightening cash management procedures. Employees attended mandatory classes to improve their sales skills." Because Polly's Gourmet Coffee took the bad news as an opportunity to improve itself, sales rose 40 percent the same year that the second Starbucks moved in.

You don't always need a consultant to do the sort of analysis that Polly's did. In fact, you can't always hire a consultant. But what a consultant does is force you to gather up all that information about exactly what you were doing when a crisis hit, what you did to turn it around (or, sometimes, what you didn't do), and how to keep refining those tactics to beat the crisis again and again. What you want to do is make that information-gathering a regular part of your crisis response and recovery, and funnel your insights straight into your new and improved prevention plans.

I like to think we turned bad news into good news at FEMA. In 1994, President Bill Clinton said, "When I took office, the National Academy of Public Administration said this about FEMA: 'FEMA is like a patient in triage. The President and Congress must decide whether to treat it or let it die.' There was even a bill pending in Congress to abolish FEMA," the president continued. "And in 1992, as I traveled the country, I never went to a place that somebody didn't say something disparaging about it. Well, the bill is gone, and it may be the most popular agency in the entire federal government."

When I was a boy, railroad crossings in some parts of the South had signs that said, "Stop. Look. Listen." That's what we did at FEMA in 1993. We stopped what we had been doing so we could figure out what was wrong about it; we looked hard at ourselves, listened to one another, and visualized what and where we wanted to be; then we mapped out a route for getting there. When we finally started rolling again, that old freight train (the one whose light we used to see bearing down on us at the end of the tunnel) was nowhere in sight.

In summary, then, how to manage a crisis to your advantage:

• **A CRISIS IS EQUAL PARTS DANGER AND OPPORTUNITY.** I'm taken by the fact that I meet people all the time who start their stories about surviving a crisis with words along the lines of "I think the storm was a blessing." Their tales usually turn to the ways that the disaster forced them to work with people they didn't know beforehand, or to find out how they or their neighbors could be heroes, or to realign the priorities in their life, or to make their town a safer place. A crisis gives your people a chance to demonstrate leadership that can be valuable not just in a crisis. It allows you to solidify relationships with suppliers, clients, or partners. It forces you to see the weaknesses in the way you do business and turn them into strengths. To make an opportunity out of the danger, you've got to think about the crisis as more than something to cover up, put out, clean up, and forget. First, you should make sure that everyone knows all the bad news as soon as you know it, so you can disarm the danger and start getting people focused on the opportunities. Once you've got the crisis under control, you should nurture the unexpected benefits of the crisis. The employee who stepped up to the plate can be placed in charge of a new project to prepare you for the next crisis or to develop new business with a partner who helped pull you through.

• **LEARN TO VIEW DOWN TIMES AS A CHANCE TO STOP, LISTEN, AND LOOK.** There are times in a crisis or at the early stages of recovery when it feels like things—especially things that are out of your control—are moving like molasses. You might take that as a sign that you should hunker down or take a breather. Take advantage of these times to ramp up. What projects have you been wishing you had the time for, but could never get around to because of other priorities? How might you get them under way so that they'll make you more efficient or more reliable when things turn around? Keep turning to your support network to look for ways you can work together after the crisis, even if you couldn't find ways to help each other out in the midst of it. What do they need to recover? What will they need after they recover? How do those needs match up with what you used to supply to them, and what you could supply to them?

• **DON'T LET YOUR MISTAKES AND SUCCESSES GO INTO A VACUUM.** Collect every bit of knowledge you can about your crisis response, how your crisis preparations or prevention plans held up, and what you can improve for the future. If your communication infrastructure stayed firm, you'll have a wealth of information in the updates that your employees provided in the moment; those reports will tell the story as it was happening, before you've got that 20/20 hindsight. Take time after the crisis to look for patterns as well as opportunities for improvement in those reports. What resources did employees need that they didn't have? Did decision-making get tangled up because it wasn't clear which project or product or client took priority? Did communication work between teams and within teams (did your employees get what they needed to know from each others' reports at the time)? Were there wrong assumptions in their assessments of their progress, of the level of crisis, or of their ability to handle the problems assigned to them? While you're spotting your patterns and fixes, ask employees to write up brief memos that give their perspective on what went right and what went wrong.

• **TO COIN A PHRASE, CRISIS IS THE MOTHER OF REINVENTION.** The recovery after most natural disasters involves rebuilding. It's a chance to lay new foundations and support beams that can weather the next disaster better. It's a chance to decide if there's a way to get out of the way of that disaster altogether. It's a chance for you to revise your crisis preparations, fine-tuning or rethinking your values, your on-hand resources, your early-warning flags, your reporting systems, your team's setup and their skills, your support network, your lightning rods and the sparks they create, and everything else I've touched on in this book.

IF THE OX IS IN THE DITCH . . .

Get Him Out—Then Build a Fence

Growing up in the country, I used to hear this saying a lot: "If the ox is in the ditch . . ." The unspoken part was, "You've got to get in that ditch and get him out." In other words, in a crisis, you have to do what you have to do to handle the situation.

I've been in and out of a lot of ditches in my life—both literally and figuratively. When the Midwest floods started washing over the central part of the nation, I needed to get to Madison, Wisconsin, immediately for a meeting with the state's governor. Flying commercial, I caught a Washington-Madison flight with a change in Chicago. Unfortunately, we sat so long on the tarmac at O'Hare that I missed my connection. I managed to book another flight as far as Milwaukee, but still couldn't fly into Madison that night. A cab driver offered to drive me for $100, which I considered highway robbery. Instead, I got him to take me to the Greyhound station. I boarded the bus at 1 A.M. and sat in the very back with a lady and her two young sons, one of whom slept the night with his head on my lap.

During that bus ride, I thought back to all the other times I've been called upon to come through in a crisis. At age five or six, I started having to protect my sister Lura from the old turkey gobbler that inevitably trapped her—and only her—in the outhouse and wouldn't let her out. I never knew why he picked on Lura. He would squawk and strut and flap his wings and peck at the door. Of course, she would scream and I would come running, waving my arms and yelling at that old bird, who was as big as I was in the early days. This went on for so long that I ceased thinking of it as a crisis. It was just life.

Because we were so poor, I worked all the time. I got my Social Security card at age twelve and went to work at a poultry company cleaning out chicken houses with a scoop, loading the stuff on a manure spreader, and carrying it out to the boss's fields. These chicken houses were laying-hen houses, so they were only cleaned out every three years or so. The ammonia smell was so strong it would just choke you. This was where I was working the day our house burned. A man named Mr. Pelt was there. "James Lee," he said, "that smoke looks like it's about where you live." We drove there in his car, and sure enough it was my house. The fire took everything we had, except for the clothes we were wearing. Dad rented a house in town. I remember some folks gave us furniture.

That's when I bought a reconditioned bike on time and began delivering the *Arkansas Democrat*. After school I bagged groceries. On weekends I pumped gas at a service station and changed tires on big feed trucks. Beginning at age fifteen, for two summers I worked in Texas baling hay for Mr. Claude Sheets. At the end of the second summer, he asked me to come back after high school and become his business partner. Life would've been a lot different if I had done it. Mr. Sheets went on and did well by inventing a spool for dispensing a mile of barbed wire.

Instead I grew up and went into the construction business, which is when I first felt the call to help people in trouble. A tornado tore through Jonesboro in the 1960s, destroying a good many houses. I offered to build some back at cost. I kept doing that for tornado and fire victims until I was elected county judge in 1978 and gave up construction. As the chief county administrator, I never knew what a day would bring—or when it might end, for that matter. My first winter in office, it snowed every Wednesday for seven straight weeks. Every road in the county fell through. One icy night I got a call at home at midnight from a man who said his wife had gotten stuck in the middle of a county road. He wanted me to bring some chains and come pull her out, which I did. It wasn't the last time, either.

Not every crisis was perilous or life threatening. After then-governor Clinton appointed me to head the state office of emergency management, but before I had officially started the job, he phoned and asked me to go with him to tour an area of tornado damage outside Little Rock. I met up with him and his entourage, which even then was something to behold, and we motorcaded out to the rural Scott community. Surveying the storm damage caused the governor to work up an appetite. He suggested we stop off at a country café called Cotham's, which was known for its "hubcap burgers," so named because of their size. We all—about a dozen of us—ordered burgers, fries, and pie for dessert. Afterward, Clinton got up and walked out, and most of the others followed. His press aide, Mike Gauldin, looked panicked. "James Lee," he said, "you got any money?" I picked up the whole tab. And because I wasn't a state employee yet, I couldn't even expense it. Live and learn.

In Washington, I learned many things, some of which didn't seem—at first—to pertain to crisis management. Washington is largely a world of posturing, positioning, and protocol. Either something happens to make some people that way when they come to Washington, or they gravitate toward Washington because they're that way in the first place. In our nation's capital, the currency of the realm seems to be proximity to presidential power (which I admittedly enjoyed). At official gatherings, where you sit, who's next to you, what row you're in, who takes the podium first—these are major concerns. Privately, which table you get in which restaurant is an overwhelmingly important consideration. I've never understood any of that. Some of my FEMA staff people were appalled at my response when, late one afternoon, someone from the West Wing called to ask if Lea Ellen and I would like to join the president and first lady for a movie at the White House that evening. "I don't know," I said. "What's he showing?" My staffers were holding their heads and mouthing, "No, no, *no!*"

But this kind of intense and overwhelming personal ambition tends to create a disconnect between the people who comprise our government and the people they're supposed to serve. I remember wondering, when I first got to D.C., if there would be any similarities between the world I had come from and the world I was just entering. Sure, the Potomac River flows through a city of marble and granite, of limos and motorcades, while my part of the Arkansas flows through rolling farmland near the Ozark foothills.

The closest thing to a motorcade you're likely to see in Dardanelle is the procession of pick-up trucks heading toward the trading barn on Saturday mornings.

And yet both places, I thought, ought to prize and reward a talent for the hands-on, for the ability to understand how things work, for knowing how to pull the levers and push the buttons and operate the machinery to get the desired things done. I was right in a way. Unfortunately, it's in the "desired things" that these two places split like a big river and go their separate directions. In my Arkansas, they still know that if the ox is in the ditch, you simply have to get in there and get him out. But in Washington, if the ox detours into the ditch, you form a fault-finding committee and immediately call a press conference.

WHEN I WAS in local and state government, we had a strong sense that "those bureaucrats in Washington" didn't spend many sleepless nights worrying about our well-being. Having been privileged to work with the career employees at FEMA, I know that's not all true. It's just that government agencies too often value their rules and regulations and programs over actually helping people. I wanted to change that at FEMA. I wanted people in local and state government to see FEMA people not as bureaucrats, but as public servants.

At the same time, I wanted to spread the word to the states and communities that they shouldn't sit around waiting for the United States government to bail them out in a crisis. If they built themselves a fence, maybe the ox wouldn't ever *get* in the ditch.

I wrote this book to continue spreading that message. I've been gratified to see that businesses and educational institutions are becoming proactive about crisis management (being proactive ought to be the *definition* of crisis management; otherwise, you're just mopping up). More and more business schools are starting crisis management courses, which means increased awareness and expertise in the business world. And more and more organizations—including governments all over the planet—are hiring consultants like me to help them develop crisis plans for that day we used to think would never come.

Unfortunately, I don't have to tell you the world has changed.

On September 11, 2001, Lea Ellen and I drove down from Wildcat Hollow to Little Rock so I could be interviewed on TV. On the drive down, I thought about some of the things I wanted to say, and that led me to recall the disasters I had worked on over the years. Oklahoma City loomed heaviest of all, and not just because it was also an act of terrorism. It was at Oklahoma City that I met Ray Downey, a battalion chief and thirty-three-year veteran of the New York City Fire Department. He and I really hit it off, and when President and Mrs. Clinton came out to Oklahoma for the memorial service, I introduced them to Ray and told them what a good job he had done for the people of Oklahoma City. "Next time I'm in New York," I said, "I'm gonna take him out for a steak dinner."

"Well," Ray told the president and the first lady, "before James Lee comes to the big city, he's going to have to get rid of those cowboy boots."

President Clinton laughed like it was the first time he had laughed in weeks. "Ray," he said, "James Lee didn't even *own* a pair of lace-up shoes before I brought him to Washington!" It was a funny moment, a nice break from the heartache and hard work we had been doing for days on end. On that September Tuesday, as I drove east on I-40, it occurred to me that Ray would've been one of the first on the scene at the World Trade Center. I said a silent prayer for him.

As I was working on these last few pages, the remains of Ray Downey were identified in the debris of the World Trade Center. I wasn't able to attend his memorial service, but I saw a picture of it in the paper—two young girls in flowing dresses, and a little boy wearing a fireman's hat, saluting. Ray's grandchildren, I'm guessing. They made me think of my own.

My grandchildren all live in Dardanelle. I'd like to think that protects them some from the kinds of crises that threaten our friends in larger cities. Even so, I know that no life goes unscathed. No one skirts all the pain. There will be all manner of oxen in all manner of ditches. There will be all manner of thrown rods. What I hope for my grandchildren, as I hope for yours, is that they'll grow up to be people of uncommon common sense—people who know themselves, who're true to themselves, who know that every crisis gives them an opportunity to become stronger, and who have the confidence to triumph at their core.

ACKNOWLEDGMENTS

This book, which had its beginnings nearly a decade ago, was helped along to fruition by a great number of people. Space prevents elaborating on specific roles, but we nevertheless want to acknowledge the invaluable contributions of Lynda Dixon, Henry Finder of the *New Yorker,* Max Brantley, Jane Bullock, Mark Merritt, Morrie Goodman, Bill Tidball, Kim Fuller, Ada Alvarez, and Chief Jim Hone.

In the chapters on individual disasters, many of those we owe are included as characters in the dramas themselves. Reliving such difficult events can't be easy, and we appreciate their willingness to share their time, their stories, and quite often their still-tender emotions. In addition, for the chapter on the Malibu fires, we want to thank Stephen Randall and Tim Weil. For the chapter on Hurricane Fran, thanks go to Carol Thiel, Brenda Coffey, Kim Taylor, Carolina Beach Mayor Ray Rothrock, Willard H. Killough III and the staff of the *Island Gazette,* and Drake Mann. For the chapter on Pattonsburg, Missouri, our thanks to Eddie Meador, the irreverently helpful staff at City Hall, and the reference department at Daviess County Library. For the chapter on the Oklahoma City bombing, special thanks to Mark Ghilarducci for his patience, his insights, and his leads to other sources. Thanks also to Dave Kehrlein and his very helpful staff.

For the Northridge Earthquake chapter, thanks to Chris Lopez, Josie Arcurio, and Linda Curtis at USGS. In Grand Forks, North Dakota, thanks to Rick

Duquette in the mayor's office and to the marketing department lady at the *Grand Forks Herald,* whose card we've apparently lost. For the chapter on TWA 800, thanks to Morrie Goodman and Leo Farber, and especially to Sean and Ann Carven, who agreed to talk with Jim about the loss of their loved ones. In Falmouth, Kentucky, thanks to the reference staff at the Pendleton County Library. Special thanks, too, to Ruby Wyatt, still a trouper despite her weekly chemotherapy treatments. And for the chapter on the terrible tornado at College Station, Arkansas, thanks go to Vera Mae King and to Tom Smucker of the Mennonite Disaster Service, and especially to Tressie Robierson for her bravery and to Hezekiah Stewart for his eloquence.

To those authors and magazine writers whose publications were so helpful in our telling of these stories, we express our gratitude for your good work. In every case, we tried to acknowledge it in the text.

—JLW and JM

Among the handful of people intricately involved in the overall book, I want to express my appreciation to Lea Ellen Witt for her abiding encouragement of this project; to editor Robin Dennis at Holt for her vision, taste, humor, and hands-on help; to my agent, Michael Carlisle, for his optimism and perseverance; to my friend James Lee Witt for his trust; and to both James Lee and Michael for stepping forward together during a last-minute crisis to make this book a reality.

Finally, to my family—sons David and Matthew, daughters Blair and Bret, and wife, Beth—I offer love and thanks. Especially to Beth—for her belief in the book, her support during its development, and her forbearance whenever my moods matched the disasters I was writing about.

—JM

I want to thank Lea Ellen for her continued support over the last forty years; Jim Morgan, for spending so much time helping me to write this book, and for all the interviews he has done on my behalf; and President Clinton for giving me the chance to serve the American people. And to the hard-working employees of the Federal Emergency Management Agency, I thank you for the wonderful service that you gave the American people while I was director, and which you continue to give.

God Bless.

—JLW

INDEX

ABOUT THE AUTHORS

A native of Wildcat Hollow, outside of Dardanelle, Arkansas, JAMES LEE WITT served as director of the Federal Emergency Management Agency from 1993 until 2001, when he transformed FEMA into a customer-focused model for crisis management. He began his career as a "master of disaster" in Yell County, Arkansas, where he was county judge, and later oversaw disaster response and relief for the entire state. An international consultant, with clients including the City of New York and major corporations and associations, and a motivational speaker, he and his wife, Lea Ellen, split their time between Washington, D.C., and Arkansas.

JAMES MORGAN is author of the *New York Times* Notable Books *The Distance to the Moon* and *Leading with My Heart,* Virginia Kelley's bestselling memoir of raising President Bill Clinton. He and his family live in Little Rock, Arkansas.